BEYOND
THE
DREAM

5/2023

Dear Henry,
I'm grateful to know you through
our son Ross
Enjoy your journey

Mel

BEYOND THE DREAM

A Family Journey
Without Limits

MEL BARON
as told to James Novack

Author's Note

This memoir is independently authored and published. It is not endorsed by or affiliated with any of the institutions or individuals with which I have been professionally associated, including the University of Southern California and its School of Pharmacy. The opinions expressed in this book are mine alone.

For information about this title or to order other books
and/or electronic media, contact the publisher:

Boyle Heights Publishing
info@BoyleHeightsPublishing.com

ISBN: 979-8-218-16637-3 (softcover)

Printed in the United States of America

To My Beloved,
A Wondrous Woman

Table Of Contents

Acknowledgment

This book would not have been possible without the contributions of Jim Novack. Writing your own memoir can be a daunting task for anyone, and in my case, especially so because my declining eyesight makes it increasingly difficult to type. Fortunately, someone connected me with Jim.

Guiding me each step of the way, Jim conducted a series of in-depth interviews—with me recounting my family history and colorful upbringing, through my becoming an adult and creating a successful career and family. An enthusiastic listener, Jim's probing and insightful questions stimulated my recollections as well as long-forgotten memories. He helped me draw connections between different events and times, and with that came new realizations.

Given the circumstances of COVID, most interviews were on Zoom, which proved just as comfortable and productive as those in person. Plus, a day or two before each interview, Jim emailed me questions about the areas we would discuss next. This gave me a chance to prepare by reminiscing on those earlier times, plus talking about them with my wife, Lorraine, comparing her memories and perspectives with my own.

From transcriptions of our many hours of interviews, Jim created a wonderful narrative, interweaving experiences, feelings, and further insights. He produced a cohesive story of my life. Moreover, he was able to write this *in my voice*: the book sounds like me, speaking to my family, friends, and colleagues.

To my delight, the entire experience has been extremely enjoyable, and even therapeutic, as I got to revisit and rediscover the many pieces that have made up my life. I couldn't be happier with the result on the pages before you now. Enjoy.

(Jim may be contacted via his webpage, www.JamesNovack.com)

Introduction

All That Is Possible

We enjoy wonderful dreams as children. Imagining all varieties of things and all kinds of adventures.

As we reach adulthood, most people embrace the security of more practical dreams—limiting our imaginings to those goals we have a good chance of attaining in our lives. Though we may still fall short of those aspirations, many times we're able to manifest much of what we want.

And sometimes . . . far more than we ever imagined.

This is my life.

My grandparents and my mother are all uneducated Russian peasants who escaped that world and made their way to America. As I think about this, I realize my mom came here in 1916—and we are now just a few years past 2016. A hundred years have passed since her family arrived on our shores with no skills and unable to speak the language. Even my father, born in the U.S., never went past the eighth grade.

Yet their son goes on to earn two advanced degrees, create a successful *legitimate* business (you'll read why "lawful" is worth mentioning), and becomes a college professor—as does my own son. My daughter becomes renown in the field of education as well. My wife, Lorraine, earns her BA in Social Sciences in midlife and becomes a Marriage and Family Therapist. Together, she and I create a beautiful family whose *many* offspring continue to impress and wow me today, with most of our grandchildren highly educated and who are, in various ways, major players in their communities.

In many respects, ours is the quintessential American story. A life beyond anything I could even have envisioned as a child.

This Gift of a Lifetime—For My Family

As Lorraine and I each enter our 90th year, I'm excited to create this remarkable telling of the life that she and I have shared together. Ours is a large family with grandkids and great-grandkids. Most of them never met my parents. Some of my great-grandkids are very young, one and two years old. How well will they get to know us? Reading this book will give them that chance.

Our family has always been eager to hear about my life. My grandkids and older great-grandkids are like, "Hold on, Papa, tell us more about what happened back then!" They feel connected to the people in my stories even as I talk of lives and times far different from today. My grandchildren still can't believe my mom got involved in illegal bookmaking, operating under the codename "Broadway."

"How could Great-grandma do that?!"

But they have only heard some of the stories. This book reveals more—and goes deeper. How and why these events occurred. My feelings about what happened. For those in the family who think they know us now . . . this book provides a fresh chance to understand us far better than they have ever before.

More Benefits

I feel there is much to be gained from discovering your family's history even beyond knowing about Lorraine and me and our forebears. It helps you *feel connected* to your other family members who share that same history. It provides you a sense of identity. It adds to your own uniqueness.

It also shows you—what can be possible.

Life always has challenges. Many people feel today's problems are greater than ever. Yet going back in time, you'll see that earlier family members faced tough times too—much different from ours—but just as hard if not more so. Even though my own life has been highly successful, there were setbacks, outright failure, and times of despair. Back then, many of these seemed insurmountable. Yet we did overcome them.

Our family stories can help you see what is achievable, and inspire courage and strength to overcome challenges in your own life.

Knowing what I and others went through—what we did for our family and for others—can encourage you to have more gratitude, empathy, and compassion as well.

Love Story

Importantly, while much of this book's focus is on me, without Lorraine, there is no story. The truth is it's not my story. It's *our* story, and as you read it, you'll start to see why she and I have been able to sustain our love and commitment over 70 years together. We are as strong a couple as we have ever been. That is not by accident.

I continue to look back on ours and my family's lives in pure amazement. To me, this really is an amazing dream. Except it's all true.

So how did it all happen?

Let's find out.

✦ ✦ ✦

CHAPTER 1

The Beginning: My Mother

Half a world away from Los Angeles, across the Pacific Ocean, beyond China and much of Eastern Europe, lies the city of Minsk in the Republic of Belarus. Part of what was once called the Russian Empire, it is here that Sadie Bauchman is born in a small rural village on December 10, 1905.

My mother.

When I am young, my mom tells me tales of her life growing up. I eagerly listen to every description of a world so unlike ours. I would say the play (and later film), *Fiddler on the Roof*, reflects the atmosphere of her life. The play describes a small Jewish village in 1905, where life is simple, almost primitive, and everyone knows everyone else.

In fact, if you live in this village, you don't know many people *outside* of it. When seeking someone to marry, you do not look to Jews or non-Jews outside your community. You rely on local matchmakers to find someone in your village who is available.

The result of such a limited pool of singles is that my grandparents are first cousins.

Life May Be Simple, But Not Easy

My mother's home has no electricity, no telephone, no indoor plumbing. For water, they use a hand pump connected to a well, or go down by the river to collect water and carry it back. There are no cars.

1

My mother shares a story that as a little girl, she must walk to a dentist for an aching tooth. It is some distance, but she makes her way all on her own. In the office, the dentist brings her toward the only source of light he has—through the window—and asks her to point to the tooth that hurts. Then he yanks it out without anesthetic, and my mother heads home. She walks there and back barefoot since she has her only good pair of shoes with her and she doesn't want to damage them.

I never get the feeling that hers is a joyful childhood. Mostly, it is full of hardship. My mother is born a twin, but the other child dies. My mother has two siblings—my Aunt Katie and my Uncle Morris—with my mom in the middle.

Though her father serves in the military, little is ever said of it. Except that circumstances suddenly change and it becomes certain that he is about to be conscripted to join the military again. This will not be good for him or for the family. To avoid this, he must flee. His destination: America. For some reason, he is not able to take his family with him.

Yet, there will soon be reasons for all of them to leave.

Pogroms

This is not a good period to be Jewish in Russia. It is the time of pogroms.

Pogrom is a Russian word meaning to "wreak havoc or demolish violently." Historically, it refers to attacks by non-Jews on Jewish people in the Russian Empire and other countries. These assailants are given free reign and sometimes encouragement by local governments and police. They rape and murder Jews, then steal their property.

Cossacks raid my mother's village, beating people and setting fire to homes. It could have been worse . . . and next time, it probably will be.

My grandfather must have been in contact with them through letter writing. He desperately wants them to flee. I don't know how he or anyone in the family earned a living in their village, or if he sent them money from America. But somehow they save enough to pay a woman to get the necessary papers to allow my grandmother and her children to travel out of Russia.

To leave their homeland.

My mother is just ten years old when she escapes with her two siblings and my grandmother. They board a train with only a few articles of clothing and begin an unbelievable journey—hoping to get to the coast of Japan, where they can find a ship to take them to America.

Strangers in Even Stranger Lands

Being Russian peasants who have never left their village, my family has no knowledge of the outside world and are now traveling through much of Asia on their own. The distance *in a straight line* between their village and Kobe on Japan's coastline is five thousand miles. But they are not flying, of course—which means the distance they actually travel overland is far greater! With no GPS to guide their way, they must cross through a huge portion of the Russian Empire . . . possibly Tibet . . . surely China . . . possibly Mongolia . . . probably Korea . . . and certainly Japan. The only languages they know are Hebrew, Yiddish, and Russian.

The clothes they have on do not match that which is worn in the communities they pass through. My mother and her family really stand out. They face daily challenges whenever they need information and cannot speak the language. Local foods are surely not kosher and far different from their own Eastern European diet. In parts of Asia, they are given only chopsticks to eat with.

"What are these used for?"

There are many questions for which I have no answers. Did they rent rooms while traveling or camp out? How did they handle money exchanges? There were no traveler's checks or credit cards. Was their money in paper currency? Did that have any value in these countries?

Were they carrying gold or silver coins? Or ounces of raw gold or silver? Or other valuables to trade?

It is so bizarre to imagine what this woman, traveling alone with three children, who has only lived in a small unsophisticated village, must have coped with during these travels.

How the hell does anyone survive such a trip?

What Is a Banana?

Somehow they make it to the Japanese coast and get on a ship heading for the United States. But that's hardly the end of their journey.

In this period, ships have first- and second-class accommodations. But in the lowest decks of the ship, where cargo is stored, there is also *steerage*. In the late 19th and early 20th centuries, steamship steerage decks provided the lowest travel cost for European and Chinese immigrants to North America. There are poor sanitary conditions and inadequate food, mostly rice, with limited privacy and safety. Yet this is where poor people are housed. My mother describes being sick during most of the voyage, and her brother often throwing up.

At some point during travel, they are offered bananas.

"What in the world is this? What do we do with it?"

They have never seen a banana before.

Somebody shows them how to peel it. But they already don't feel well from the travel (likely seasick as there is little ventilation deep in the ship). The banana is a taste they have never encountered.

They hate it and throw the bananas away.

Their travel conditions are so harsh, the destinations and the futures ahead of them so unknown, that to give up everything and make this trip is still mind-boggling for me to this day. They are on a boat in the middle of an ocean. They have never even seen an ocean before! There is no land anywhere in sight. Just endless water and waves and a vessel that doesn't stop rocking for weeks.

Their courage and the strength of will to survive is beyond anything I can imagine.

Land Ho!

After this arduous sea voyage, my mom and her family land in America! The ship's manifest reports their arrival at Seattle, Washington on December 24, 1916.

Even though this is not Ellis Island on the East Coast where most immigrants arrive, they still go through an immigration process. The family's last name is Bauchman . . . or more likely, it *becomes* Bauchman. With immigration back then, the arriving person states their name in their native tongue, in this case Yiddish or Russian, and the immigration officer writes it down the best they can spell it. So is Bauchman their name's actual spelling? My sense is that's just how it sounds to the official. But that's what gets scribbled down and it becomes their new name.

Though I know my grandmother called my grandfather "Neasil," the immigration officer gives him the name of Sam. My grandmother's name becomes Cecilia—an American name made up by some official. Since my mother arrives when she is only a young girl, by the time I come around, she is not able to accurately recall how to spell the names they had before.

But one thing they don't forget is the oppression of the world they left. They hate Russia, and once in America, vow never to speak Russian again. They speak only Yiddish. Of course, my mom is young and learns English. My grandparents learn English too, but not well.

They don't remain in Seattle. They travel to Cedar Rapids, Iowa, most likely by train. But why Cedar Rapids? There must have been some relative or the promise of a job opportunity there for my grandfather.

West to California: Boyle Heights

At some point, they leave Cedar Rapids to head back west, to Los Angeles. Once here, they settle in Boyle Heights, an area much like a Jewish shtetl (the name for Jewish villages in Eastern Europe).

Neighborhood streets are lined with storefronts, fruit stands, and people selling from pickle barrels (you reach in and pull a pickle from a barrel). Some locals peddle wares from pushcarts. All are run by Jews. They speak a variety of languages from Hungary, Czechoslovakia, Russia, and more—with Yiddish being the one common language to all Eastern European Jews. Pretty much everybody knows everybody. It is the largest Jewish community west of Chicago.

Many decades later, I ask a USC photographer to take a picture of me in front of this pharmacy on the corner of Brooklyn and Soto in Boyle Heights for a USC magazine. Being there feels like returning to my roots. Interestingly, the Ramirez brothers, who now run it, were my students.

In fact, Canter's famous delicatessen, which still exists today on Fairfax, originally opens on Brooklyn Avenue in Boyle Heights in 1931, a couple of doors down from Soto Street. This corner of Brooklyn and Soto is a hub of Eastern European Jewry at the time. People wanting to get together say, "I'll meet you at Brooklyn and Soto."

When her parents send my mother to school, they place her in a first or second grade class since she has no prior education. My mother is older and bigger than her classmates. She doesn't fit in and doesn't want to be there.

She drops out and educates herself, as she becomes an adult in America.

✦　✦　✦

CHAPTER 2

Arrival of Melvin F. Baron

Growing up in a safer, more stable environment in Los Angeles, my mother matures into a young woman.

One day, she meets Al Fink and is swept off her feet. He is a good-looking guy, dashing and colorful. Women of this time tend to marry young and my mother is no exception. She gets married at 21 years of age.

Al Fink and Sadie Bauchman are together six years before I appear on the scene July 29, 1932. I am born at California Hospital in downtown Los Angeles.

My 27-year-old mother excitedly names her boy Melvin Farrell Fink. I don't have any say about it. But once I get older, I express that I am not too happy with this.

"Melvin Farrell? Mom, where did you come up with those names?"

Apparently, not a lot of deep thought went into this choice. *Melvyn* Douglas and Charles *Farrell* are the matinee idols (movie stars) of the time. That's how I get my first and middle names.

Al Fink and Sadie

"Really, Mom? *Melvin? Farrell??* Those are the worst!"

My mom is fascinated by movies. She excitedly tells me of once going to an open studio casting call for extras (nonspeaking background actors). She is selected to be in the film and even gets a few lines to say during a scene. This is a fantastic moment for her!

Later on (after she remarries, to Leo Baron), I decide to sign everything simply Melvin F. Baron. I never tell anybody my middle name is Farrell. If someone asks, "What does the F stand for?" I answer, "Frank."

I eventually eliminate "Farrell" entirely and even the Melvin, and commonly go by Mel Baron. That is how I am mostly known in my field. A much easier name to live with.

The Fink Is Gone

Unfortunately for my mother, Al Fink has an affair early in their marriage. The woman's name is Mae. She is a waitress at Brooklyn Avenue Café, a popular restaurant I remember later going to as a kid.

Everything I learn of the affair is from my mother's telling, as I am only an infant when she has the courage to dump Al. Divorce is not nearly as common then as it is today—especially instigated by a young woman with a child. Being a single mother divorcee carries a certain stigma.

This takes guts on her part. She is young herself, facing an uncertain future raising and supporting a child. She has no reason to expect that Al will offer financial support and he never does (federal laws requiring child support don't exist until 1950).

My mother and I are on our own.

Fortunately, though not highly educated, my mom is street-smart. She knows how to survive and make things happen. Remember, this is an era where there are no iPhones, iPads, or Google searches to provide answers to life's problems. You have to figure it out.

She gets a job working at Bishop's candy factory doing piece work, meaning she doesn't get an hourly salary, but is paid based on how much product she produces. Of course, she isn't alone in doing whatever she can to make a living and survive. Generations of immigrants do this. My mom supports us.

I am well-fed, well-clothed . . . and apparently *quite cute.*

✦   ✦   ✦

CHAPTER 3

Leo Baron Appears

I am an infant sitting with my mother in a restaurant when a man comes over to our table and invites himself to sit with us.

His name is Leo Baron.

Apparently, much of their discussion revolves around me, though I am hardly aware of it at this time. But according to my mother, Leo falls in love with *me*. Obviously, I must have been adorable!

That starts their courtship, and when I am three years old, they marry.

Leo has been married before. Apparently, his prior wife took all his clothes, cut them up, and threw them out the front door. There was some drama in that relationship.

Leo Baron

Fortunately, Leo's marriage to my mother goes more smoothly. I hardly recall any arguments between them. Nobody throws anything. It all seems quite pleasant growing up. I always feel cared for.

I'm still overjoyed that Leo chooses to adopt me. Among other benefits, it erases the Fink from my name so I don't have to be Mel Fink my entire life! I become Melvin Farrell Baron (a positive step name-wise). In

11

fact, if you look at my birth records, it *only* reads Melvin Farrell Baron. You can't find "Fink" anywhere.

Early on growing up, I don't know about my biological father, Al. I have no memory of him. Leo *is* my dad and his whole family embraces me as one of their own. It never feels like I am adopted.

When I eventually learn of Al, I only hear bad things about him from my mother. She calls him "the Kaiser"—after Kaiser Wilhelm of Germany—an awful man whose thoughtless actions led to World War I.

It is not a great endorsement.

Life with Leo

My father Leo is a great storyteller.

But the family stories that he told are only of him as an adult. He does not recount tales of his early childhood or about his mom or dad. Looking back, I now find this kind of strange. My kids and grandkids love my early stories. I would have cherished learning those from my dad.

So I know little of Leo's family or their history. I do know he has two siblings, Betty and Sid. Another brother named Archie drowned from diving into the "Ocean Park Plunge" when he was just seventeen years old. (Ocean Park Plunge was one of several massive indoor seawater swimming pools near the ocean at the time).

I think Leo and his siblings are born in this country since they all speak English well. They relocate from New York to Los Angeles, though I don't know what's behind the move.

Is "Baron" even their real name? I have no idea.

Not Typical

Leo is not a typical father—not the kind of dad to toss a ball with his son or take him fishing on a boat. But I don't feel shortchanged by any of this. I feel loved my him, and I can do those other things with my friends.

Leo's Parents with Leo, Archie, and Betty. Sid is not yet born.
Notice Leo's outfit and Archie's long curls—typical for the time.

Leo more than makes up for this by being larger than life and incredibly fun to be around. Frankly, he is outrageous in many ways!

He and my mother are an interesting match. In contrast to him, my mom is quite conservative, a quieter private person. and not at all showy like Leo. Mom has a great laugh, but she won't make a joke or tell a funny story. That isn't her. That is Leo.

Mom doesn't initiate a lot. She won't suggest places for Leo and her to go or things to do with the kids. But if Leo calls on his way home from work and says, "Hey let's go out to the XYZ tonight," she'll be ready and waiting.

Leo takes my mother to new places—both to physical locations *and* to parts of her personality that she otherwise would never visit. Looking at pictures of them, you start to see something surprising.

Sadie and Leo at Santa
Anita Racetrack

Their life together is flamboyant, even when times are tough and money is hard to come by. Leo has eight seats at the Hollywood Legion Stadium. Prizefighting (boxing) is a huge thing during this era and my mother and I join Leo at these matches. Leo and my mom even fly from Los Angeles to Chicago to watch Rocky Graziano battle Tony Zale for the middleweight boxing championship.

That is pretty extravagant.

Leo also has box seats at Santa Anita racetrack. I have pictures of my mom posing in winner's circles wearing hats and furs. Though reserved at home, she is like a different person living this flashy lifestyle.

The truth is, even when not going out to glitzy affairs, she is always well-dressed, always has her hair done. She is always fastidious about all of it.

This is so interesting to me, considering that she grew up dirt poor in a poor village in a poor country. And it's not just about how *she* looks. It's also how my sister and I are dressed. Though I am too young to notice at the time, my mom later tells me that when I was a little kid

14

taking naps, she removed the shoelaces from my shoes, washed them, and put the clean laces back in. My mother irons my underwear and socks when I am a kid.

Who the hell does all that?

Clothes Make the Man . . . and the Man Has Clothes Made

Without a doubt, Leo has his own snazzy sartorial style.

When Leo enters a room, he commands attention. A big man with an even bigger personality, he wears a large ornate belt buckle. I don't know if he made it himself or has it designed . . . but there are jewels on it.

He has shirts made by a Chinese company called Sunsun: wool shirts that look like cowboy shirts in solid colors but with fancy fringe on them. All long sleeves. My father is embarrassed by a tattoo on his arm. I don't know how he got that tattoo or what it is supposed to represent, but he never wore short sleeves. People today use lasers to remove tattoos. Leo tries having it removed surgically and this leaves a huge scar.

Leo cares how I dress too, but in a different way from my mother. When it comes time for my ninth-grade graduation, he has a suit made for me to wear at the ceremony. Not off the rack. I have no idea what this cost, but at fourteen years old, I go to a tailor shop for a fitting. I doubt anyone else at our school gets custom suits. It boggles my mind when I think of this.

But that is Leo.

No Longer an Only Child

A few years after she and Leo marry, Sadie gives birth to another boy, Arnold. Sadly, Arnold dies from pneumonia when he is less than two years old. I have no memory of him.

Later, when I am six, my sister is born. Named after Leo's dad, Max, she is given the name of Maxine. My first memory of her is on her second birthday. My parents throw a party and Leo carefully spells out "Maxine" on a bowl of potato salad using green peppers for letters. Who needs a decorated cake when you've got potato salad?

But I have my own idea about my little sister's name.

I call her Doo-Doo.

Surprisingly, she never hated me for giving her this charming nickname. Even throughout our lives as adults, I sometimes greet her on the phone with: "Hey, Doo-Doo."

Doo-Doo and I have a fun childhood together, which included sharing a bedroom with twin beds. As her big brother, I often take care of her in some way or another.

Strangely, my sister is in her late teens or early twenties before she finds out that she and I have different fathers. At my mother's bidding, Al was an unspoken family secret. I never say anything to Maxine (or anyone else) about him. As a kid, I don't question this instruction.

Maxine finally learns the truth when a relative lets it slip. Not understanding what the heck they are talking about, Maxine asks our mother and is shocked to learn the truth. Yet this remains something that she and I never talk about. She knows that I know. But as far as we're concerned, there is never a time when we refer to each other as half-sister or half-brother. She is my sister. I am her brother. That's all there is to it.

✦ ✦ ✦

CHAPTER 4

My Mother's Parents

Beside my own parents, the other two adults most involved in my life are my mother's parents—my grandparents.

Growing up, I have no idea what my grandfather does for a living in Russia or what kind of work he does when first arriving in Los Angeles. As with many immigrants, it is possible he couldn't use the skills he had back in Russia to earn a living in America. I don't think he has any tradesman abilities that would allow him to be an electrician or plumber or cabinetmaker. Where he came from, there was no electricity or plumbing and likely nothing resembling fine cabinetry.

By the time I come around, the family has been here a while. Grandfather owns a pickup truck and does hauling and odd jobs. Every morning, he drives his truck downtown to Los Angeles Plaza Square, seeking to be hired, much like modern day laborers who hang around places like Home Depot. The fact that he has his own truck gives him an advantage, as I remember him as always working. He continues this through most of his life. I don't recall my grandfather ever complaining about illness or being in a hospital.

For me as a kid—his pickup truck is also great fun. He lets us sit in the truck bed as he drives to Ocean Park and the beach.

This is big time excitement!

Grandparents' House

I often visit my grandparents at their home on Chicago Street, right off of Brooklyn Avenue. It is a nicely furnished house with crocheted doilies (handmade by Grandmother) on all the armrests of chairs and the couch so they won't wear out. There is indoor plumbing (a bathroom!) in this home. On the porch is a swinging seat suspended by ropes. There is a large fig tree, plus a shed in the back to store Passover dishes. I expect all of this is a big step up from what they had in their Minsk village.

Wearing a mustache, my grandfather is an easy kind of guy who I always feel comfortable around.

In contrast, Grandmother is a bit tough. You can't get away with much with her! She is not the sweet, kindly, and affectionate grandmother that my future wife Lorraine is to our grandchildren.

I also have to say, though my grandparents live nearby, my mother isn't so fond of her mother (my grandmother). I'm sure my mom loves her mother, but I don't think she *likes* her very much. The woman just isn't warm and fuzzy. This may be due in part to the harshness of life in Russia and the difficult journey to America. Survival, not tenderness, may be utmost in my grandmother's mind. Life in Los Angeles continues to be a challenge for my grandparents as they do not have two extra nickels to give their grandchildren. Though we visit my grandparents and are all together on holidays, it never feels like a joyous time.

Still, during the early days of television, I vividly remember my grandparents driving to our house on Tuesday nights. My folks set up chairs in the living room like a theater to watch Milton Berle. Though my grandparents haven't learned English very well, they know enough to enjoy Uncle Miltie. Of course, the novelty of television at this time is pretty enticing too, even though our television is probably the size of my iPad and all the shows are in black and white.

Yet I have very fond memories of this.

Cuisine of the Old Country

Growing up, red meat and potatoes are the food staples, along with chicken. It is ironic today at restaurants that fish is so expensive. Everybody wants it! When I was young, only the poor ate fish.

We have fresh vegetables, but you have to purchase them almost daily. The old iceboxes aren't cold enough to keep food very long. Early refrigerators are better, but not as effective as those of today. There are no freezers at all—so you aren't defrosting snow peas and putting them in the microwave. Those don't exist yet either! The result is that many vegetables are canned.

One thing my grandmother brings from the motherland is its regional cooking. My mother uses a lot of those recipes as well. I still recall my mother and grandmother making sweet-and-sour cabbage borscht.

Basically, it's cabbage with some meat in it, with a kind of sweet-and-sour taste. My mom makes it with gingersnaps. Many years later, Lorraine tries to cook it, as does my daughter. But they can never quite capture the flavor. Then one day we are in Fromin's Deli in Santa Monica and I see sweet-and-sour cabbage borscht on the menu! The first time I eat that dish, I start to cry. It tastes exactly like my mother's recipe! Whenever I'm there, I get that bowl. With tears as my "side dish."

There exists another dish called beet borscht, but that's different. It is made with beets, though a lot of people also put a potato in it. You can serve beet borscht warm or blend it with sour cream to make a fabulous cold drink. But sweet-and-sour cabbage borscht is more like a bowl of hearty soup.

Mother's Siblings

Other adults in my life on my mother's side are her sister and brother. Aunt Katie is a lot of fun. She is kind of like Auntie Mame—eccentric, showy, and a free spirit. A real character: ostentatious clothes, makeup, and big hats. Never too serious, there is always a lightness to her. Sometimes my parents go away and Aunt Katie stays and takes care of us. I really enjoy that!

She gets married, but divorces early and never marries again. I don't even remember her husband. But he leaves her with their three kids—Millie, Willie, and Eddie—born in that order. As Eddie is the youngest, they call him Babe throughout his life, even as an adult! Somehow Aunt Katie raises all three of these children on her own.

How she does this is the source of rumors.

There are whispers that at one point, Aunt Katie was a madam with an "operation" around 7th and Alvarado in Westlake Park. That would certainly be one way to survive economically. While I'm not sure if it is true, I do know that she had a series of "men friends" who went in and out of our lives. Sometimes as "chauffeurs." I never really knew who they were.

My mother's brother, Morris, marries a woman also by the name of Sadie, but she is not very pleasant. Uncle Morris drops by occasionally to see my mother by himself. He is a good guy and always kind to me.

Uncle Morris is a caddie at Hillcrest Country Club. One of its members takes a liking to him and gets him a job as an assistant cameraman at Columbia Studios. That changes the trajectory of his life. Uncle Morris remains there until he retires, working on a wide variety of movies, from *Fort Ti* (with George Montgomery) to *They Came to Cordura* (Gary Cooper and Rita Hayworth) to *The Outlaws is Coming* (the Three Stooges) to *The Harrod Experiment* (Don Johnson and Tippi Hedren).

Uncle Morris is our Hollywood connection.

✦ ✦ ✦

CHAPTER 5

All the Comforts of Home

The world I am born into is far different from today's in all sorts of ways, many that younger people might not imagine.

One of these is what could be called "home conveniences."

Right to Your Door

It may surprise many people that *long* before modern grocery stores make home deliveries or Amazon drops off packages on your porch, we have an array of home delivery services.

On Mandalay Drive, a milkman delivers directly from a local dairy. This type of service originated out of necessity before homes have reliable refrigerators. Milk (especially before pasteurization) is very perishable. So daily delivery is needed to prevent it and other dairy products from spoiling before people can consume them.

Usually adorned in a white uniform, cap, and bow tie, the milkman drops by nearly every day. We leave a note saying what we need, and he leaves the requested milk, cream, butter, or cottage cheese in a metal box or grate on the back porch. Once we finish the milk, we put the empty *glass bottles* back on the porch to be picked up. The dairy cleans and reuses them—early recycling in action.

This is not the only such service.

Helms Bakery trucks come to our street as drivers blow a whistle to let residents know they are there. Parents buy rolls and loaves of bread while kids get jelly donuts. I still remember the long metal trays of newly baked bread on the truck. Fresh and fantastic!

We also have a produce truck come by, from which my mom purchases fresh tomatoes, lettuce, and other locally grown vegetables.

Believe it or not, there is also *a seltzer man*. He delivers bubble (carbonated) water in a pressurized bottle—you press a button and out it squirts. Many Jewish people get seltzer delivery. To illustrate the popularity of this drink at the time, waiters in restaurants typically ask, "Would you like seltzer or regular water?" Today, you're asked if you want a bottle of Perrier or San Pellegrino—essentially the same thing.

Of course, we also have the Good Humor Man driving through neighborhoods selling ice cream, mostly to kids. One of my favorites is a milk-nickel: an ice cream bar on a stick that costs five cents.

The Iceman Cometh

I would be remiss if I didn't describe one of the earliest and most important delivery services of all.

The ice delivery man. When I am very young, he isn't delivering bags of little ice cubes for drinks. He brings huge square blocks of solid ice (25 to 100 pounds!) to keep our food cold, using large sharp metal tongs to carry this very slippery heavy block!

Electric refrigerators aren't common until the late 1940s. Before that, we have iceboxes: large, standing refrigerator-size boxes made of wood. The ice block is placed in the upper section while the food is stored in the lower portion. This keeps food cold . . . sort of.

There are no large supermarkets when I am growing up. Just little neighborhood grocery stores where everybody knows everybody, plus a few of what we might today call "specialty stores"—local bakery, butcher, even a butter-churning shop. To supplement our deliveries, my mother visits stores pretty much every day, especially when we have an icebox since they do not keep foods as cold as a refrigerator. It isn't even close.

Fresh foods only store safely for a couple of days. Not only that, when refrigerators first become widely available, they don't have freezer sections, and there are no standalone freezers.

So my mother walks the couple of blocks from our house to the little Plaza Market grocery. While living in City Terrace (an area of Los Angeles just east of Boyle Heights), we have one market, one five-and-dime store (much like dollar stores of today but with much lower prices), one drug store, one cleaner, one gas station, a library, and the Terrace Movie Theater. That is it!

Modern Appliances

Life in our home is far easier than it was for my mom growing up in her small village. We have electricity and electric lights. We don't have to go to the local river to fetch water or to wash our clothes.

When we live on Mandalay Drive, we finally get a refrigerator—and even a clothes washing machine! But there are still no clothes *dryers*. Once wet clothes come out of the washer, we hand-feed them one piece at a time between two heavy rollers mounted on top of the washer. You crank a big handle to turn the rollers so the article of clothing moves between them to squeeze out excess water.

Then you go outside and hang the apparel on a clothesline to dry in the sun. My mom wears a special apron with pockets to hold the clothespins that she uses to attach our clothing to this rope. Fortunately, winters in California are not too cold. Clothes are hung out year around.

We also have our own backyard trash incinerator in which we burn our garbage. Common in Los Angeles (though rare in other parts of the country), backyard incinerators allow people to avoid paying for trash pickup service—but they greatly add to pollution. The city finally bans incinerator burning in 1957.

✦ ✦ ✦

CHAPTER 6

Home Entertainment

It's interesting that so much of today's modern entertainment is electronic. People don't feel the need to go outside their homes like they do just a short time ago. Of course, we have our own types of home entertainment when I am growing up too.

It is just a bit different.

Our "Internet"

Long before computers or even television, our primary "electronic" connection with the greater outside world is by radio. But these are not little portable units. They are big, usually wood-encased radios with multiple dials that you turn to find reception on different stations.

On Sunday, there are programs we listen to as a family: *The Jack Benny Show, Fibber McGee and Molly*—all high entertainment!

As a kid, I listen on my own to shows like *The Green Hornet* or *The Shadow* mysteries or *Jack Armstrong, the All-American Boy*. As these programs are only voices, music, and sound effects, they make full use of your imagination. You might be underneath the covers, envisioning all kinds of escapades as you listen to engaging stories. You can even join their "clubs" that are tied to the shows, as they offer "extras" to hook kids into being loyal listeners—*like secret decoder rings*—inexpensive promotional toys you buy to figure out secret codes mentioned during a show, or to send hidden messages back and forth to friends. It is very cool to a young boy at the time.

The Sound of Music

Long before audio cassettes or CD players or Spotify, we have a record player in the den. I love listening to music and playing drums along with records. I especially like what we call swing jazz. The famous Benny Goodman song, "Sing, Sing, Sing," is recorded in 1938 at Carnegie Hall. This concert is important in jazz history as it is the first time people sit in a concert hall to *just listen* to swing music rather than dance to it. When you hear this song today, it feels contemporary. It's terrific.

The drummer is the famous Gene Krupa. His drum solo during this song is fantastic and changes the role of the drummer from just an accompanying musician to a solo performer in the band. By this time, I have my own drum set and I probably play along to this Gene Krupa solo a thousand times trying to duplicate him. There is also Ziggy Elman on trumpet and Kenny Wilson on piano—a whole array of incredible players, especially notable as Benny Goodman has both Black and White musicians in his orchestra—starting in 1938!

As you can tell, music excites me!

But not just me. Our whole family plays records. This leads to a standout afternoon for my mom when I am a teenager. Milt Chortkoff, who owns the local cleaners, also teaches dance at an Arthur Murray studio. He and his wife are neighbors and family friends. Milt is also kind of a ladies' man, and one day when delivering our laundry, he puts on a record and dances with my mom. I mean—*they really dance*! Even I can tell he is good. She loves it! A wonderful moment for her—and for me to witness.

Years later, I get involved with Milt Chortkoff in a business venture. Recently, I reconnected with his brother Bert, who lives in Santa Barbara, for his virtual 90th birthday party!

People that I grew up with in City Terrace in the 1940s continue to be part of my life.

It's All in the Cards

Card playing is very popular with adults when I am growing up. One of my parents' favorite social activities is playing with other couples in homes. In one room, the women might be playing mahjong (a tile-based game out of China popular in the U.S.), while the men are playing cards in another room. But it isn't just a game of bridge with some pals. This is gin rummy, poker, pinochle—serious stuff with money wagered. My father plays a lot. I don't know how good he is, but a lot of money is bet.

My sister and I are around to watch all of this. Nobody cares. All the adults are smoking (including my parents) and everybody smells like smoke. One interesting thing is that while there is alcohol, nobody drinks mixed cocktails. Instead, it might be a bottle of bourbon or the like. They fill a shot glass, say "L'chaim," down it, and then no more drinking. That is so different from today when we go to someone's house and enjoy cocktails throughout the evening. For my parents, it is one bottle. One shot. You're done. I never see anyone drinking wine other than Manischewitz on the Jewish holidays. That is not a popular thing at the time.

Staying on Track

Though kids don't really play cards, Monopoly is a very popular board game at the time (still played today!). But my favorite is the electric train. Lionel model trains are very popular. Heavy and extremely well built, they run on electricity conducted through their metal tracks.

I connect all the tracks together and mount them on a plywood board, since it is hard to run on carpet or the bare floor. You have different types of cars that you make go fast or slow using a handle on a big electric transformer wired to the tracks that powers the train's locomotive. Well before the days of "safety councils," kids get lots of shocks from these setups!

Dog Days

While we live on Mandalay, we have a dog. I wouldn't say "my" dog as I am not a dog lover (years later, our kids will have cats). I don't even recall our dog's breed. Though later when I am in high school and preparing for college, my mother gets a chihuahua.

I am no fonder of that dog than the first. Chihuahuas are scrawny little creatures and not much fun. But my mother loves it as does my sister. Its name: Tito, of course.

✦　✦　✦

CHAPTER 7

Life for Mel: The Golden Child

My mother considers me "The Second Coming." I have no idea why. But in her mind, I am perfect and can do no wrong. Praise forever comes my way.

God bless her, Mom is unrealistic about who I am. We all have frailties and warts. We might be a super nice person and doing great things, but "perfect" isn't possible. Frankly, it is a heavy weight to bear to always live up to this image!

It is true that I am a pretty easy kid growing up. Pretty compliant. Not belligerent or defiant, I get along with people. This is my nature and how I still am with most people today.

Part of my agreeable behavior back then may be attributable to seeing my parents going through plenty of challenges, considering the Depression, World War II, etc. Everybody is having a tough time making ends meet and making life work. Some part of me doesn't want to add to their troubles.

For some people, a "perfect child" is simply one who doesn't cause problems. To better understand this, it helps to realize that the philosophy in many homes at the time is that "children should be seen but not heard." That doesn't mean my parents don't love me or shove my concerns aside. But what I have to say and my wishes are not the big priorities for them.

What *is* important to my parents is raising good kids. When I get a report card, my parents are more concerned with my "citizenship grades" than my subject grades. My report cards assess students in two parts: the first lists the typical subjects and a letter grade of A, B, C, D, or F. Another section concerns citizenship: behavior at school, in the classroom, and with other children. If I were to come home with bad citizenship reports or they get a call from the school about my behavior . . . that would not go well.

As I get older and enter those "rebellious teenage years," my behavior still remains mostly cooperative, though my folks do call me a "secret agent" when I am in my teens. They ask me a lot of questions but my answers are quite brief: "Yes . . . No . . . I don't know"—typical teenage replies. I don't want to tell my parents things that may not fit their idolized picture of me, including my feelings on different topics.

Of course, I am a teenager, so I am still going to do what I'm going to do. They just don't know. So in my mother's eyes, I am *still* perfect.

In fact, many years later when my mother is quite ill in the hospital and I think she is dying, I go in the room to be alone with her and pour my heart out. I tell her that I'm certainly not perfect. I'm mortal with faults like anyone else. I've made a lot of mistakes. I stumble.

I wish to relieve myself of that burden and figure this may be my last chance. As it turns out, she doesn't die and forgets everything I tell her! She lives a long time, and in her eyes, I remain the flawless son. He who walks on water.

Somehow, my sister has held onto similarly inflated views of me. Honestly, I'm still astonished she has stayed so fond of me. While I was showered with Mom's praise, and have had successful careers along with a great marriage and children, Maxine endured some struggles. Yet she has maintained wonderful feelings toward me. I mean, I am a good brother. But I'm not *that* good.

Confronted by Contrast

Of course, my upbringing seems entirely normal to me. It's the only way I have ever known. That's why it is so startling later when I see the contrast between my family and Lorraine's interactions with her folks.

Growing up, my parents and I have conversations and disagreements—to a degree. Certainly, if I ever raise my voice, my mother insists, "You can't speak like that to your mother."

That's why witnessing Lorraine and her family interact is both a breath of fresh air and shocking. After one of their exchanges, I pull Lorraine aside: "What are you doing? You're *talking back* to your parents?"

I always imagined that if I ever did that, my whole world would crash down. Maybe my parents would get divorced or they would throw me out! As a kid, I don't actually think through what disasters that might realistically occur. I am just sure that life will end as I know it.

To this day, I'm not a confrontational person. I work well with people. I have a good sense of what "game" I'm involved in. I call it a game, like academia is a game. Corporate America is a game. Being an entrepreneur is a game. You navigate all of them and the people involved once you figure out the "rules" of each world. I'll speak more on that later.

Big Brother

I enjoy the role of big brother. As children, Maxine and I have a really nice relationship and a lot of fun together.

One such amusing time is when the whole family goes to Pop's Willow Lake. This is a resort in northeastern San Fernando Valley. Pop's Willow has boating and swimming, a café and dance hall.

My sister, then a toddler, steps into the lake water, looks around puzzled and says, "Where's the shoap?"

Maxine thinks she is in a giant bathtub. We all crack up! This becomes a family joke that has endured ever since.

Of course, later on, my sister always wants to tag along when I am a teenager hanging out with my buddies. In fact, my mother commands it: "Take your sister."

I don't want to, but I am stuck with her. Otherwise, I can't go out. This happens so often that she gets to know all of my friends. Yet this isn't exceptional in our community. If somebody has a younger sister or brother, they come along.

I am always protective of my younger sister, though it is seldom needed. Everyone knows and respects each other. Still, by the time she is in junior high and I am in high school, if she ever is having an issue, whether academic or personal, I help smooth things out.

Lady of the House

Raising kids and running a household is never easy, especially back then. I don't think my mom ever works outside the home once she marries Leo. She is a housewife, which is typical at that time. All the fathers that I know work. All the moms are at home. Very different from today when husbands and wives frequently both work and can have careers.

In the home, my mom is in charge. Certainly in her managing me and my sister. Of course, if you get out of line, you hear the classic warning: "*Wait till your father gets home!*" But it is more a threat than a real promise of punishment. I never get spanked or anything like that. That doesn't mean I don't get grounded. "You can't go to the movies for six months!" Or "You can't use your bike for a month!" This is a pretty big threat since the bike is *the* major mode of transportation for a kid. But usually after a week, my parents forget about the punishment. Generally, the threats are huge and the penalty much lighter.

Housework Is Real Work

Of course, once my sister and I are at school, Mom doesn't have to take care of us full-time. But she still takes care of the house and that is a lot more work than it is today.

Like I said, there are no frozen foods that you can thaw or micro-wave. You go to the market daily. Since most women don't have cars, they either take a streetcar or walk to a local grocery store. You can only carry enough food for that day.

You're shopping more. Cooking more. Cleaning more. Appliances are not as efficient as they are today or simply do not exist. You don't have a freezer. You don't have a clothes dryer. Vacuum cleaners aren't commonplace until after World War II.

On Fridays, the floor is always freshly washed for Shabbat. In fact, my mother places papers on the floor for us to walk on so we don't bring schmutz into the house.

That doesn't mean my mother won't have help at times.

We have various housekeepers over the years, none memorable except for a young Japanese girl who lives with us on Mandalay. Hiromi is both a housekeeper and a nanny for my sister, who is between six and eight at the time. This is interesting since this Japanese girl comes to live with us soon after WWII. Obviously, my parents' view of the Japanese is more open-minded than those who want them confined in internment camps because of the war (more on that later).

Independent Woman

My mother teaches herself to read, eventually studying and passing the test to be a U.S. citizen. It is fascinating to me what people with so little education can teach themselves. Figuring out how to survive and succeed!

Growing up as she did, my mother learns to fend for herself. Sometimes far more than we might expect. One day when I return home from school, I am shocked to learn what she chooses to do that day.

While my sister and I are in classes, Mom takes a streetcar by herself to a dentist. While there, she has her teeth pulled and replaced with dentures (false teeth). What the need is for this, I have no idea.

My mother's petition for citizenship. You'll note
whoever filled out the form got some information wrong
(marriage date, name spellings, U.S. arrival date).

But let me be clear: she has *all* her teeth pulled. In one appointment! I doubt you could even find a dentist today willing to remove all of somebody's teeth in a single sitting! If my kids ever have even one tooth taken out—Lorraine and/or I are always there with them for support. Yet my mother does this all on her own. Even if that dentist administers some kind of anesthetic, the medication wears off at some point. She has to be going through some serious pain!

My mother was one tough lady.

Most people never knew she had false teeth. She was not the type to remove her teeth in front of others to place the dentures in a glass of water like some people do.

Apparently, my mother still had a certain level of vanity. Even if she didn't still have teeth.

✦ ✦ ✦

CHAPTER 8

Kids: Life on the Street

We live on quite a few streets when growing up: Eastern Avenue, Connor Place, City View Street (that does *not* have a view of the city), McConnell Place. . . .

Of all of the places we live, my most vivid memory is the house on Mandalay Drive in City Terrace, which my parents buy when I'm in third grade. We like to call City Terrace "the Beverly Hills of Boyle Heights" as it is a little upscale. I think my parents pay between $8,500 and $9,500 for the house—a comfortable home with a large bay window in front.

Situated on a very narrow street, there is barely room for two cars to pass each other. But for neighborhood kids—the street is our playground.

On Our Own

Our play is nearly all outside. That's where we *want* to be. All the kids from the neighborhood are out. We are simply told to be back by dinner.

There are very few organized sports at this time. Instead, we "organize" our own games and teams, and neighborhood kids of all ages play together. We play baseball. We play touch football. We play basketball. Near our house is a Jewish center with a basketball court. We can usually go there to find a pickup game.

Sometimes we add our own narration as we play different games. Like I am a radio announcer: "Okay, Mel Baron is up at bat. It's the ninth inning, with two on base. Everything depends on him! He waits for the pitch. . . ." This only adds to the fun!

We also play games that are less common today, like Three Feet Deep in a Mud Gutter. Despite the odd name, it is really a tag game that involves jumping over a wide strip of ground. The person that is "it" is stuck in the "mud gutter." Of course, we still enjoy the classics: hide and seek, Simon Says, hopscotch, jacks, and marbles.

Marbles is a big thing. Players sit on the sidewalk and line up marbles in a circle. Then each player takes a turn flinging their marble with their thumb and forefinger to hit a marble out of the circle. It is competitive with different kinds of marbles used, some made of glass or agate, some in special colors, some steelies (metal). You shoot with the agates or steelies, and win each other's marbles. Many years later, my buddy Lazar gives me a whole bunch of marbles to nostalgically call back those games we played when we were young.

I still have them in a jar.

Where Everyone Knows Your Name

As you might guess, things are simpler. Even though it is Los Angeles, life during this era resembles small town living as portrayed in movies where everybody knows everybody.

If you are behaving badly—being a jerk creating noise and havoc—somebody will call your mother because they know who you are and who your parents are. Your mother comes and drags you home!

Not a pretty sight.

Boys into Men . . . Not Quite Yet

Weightlifting is a big thing. Charles Atlas has an exercise program and a big advertising campaign that declares, "Don't be a 97-pound weakling and let somebody kick sand in your face. Become a strong man like me."

We see these enormous tough guys in our neighborhood lifting weights. They are our heroes.

At eleven years old, my friends and I decide to work out too! We will become impressive bodybuilders. Everyone chips in to buy a set of weights that we set up in my garage: our weightlifting club. Everybody encourages each other to lift bigger and heavier weights. We feel pretty good about ourselves.

Then one day in the middle of our workout, my mom comes in while we are grunting and groaning as we vainly struggle to lift a barbell. She watches us a moment, then walks over, bends down . . . and easily raises the barbell over her head. She then drops it and walks away.

We all just look at each other. We finally say, "Okay, we're done."

And that is the end of our weightlifting club.

Scoop of Vanilla

Children's love of ice cream seems timeless. Even when the choices were far more limited than today's.

Our special place is Currie's Ice Cream on the corner of Brooklyn and Soto. On top of the building is a giant fake ice cream cone they call a "Mile High Ice Cream Cone." Great advertising! Though unlike Baskin Robbins and its 31 flavors, Currie's has just three: vanilla, chocolate, and strawberry.

There is also a drug store on our corner with a soda fountain where we can get drinks and ice cream as well. Drug stores back then might serve sandwiches, pies, soft drinks, and milkshakes. You sit at a counter, as there are no tables. It is a common place for people to get lunch.

In fact, a large percentage of neighborhood pharmacies have soda fountains that dispense sodas into a glass or combine it with ice cream for an ice cream soda. Even when I work at Major Drug many years later, people call and ask us to hand pack the ice cream, as this is "fresher" than premade prepackaged pints.

Downtown with a Difference

Though not a place where most young kids hang out for fun, LA's downtown is a very different place when I am growing up.

Back in the mid to late 40s, downtown Los Angeles is the hub of social life and shopping. Near Union Station, where Broadway is the main thoroughfare, are all the big movie theaters, plus plush places like Bullock's downtown and Desmond's. These last two are upscale department stores for men's and women's (and kid's) clothes.

There is no internet shopping. A few mail-order catalogues exist (like Sears), but they are mostly used by people living outside the larger cities who have few local stores.

Today, most people live near a shopping center or mall. But when I am young, these don't exist. We take the streetcar to downtown to shop. I remember going to the fancy Bullock's downtown with my mother for clothes before my junior high school year starts. Then we eat at one of the nearby coffee shops or restaurants. Clifton's Cafeteria is always a favorite. Its interior looks like a mountain lodge, with a fake 20-foot waterfall emptying into a small "stream" running through the dining room past fake redwood trees! A life-size forest mural covers one wall. The place is like a rustic indoor mini-Disneyland long before Walt Disney ever builds his park. You can imagine how much fun this would be for a kid!

In fact, I decide to find out.

Some years ago, they reopen Clifton's after restoring it to recapture much of what it was like during that time. I go with my grandson Jack, along with my daughter and Lorraine. It is wonderful.

Early Explorers

We talk today about helicopter parents. There are no helicopter parents when I am growing up.

Kids roam around on our own. We ride our bikes all over. We get on street cars. For those who don't know, a streetcar is a wooden doorless train car that travels on metal tracks laid in streets. Each one has its own electric motor that gets power from a trolley pole that connects to an overhead wire. It is a terrific way for people to get around as it crisscrosses the city. (Streetcars later become enclosed and streamlined to look more like buses, though still electric.)

I take streetcars all over. I go downtown. I ride to my drum lessons in West Los Angeles all on my own.

This is all fine with my parents. They don't worry like parents do today even though, back then, if your child doesn't come home on time for some reason, parents have no idea where their kid may be! There are no cell phones. The best a kid can do is try to find a payphone and some chump change to call home.

For various reasons, streetcars eventually get replaced by gas-engine buses (all Los Angeles streetcars are gone by 1963). Ironically, what is Los Angeles doing today? Building all-electric Metro Lines.

Crazy Kids

Our independence doesn't mean we are always responsible. Sometimes we do goofy young kid stuff. That occasionally includes harassing people.

A woman on our street has a car, but doesn't drive well. For some reason, we think that gives us cause to hassle her. Her car has running boards (a narrow platform attached under the car's doors to help you step into a car, back when cars were higher off the ground than today). As she slowly drives down the street, boys jump on the running board for a "ride along." She doesn't crash into anything, but it freaks her out. And the boys get a good laugh.

Of course, as teenagers, we think smoking is cool and give that a try. But I can't stand the smell of it on my fingers. I figure, "This is stupid." Thank God I never become a smoker.

As we get older, our mischief turns to crashing parties. A bunch of us guys just show up and go in. We think we are hot stuff to do this. Our hope is to meet girls and maybe make out.

I remember going to one such party uninvited. Worse, I remember going in the bathroom—and peeing in somebody's perfume bottle! Why I think this is clever, I have no idea. Unbelievable.

Of course, there are many more escapades when I am a teenager. But I will save those tales for later in my story.

The Magic of Motion Pictures

In City Terrace, we have one movie theater: the Terrace Theater. This is *the* spot to go on weekends. Many times, we know the people selling tickets and sneak in. There is usually a double feature, which means two movies for one price! Plus, there are cartoons, and maybe an additional featurette. It can be a long afternoon in the theater!

A lot of the movies we see are *serials*—continuing stories with a new "chapter" shown each week. *Flash Gordon, the Green Hornet, Zorro,* and westerns like the *Lone Ranger, Roy Rogers,* and *Hopalong Cassidy.* Each episode ends in a cliffhanger. It might literally be someone hanging off the edge of a cliff, with you wondering if anybody will save them or will they perish? Or there might be a gunfight and you don't know who wins until you come back next week. Of course, after World War II, a lot of films are war movies that portray the Americans as wonderfully heroic.

The Terrace Theater is a hub for young people to hang around outside as well as inside the theater. As we get older, guys take girls there on a date. You can make out in the theater when the lights go down.

Yet even when I am really young, I walk to the Terrace Theater by myself just to watch movies. As I get a little older, I sometimes go downtown to the Orpheum Theater with my parents or just my mom. By the time I am thirteen, I take a streetcar to go there on my own.

Why? Because the Orpheum is a very special place.

Movie and a Show

The Orpheum Theater is very ornate with Art Deco decor. If you've been to the Grauman's Chinese or Pantages theaters in Hollywood, that is what movie theaters look like during this time. There is one large room with a big screen, not a bunch of smaller rooms with a different movie playing in each like today.

But the real magic here is when the Orpheum Theater not only shows a movie, but afterward has a live band orchestra play with major talent: Harry James, Cab Calloway, Gene Krupa.

The big curtains close after the movie is over. When these curtains open again, the band is already playing as the stage automatically moves out toward the audience! It is stunning to see! These are big full bands with twenty or more people. Sometimes with a singer at night. It is a real show.

I sit through the movie just to see the stage show. Then sometimes I stay in my seat to watch the movie replay again and hours later see another band. Downtown's Paramount Theater also has live shows.

This is big-time stuff for me!

Staring at the Heavens

As a kid, I go to the observatory in Griffith Park. It has a planetarium (only the third to be built in the U.S.) and a big telescope you can look through. We see amazing stuff as kids! It really excites our sense of wonder.

There is also the Griffith Park Zoo with animals from around the world. You must remember, this is before television and nature shows. Can you imagine what it was like for a kid to see all kinds of strange exotic animals for the first time—like an eighteen-foot-tall giraffe?

Griffith Park also has a big fancy merry-go-round. (Many years later, we take our grandchildren to pony rides there too.) As a kid, I don't go to the park on my own since it is too far out of the way.

The Pier that Used to Be

While Griffith Park's carousel is great, there is a carousel at the beach too, on the Ocean Park Pier. Though no longer there, this pier is much frequented at the time.

The pier is surrounded by a Jewish area that is a popular place to stay for a week during summer. Taken here when I am young by my grandparents, we stay around Rose Avenue and visit other people staying at the beach.

The pier is big, with a full array of rides and booths. In a way, it is sort of like a Disneyland over the water. The ride I like most has cars you sit in by yourself or with a friend as you ride around on the rink's slick metal flooring. A rod extends upward from each car to touch electrical wires that power the vehicles. Very environmentally friendly!

You are *supposed* to drive in circles around this rink. But most people purposely ram their car into everybody else's! These are *bumper cars* and you are always in crash mode. Each car has thick bumpers on all sides so they are never damaged . . . though drivers do get knocked around. It is the coolest thing!

This is the highlight for me, even more than the big Ferris wheel. Or the even bigger *double* Ferris wheel that is on the pier at one point. With tons of lights strewn all over the metal structure, it is very cool-looking at night and takes you high up for great views of everything! There is also a wooden roller coaster, far larger and faster than the mini version on the Santa Monica Pier today. The roller coaster is always fun and a little hair-raising. But with both it and the Ferris wheel—you just sit in them. You don't *do* anything. Driving the bumper cars is the thing for me.

My other favorite activity is getting corn on the cob. I don't remember ever having this at home, as our corn is already cut off the cob and served on plates like other vegetables. Eating off the cob is a new experience for me and each cob comes on a stick—easy to eat with no mess on your hands.

As teenagers, we spend a lot of our summertime at the beach. You just grab a streetcar at City Terrace and transfer to the Blue Bus to go all the way. You bring your bathing suit and towel and look for girls at the pier attractions and on the sand.

While my and my friends' own weightlifting careers are short-lived, lots of people watch the bodybuilders heft big weights at Muscle Beach—an outdoor gym area on the sand. Famous bodybuilders like Jack LaLanne and Joe Gold (who lives in Boyle Heights and later starts Gold's Gym) work out here. It is an exhibition—you go to watch them do all their stuff.

I also like to body surf in the ocean. Real surfing hasn't really arrived yet, so we jump in the water, swim out, and ride the waves back using our bodies like surfboards. Of course, getting a tan is essential even then. Dermatologists today would cringe at us! Now they want you out of the sun, but we couldn't get enough of it. There is no such thing as sunscreen. In fact, we put on oil to help us tan *more*. We even add iodine to the oil to darken faster! Both girls and guys get sunburned badly. God only knows the damage we do.

Hanging Out in Alleys

Starting around eighth grade, a bunch of us guys living on Mandalay spend time at the bowling alley. It is a pretty popular pastime.

But those bowling alleys are different from today's. We don't have elaborate lighting like there is now, and bowling lanes are not automatic. When you knock over pins, *workers* roll your bowling ball back to you down the alley and physically remove any fallen pins. After your second try, they roll the ball back again and reset all the pins back to their standing positions by hand. They run up and down between different lanes to reset pins! Sometimes you wait a bit before they get to yours.

Interestingly, I never really bowl again as an adult. Some of our friends are in bowling leagues, but Mel and Lorraine are not. I peak when I am in eighth and ninth grades.

Professional Sports

Professional sports? There are none! When I am growing up, Los Angeles does not have *any* major league sports teams! In fact, the National Football League (NFL) doesn't even exist.

Instead, we focus on *college* football.

I spend a lot of time watching USC play at the Coliseum. That is a big event. As with professional sports, you buy a ticket for entrance. Except I never do.

I sell newspapers outside the stadium. Costing just seven cents, the papers list the players' lineup on the front page and are cheaper than buying a program inside. So it is a great place to sell papers. Of course, when somebody hands me a dime, I fumble desperately as "I try to find" three pennies to make change. Because people are rushing to their seats for the game, they usually say, "Oh just keep it." So I create a profit margin. I already have some of my father's entrepreneurial skills!

But the best thing about selling papers is we are allowed into the stadium for free toward the end of the first quarter. We can watch until near the end of the fourth quarter when we have to go out to sell papers again after the game. That's how I watch college football.

The National Basketball Association does not exist, either. However, there is major league baseball by this time. But with no major league teams in Los Angeles, we listen on the radio to the Yankees and (Brooklyn) Dodgers games on the East Coast.

Fortunately, Los Angeles does have some minor league baseball teams: the LA Angels and the Hollywood Stars of the Pacific Coast League.

And again, I don't pay for tickets.

At fourteen I get a job selling at a hot dog stand at Wrigley Field (near the Coliseum) where the Angels play. That's how I am able to see them. I still remember some of the players' names: Broadway Billy Schuster and Alban Glossop. These are terrific games!

Big-Time Racing with Small-Time Cars

Also popular during this period are midget auto races. Though the cars are small, the engines are powerful. I watch them at Gilmore Stadium on Fairfax, where CBS is now located along with the Town and Country Market. Because Gilmore is the first venue built solely for midget cars (in 1934), some people credit Los Angeles as the birthplace of midget racing. Gilmore racing lasts until 1950.

Cars speed around an oval *dirt* track. While nothing compared to Indy 500 races, we love it! A neighbor shouts, "Hey, we're going to midget auto racing. Wanna come along?" And I go! Star drivers have their own following and I still remember a few of their names too, which is weird.

So no, we don't have TVs. There are no computers. Social media and iPhones do not exist.

But we do have a lot of fun.

✦   ✦   ✦

CHAPTER 9

Religion

Though my mother's family is Orthodox in Russia, I don't recall my grandfather wearing the traditional undergarments here. Of course, he wears a yarmulke.

He and I go to services in Boyle Heights, where all the synagogues are Orthodox. Though I like spending time with my grandfather, I pretty much just sit there during these services—having no idea what is going on since every word is spoken in Hebrew.

Of the three different shuls I attend with him, the most famous is the Breed Street Shul. It has this Eastern European architecture, topped by a Russian dome. Apparently, it's built in "the Byzantine Revival style"—with round arches and patterns formed by two alternating colors of brick. Interior wall illustrations call to mind Eastern European folk art. It has a real old-world sensibility, which must be comforting to the mostly immigrant congregation. It is *the* spiritual place for the Boyle Heights community.

To attend, everybody dresses up. No Levi's and casual shirts. You have on slacks, shirts and ties, and dresses, especially on high holy days. Unfortunately, what Breed Street Shul doesn't have is air conditioning. The Orthodox men pray in heavy woolen clothing. It is a hundred degrees outside and they are wrapped in old wool tallises, not the thin silky ones we have years later. As a result, it sometimes smells a bit—and not in a good way.

On Yom Kippur, people are fasting in there all day. Today, if you go to temple, there is air conditioning and you're there only an hour or two.

Even though I don't know what anyone is saying, it all makes quite an impression on me. Men and women are seated in separate sections, with the Rabbi and cantor in the center. This is real theater. The cantors, called hazzans, wear the big hats and boy can they bellow—with no microphone! And this is a huge facility. I've heard it is *the largest* orthodox synagogue west of Chicago between 1915 and 1951. I believe it! Today it is the Breed Street Community Center.

My grandfather and I also attend a smaller nearby synagogue called Cornwell Street Shul. Though they have an upstairs balcony where all the women sit, it is more mundane compared to the Breed Street Shul.

When I am bar mitzvahed, it is at the Miller Street Shul in City Terrace. A small wooden building with a room in the back that functions both as a kitchen and a school room.

It is interesting to realize all three of these shuls are named after the streets where they are located—very different from how most schuls are named today.

Passover Passing Out

Though I don't know Leo's religious upbringing, he does not seem as devout as my mother's parents.

I still recall Passover at my grandparents' house. My family is there, along with my Uncle Morris and his two children, Morty and Marsha. We are all little kids, giggling and talking, while my grandfather performs *the entire full-length Seder*—in Hebrew. This goes on for hours!

Eventually we kids are falling asleep. Slipping under the table. Desperately wondering, "Where is the food?!"

Seeing this, Leo prompts my grandfather, "Come on. Let's move it along and skip a few pages. It's time to eat."

Grandmother is off in the kitchen focused on preparing the food. But when my grandfather skips *even one paragraph*, we hear yelling from the kitchen: "What do you think you're doing? Read what's in the Haggadah!"

Frankly, we find this pretty funny. More giggling for the kids!

"Bring Me a Velchade"

Hebrew school at Miller Street Shul is overseen by Rabbi Rosenfeld, a much older man in a dark blue suit and vest. He has a club foot and wears a special shoe.

He also has one other noteworthy fashion accessory: a yardstick. Your knuckles know it whenever you are fidgeting in his Hebrew class. That's when Rabbi Rosenfeld raps you!

We are all learning Hebrew and our Torah portions. We learn our haphtara. It is not where we 12-year-olds want to be. We have to attend because our parents send us. But at least I am with my buddies so we are hanging together.

While I forget most of what the rabbi teaches, my friends and I certainly remember the phrase when he yells: "Bring me a Velchade!" Somebody then has to jump up, race out of the school, run to the corner store, buy a bottle of Welchade grape juice, and rush it back to the rabbi. There is no air conditioning in the classroom, so he starts to overheat. For some reason, he never thinks of getting a bottle ahead of time.

For years after, when I am with friends from this class, someone will suddenly call out, "Bring me a Velchade!" We all crack up at this inside joke while no one around us has any clue what in the world we think is so funny!

Bar Mitzvah Boy

Even though my dad isn't so pious, my parents think it is important for me to be involved with Judaism and get bar mitzvahed. I'm guessing this is in consideration of my mother's parents.

That's one of the great contradictions of Leo. Though religion means little to him, he not only encourages me to be bar mitzvahed, we have a huge bar mitzvah party! It is gigantic! It is catered! Along with that, he also makes sure we celebrate the high holidays with my grandparents. But when Christmastime comes, he celebrates that too. I am eleven when we get a small tree plus presents from Santa. Even though we know we are Jewish, my sister and I are not against this. We get Christmas presents. Hanukah presents. The best of *both* worlds!

I don't think my grandparents ever knew about it. Of course, when Lorraine finds this out later on, she is aghast. "Are you kidding me?"

After Leo passes away, there are no more Christmases at our house. And there hasn't been any since.

✦　✦　✦

CHAPTER 10

World Events: Great Depression and World War II

While my stories have thus far centered mostly on life in the Baron household and my youthful adventures, I cannot ignore that all of this is taking place concurrently with some of our country's most difficult times in history.

Two major events happen while I am growing up: one that begins before I am born (The Great Depression) and the other that starts when I am just nine years old (World War II).

The intense drama of these occurrences may be hard for younger readers to imagine today, though the COVID epidemic certainly has impacted our country on a national scale.

But these are different.

Stock Market Crashes

The stock market crash of October 1929 wipes out millions of investors and sends the country into a panic. It triggers the worst economic downturn in the history of the industrialized world. It lasts ten years.

Businesses close. Massive numbers of people are without jobs. Savings are wiped out by the dual collapse of the stock market and nearly half the nation's banks (bank accounts are not insured against loss then).

Hungry people stand in long food lines down sidewalks, waiting for a free meal from charities because otherwise these people have nothing.

The Great Depression reaches its worst point in 1933, one year after I am born. Taking office in 1933, President Franklin Roosevelt conducts a series of "fireside chats" in an effort to calm panic and restore confidence, broadcasting his voice over the same radio stations that only a short time before were mostly sources of music and entertaining shows.

Given all this, it is curious that our family is never without food. Nor do I ever hear any discussion about not making rent or having enough money. If my parents talk about this, my sister and I are never party to it.

My father is a "street person"—a survivor—who is always hustling. He finds ways to make money and take care of us.

Boyle Heights is a Jewish community where everybody knows one another, and there is a lot of sharing. This certainly is true with family. If a relative is traveling, they stay at our house. They might stick around for weeks, but nobody puts people up in hotels. Guests sleep on the porch or couch.

While The Great Depression doesn't have a big impact on our lives, what follows it certainly does: World War II. American involvement in the war starts around the same time The Great Depression ends. There is no breather. World War II impacts the entire world in vast and horrible ways.

It Begins

I have a vivid memory of December 7th, 1941.

I am in the car with my mom and dad, driving toward Riverside. We are listening to music on the car radio when an announcer interrupts to report that the Japanese have bombed Pearl Harbor.

I am nine. I don't understand the significance of this. But I can tell my parents are frightened.

While the war is fought far away overseas, most everything at home is dedicated to the war effort and producing whatever is needed by our troops. Those reading this book need to understand, *the world is at war.* Not every country participates in the fighting, but every country knows they will be affected by the outcome.

The future of the entire world is literally at stake.

War Bonds

The war won't be funded simply through taxes or printing dollars. People are called upon to buy war bonds.

Though you are *buying* the bonds, it is more like you are loaning money to the government and will be paid back with interest. Much like a savings bond, you buy it at a certain price, say $18.75, and it accrues value over a number of years until it "matures." Then you can turn it in and get $25 back. I'm sure the idea is that by the time people turn them in, the war will be over and we (hopefully) will have won. Even as a kid, you might save up until you can get the $18.75 together and go buy a bond.

There are posters and appeals at movie theaters and on radio to buy war bonds. Hollywood celebrities like Cary Grant, Laurel and Hardy, Bob Hope, Humphrey Bogart, James Cagney, Barbara Stanwyck, Bing Crosby, and Carole Lombard travel the country encouraging people to purchase bonds.

When I am bar mitzvahed during the war, instead of money as a gift, people give me war bonds.

Saving for Our Future

While we are encouraged to *spend* money to buy war bonds, we are encouraged to *save* other items.

I recall saving the foil from inside packages of cigarettes. Both my parents smoke and I roll the foil into little balls to turn in. This foil back then is made of tin, which is desperately needed in the manufacture of things for the war. Tin cans are also saved.

We tie our newspapers into bundles and bring them to school for paper drives. Similarly, we turn in bacon grease that we pour into jars.

Victory Gardens

In the city, most people don't have giant yards, but if you have even a little bit of land, you are encouraged to plant a victory garden. Radishes, carrots, whatever you can grow. Posters urge people to can their own vegetables to free up factory-processed canned foods to be used by the military.

In fact, there are limits on how much food people can buy in stores.

Rationing

There are limitations on what people can purchase during the war, as so many things are repurposed to help win the global conflict. This includes food. You get ration cards and use up precious "ration points" to buy things like butter, sugar, coffee, fats, cheese, canned milk, and meats. In fact, some restaurants start meatless menus on certain days to help protect the country's meat supply. Macaroni and cheese becomes popular at home, since it is filling, inexpensive, and requires few ration points.

Some unexpected items become rationed, or rather, unavailable. Like nylon stockings for women. Suddenly nylon is needed for military parachutes, rope, flak jackets, shoelaces, and even the fuel tanks for aircraft.

Gasoline is rationed too. You place a little sticker on your car that indicates how much gas you can buy, depending on what it is needed for. If you are a doctor or in some other vital profession, you are allowed to purchase more. I find it odd that my father regularly goes on long drives to Caliente in Mexico to race horses. How he gets gas for those trips, God only knows.

Spirit of the Times

A patriotic spirit takes over the country during World War II. Very different from all the divisiveness during Vietnam and later wars, and what we witness in our country today.

Everybody is working together to make victory happen. Joining the military is an honor. Some are drafted but many volunteer. I vividly remember going down to Union Station in downtown LA and seeing family and relatives being shipped out. People do not fly much in the early 1940s. Trains are the major transportation moving people across the country.

These departures are very difficult. When a loved one goes off to war, people aren't sure if they will come back.

Limited Information on the War

People are desperate to learn how the fighting is going overseas and who is winning. But there is no internet, no social media, no "instant" reporting. There isn't even television!

The only footage of the war effort is at movie theaters.

In addition to their scheduled movies, theaters show newsreels. These ten-minute mini-documentary movies screen actual footage of Allied military operations, as well as other events on the home front. They might show you a short clip of a battle or a naval ship in action. Nothing too graphic, but enough to give some sense of what is going on.

In reality, these aren't always entirely truthful. The government wants to keep up American optimism. The short films tend to be upbeat with rousing narration and music, like "we're winning" and "go team!" When battles go badly, the newsreel may still mention it. But it is under-reported for sure.

Also, what is depicted and described in those movies is weeks old, since it has to be filmed overseas, then edited, and have narration and music added before being sent to theaters. For more up-to-date information, people rely on newspapers and especially radio. Families sit around large radios in their living rooms, hungry for news. Again, some of it is propaganda designed to keep up morale at home.

In fact, most of us do not learn of the Nazi atrocities against the Jews until after the war is over. I do not know if this is kept hidden from us by our own government, or if they don't know of it until the war is nearly over. But few people know that Nazis put Jews and others in concentration camps and gas chambers.

War at Home?

Even before the United States enters the war, we are hearing about the global fighting. There is great fear here that the U.S. can be attacked. There are supposedly even sightings of submarines off our coasts.

After the Japanese attack Pearl Harbor, things intensify. There is a sizable Japanese population in Los Angeles, and our government worries that these Japanese Americans will join the Japanese aggressors. The government begins rounding up Japanese people and putting them in internment camps. Oddly, no Germans are taken. We're in this massive war with Germany, but we are not putting Germans in camps? They are a bigger threat, in my opinion. Hitler is rampaging through parts of the world, taking over countries like Poland, Czechoslovakia, France. Of course, as a kid, I am not savvy enough to understand it all. But thinking about it now: Germans are White. Japanese are people of color.

While I do not know anyone personally who is put into those camps, there are many Japanese families living in Boyle Heights and City Terrace. We see them all the time. We also live close to Little Tokyo, a ten-minute drive away. Many of those taken away lose their homes and businesses. It's terrible. I remember my dad coming home with a car loaded with groceries, canned goods, and more because Japanese merchants in these neighborhoods are liquidating their stores before they are taken away to camps. There is already rationing at the time, and my dad stores the canned goods and other items out of sight in our garage.

Many people are upset that these people are being interned, including my parents. But others accept the U.S. propaganda that we should be fearful of anyone Japanese. As a country, this is a blot on our existence.

I later have a Japanese secretary at USC who was interned as a child. A lovely woman, both she and her husband received some funds during their lives as a form of restitution.

Keeping Us in the Dark

There is great fear that our coasts might be attacked and bombed by aircraft, just like what happened at Pearl Harbor.

My mom is a block warden, managing our street. She reminds people to pull down shades at night and turn off lights. Same as they are doing in Britain, where all windows and doors are covered at night so no light is visible to enemy pilots. Besides being inconvenient for us, it only feeds our fears.

Of course, that doesn't stop some people from taking advantage of the situation. Like my father.

There is a family down the street that my father intensely dislikes. I don't know why. But my father calls them one night, since my mom is a block warden, and "reports" that we can see this family's stove pilot light is on. Now, it is entirely unrealistic that this could be seen (either by my father or an attacking squadron of airplanes). But my father insists that they must turn it off every night.

Of course, Leo being Leo, he doesn't stop there.

Leo also orders them a grand piano. I don't mean he buys it for them. He orders it *as if he is the husband*. The company delivers this big grand piano to this neighbor and tries to collect payment.

"Hey Mister, I'm just a delivery guy. You gotta pay me for this piano."

I don't know how this family finally gets out of it, but I do remember it causes quite a loud commotion!

War Finally Over!

When we get word that the war is finally over in 1945, people are literally celebrating in the streets! Everyone is out with each other, smiling, dancing, hugging!

I am a teenager and see the immense feelings of relief for everybody. I, too, am very happy the war is over. Happy that family and friends will be returning home. This is a huge deal.

My father is never drafted. There is a tier system determining who gets drafted: single men go first, married men without children next, and married men with children are third. That's probably why my dad never goes.

Leo's draft card. I am surprised by his elegant signature!

There is a similar tier system later during the Korean War as well. Exempted people at that time includes those in college. If you are enrolled and maintain certain grades, you won't be drafted. This affects the course of my life, as I am then of draftable age.

◆　◆　◆

CHAPTER 11

Leo's Careers: Wild and Crazy

Despite living through the Depression and World War II, I never feel our family was wanting. That is a testament to both of my parents, especially my father's ability to make a living.

He really cares about our family. Yet like I said, Leo is not the kind of father who plays catch or fields grounders with his son. There is no getting in the street and tossing a football. I'm not sure why he is never part of that type of play since he is very involved in most other areas of my life and is always interested in whatever I am doing at school. Both parents attend every event I am involved in, whether playing my drums or acting in a school musical (yes, you read that right—Mel was in a musical!).

Once I am a little older, he brings me along on many of his work adventures, so we have that precious time together.

Early Employment

My father never completed high school. His education stopped at the eighth grade. As with many families back then, Leo and his siblings may have been encouraged to find work early on to help their immigrant family survive.

My first knowledge of Leo's working life is a photo I see of him with other men dressed in suits at what looks like a holiday party for Globe Bottling Company. The fact that Leo is wearing a suit shouldn't mislead one into thinking he has some nice white-collar job. All the men wear suits at such a celebration. That's how people dressed at the time. My guess is Leo was more likely driving a truck or selling their soda pop.

I am told that Leo later worked for a company selling auto insurance. Since the first auto insurance policies originated in 1897, this is certainly possible. The next story I heard was that Leo sold used cars. This might be at a used car dealership or he may have bought and sold them on his own.

These would mostly be basic cars. There isn't the variety of luxury cars (and certainly *no* foreign cars) like those that serve as status symbols today in cities like Los Angeles, where people trade in vehicles every few years for new ones. During the challenging times of the Depression and the second world war, most people just need transportation. And most families I know that own cars, own only one.

There are exceptions to this, of course, and Leo is one of them. I remember him driving a 1946 Buick Roadmaster. This is the first production year after the war ends, when automobiles become more available again. The Roadmaster is a striking car with a streamlined bullet shape. People stop on the street to look at it. For a flamboyant man like Leo, this car is a perfect fit.

Then as now, automobiles play important roles in people's lives . . . even for kids when they become of driving age. Yet as I get my first one, it will hardly be a status icon. Leo brings home a surprise gift for me: a car! I can't believe it.

Especially when I see it. I wouldn't call it a head-turner. At least not in a positive way. It is a *very used* Model A Ford. Ford only built them between 1928 and 1931, so this car was made before I was born.

Naturally I inquire, "How did you get this?"

"Oh, I flipped some guy for it."

Apparently, somebody owed Leo money and rather than being paid, Leo offers to flip a coin for "double or nothing." If the other person wins the toss, the debt is erased—a tempting prospect for that person. But if Leo wins, the debt doubles.

Leo wins and takes the car as payout. Again, this is Leo.

Truth is, it is a fun car, but very basic. It has an accelerator, brakes, an engine. With a manual clutch transmission. It seats two—inside. It also has a two-person rumble seat—an upholstered outside seat that unfolds from what normally would be the car's trunk. The car is not particularly comfortable.

I only have it a short while. It always needs work and I am not a person who tinkers with cars. I might appreciate having one today as a novelty, but at the time, it just seems like an old car to me.

Earning Green with Oranges

The first of Leo's businesses that I recall is when I am about seven or eight. We are living in an apartment around the Coliseum area of Los Angeles, when Leo comes up with a venture involving orange pulp.

There is a Sunkist plant in Ontario, California where they make orange juice. A lot of farmland surrounds Los Angeles and these orange groves are a major industry. You can drive miles and miles and see nothing but orange fields!

The Sunkist plant squeezes juice from the oranges and discards the pulp left behind as waste. Somehow Leo learns that if you feed this pulp to cows, it raised the butterfat content of their milk.

So he buys a dump truck and starts making drives to Ontario. I remember going with him: he pulls the truck into a specific spot next to the Sunkist building. They open a chute and all this pulp scoots down it into his truck. I don't know how much he pays for this or if he pays at all. They are probably just happy to get rid of it!

Then he drives to dairies. He convinces the owners that this pulp is going to increase their cow's milk butterfat. Leo is gregarious and a good salesman. Also a smart one. He says, "Let me deliver you the first load at a discount (or for free) and you try it."

Leo creates a thriving business of delivering orange pulp to dairies. He makes a ton of connections and gets numerous accounts!

But he is driving from the Coliseum area to Ontario to pick up pulp. This is a very long drive and there are no freeways. This prompts the family's move to City Terrace because it is near Garvey Avenue, a better route to Ontario that cuts off 40 to 60 minutes of travel time.

Once he makes the pickup in Ontario, he delivers to the dairies, dumping his truck's whole load of sloshy pulp at one dairy. I still remember the pulp's intense orange smell. Wonderful! On the other hand, if you've been around dairies, you know they have a very different odor—of manure. A spectacular contrast.

Leo makes several pickups and deliveries in one day. Though a lot of dairies are close to Los Angeles, I sometimes go with him as far as the Roger Jessep Dairy in Bakersfield—a whole day's drive by itself. Leo makes good money as the dairies really appreciate what he is providing to them.

I love being with him on these trips. I am like a big boy, driving around in a truck. It is a real day's work! And I get to spend time with my dad.

. . . And an uncle I have never met before.

✦   ✦   ✦

CHAPTER 12

Leo's Siblings: Betty and Sid

I have no recollection of ever meeting Leo's mother or father, Mary and Max, or much of the rest of their family other than Leo's siblings, Betty and Sid.

The oldest of the siblings, Betty marries Phil Winnick, a jeweler. Even though he is in the jewelry business, they have a modest lifestyle and home. When I visit, I love playing with my cousins Marilyn and Milt.

Then there is brother Sid, a true character, like Leo.

Neither Leo nor Sid have much formal education. I consider them street people because they survived on the street—figuring out how to make a living and to make life work for them. I even saw a photo of Leo and Sid as young kids, standing in the back of an open bed truck selling watermelons.

Truth is, I don't meet Sid for the first eight years of my life.

As the two brothers grow up, Sid takes a bit of a detour and ends up someplace out of town that isn't talked about. Not until I am eight years old. I know that's my age because we had just moved into a house on Eastern Avenue in City Terrace and I wanted to be a Cub Scout. But I am not allowed since you must be nine to join.

One day my parents announce: "Uncle Sid is coming to live with us."

Turns out the reason I've never met him is that Uncle Sid has been residing in the "big house" (prison). He was sent there because of check kiting—writing bad checks while you know you don't have money in the bank to cover them. I am not sure how long Sid has "been away."

My parents take one of their few trips: to San Quentin prison, just north of San Francisco. A condition of Sid's parole is that he is placed into my father's custody and my father gives him a job. Families were closer-knit at this time and these two brothers loved each other. There is no doubt in Leo's mind that he will take in Sid. Nor does it feel strange to me to have Sid live with us and work in my dad's business. Sid rides in the truck with my dad, and with me when I go along.

Sid and Leo

Brothers: A Matched Set

I really like Uncle Sid. He is gregarious like Leo and very loving to me. I always feel close to him.

Both he and my dad were large and not what I'd call "refined men." These are two guys trying to survive day to day. Kind of like gunslingers—they take on whatever challenges and opportunities that come their way. There is no grand plan.

Being rough and tumble, they don't hesitate to get in fights when called for. I hear of one time when Leo and Sid are walking down the street and a guy in a car shouts some anti-Semitic slurs at them. Leo and Sid pull this guy out of the car through his window, beat him up and leave him there. Fortunately, I never actually see my dad get into a fight. I also don't know if he had a gun, but I would guess so.

Not long after Sid comes to live with us, he meets Pebe. They really like each other, though not everything in their courtship is without mishap.

Sid is excitedly getting ready for one of their early dates. In the cupboard, he spots some kind of powdered talcum deodorant and puts it under his arms. At least Sid *thinks* it is talcum deodorant.

It is actually my mother's denture powder, used to hold my mother's dentures (false teeth) in place on top of her gums. When you add water to the powder, it activates a strong adhesive.

So Sid goes on his date and naturally, he perspires. All of a sudden, he can't move his arms. The adhesive of the denture powder has been activated and is cementing his arms to his side! Sid has no idea what is going on. He thinks he is dying of some terrible disease!

Fortunately, this doesn't create a lasting obstacle in their courtship. Sid gets back the use of his arms. In fact, things go so well that Sid marries Pebe. They move in together near us in City Terrace.

Sid Out on His Own

Dad doesn't have the orange pulp business long before World War II breaks out. When this happens, Sunkist comes up with a way to use the orange pulp for the war effort. My father's orange pulp business is over.

After this happens, Sid drifts away from working with my dad and tries his hand at his own businesses. Eventually, he creates the Baron Bag Company. He doesn't manufacture the burlap bags, but either imports them or has someone else make them. The business grows very successful. The bags have many uses, such as holding produce picked in the farm fields surrounding Los Angeles. Though my father and Sid are no longer in business together, they remain close. In fact, the families of all three siblings spend much time together at each other's homes. Sundays are our big family days. Lots of "Let's take a ride and go to Aunt Betty's house" or "Let's go to Uncle Sid's for lunch."

Uncle Sid and Aunt Pebe

Aunt Pebe is a welcome addition. A lovely woman who is so kind to me. When I am thirteen and trying to sell different things to make money—be it peddling newspapers, or subscriptions to the *Ladies' Home Journal* or other magazines—Aunt Pebe will buy it. When hustling something, I can always count on her!

Sid and Pebe have three daughters. The oldest is Mary Lynn. She is the most like Sid in personality: outgoing, bigger than life, full of laughter. Mary Lynn has since passed away.

I am still in touch with their second daughter, Barbara, as I am with their third daughter, Kathy.

✦　✦　✦

CHAPTER 13

Side Business: Prizefighting (Boxing)

Leo has eight seats at the Hollywood Legion Stadium where prize-fights take place on Friday nights. Boxing is a big deal in Los Angeles when I am growing up and having reserved seats is almost like someone today having Los Angeles Rams' season football tickets. Our phone often rings early on fight day with someone asking, "Hey Leo, any of those seats available?"

They are good seats, too, right in front of where the band plays between matches. Prizefights are big-time events and people dress up. It is also very social, with people walking the aisles to stop and talk with Leo. When you go regularly, you see the same people around you all the time. They become friends.

Women attend along with men *and their children*. I know because my dad and mom are taking me by the time I am ten years old! Any concerns about boxing being too violent for women or kids don't exist, even with our seats being so close that you see all the action and the sweat.

Yet for my father, the largest appeal of these matches is the wagering.

My father is not one to shy away from gambling. Just the opposite. It is a steady (sometimes) source of income for him. Bets on fighters are not made at some stadium window. People bet with each other. It's like, "Hey Leo, I'll give you twenty bucks on that fighter" or "I'll take the white corner for fifty." There are different ways to wager.

Leo takes bets himself. No receipts are given. It is an honor system. Of course, I hear who my father is betting on, so I know who to root for. People scream as things get exciting! Before the evening is over, Leo is collecting money. Or paying it out.

But he takes all this one big step further.

Leo "owns" some fighters, meaning he has invested in them. When they win, he wins. Sort of like having a winning thoroughbred in a horse race (in fact, some boxing and horse racing terms are similar: an "owner" might say he has three fighters in his "stable").

I don't know if this actually means my father is the boxer's manager or what. He certainly isn't a trainer, though I do remember going to gyms where fighters trained. Leo hangs out at places populated by what I call Damon Runyon characters—gamblers and hustlers—who often go by colorful monikers like "Rocky" and "Lefty."

Though I happily go with Leo to these locales, all of it is very alien to my later life as an adult.

The Pugilist Prophet

Occasionally, Leo's worlds overlap.

At my grandparents' house on Pesach, we open the front door at a certain point in our service as per Passover tradition to welcome in the prophet Elijah. Of course, no one is ever standing there.

Except this one time.

One of Leo's fighters, Bradis Flowers, arrives to see my father for some reason—just at that moment. He is standing at the doorway and figures we've opened the door for him. Bradis waltzes right in. It takes a moment for everybody to realize what has happened and then collapse in laughter!

Leo only has fighters for a short period of time. But the reserved seats and our attending matches continues for many years. I know the championship fight between Rocky Graziano and Tony Zale in Chicago that my parents attended took place in 1947.

Professional Wrestling

Along with boxing, professional wrestling is very popular. In the 1940s, Gorgeous George is one of its biggest stars, having created an outrageously flamboyant and charismatic persona. He has long platinum-dyed hair, with gold-plated bobby pins (called "Georgie Pins") that he tosses to the audience. He makes a grand entrance to the ring by parading down his own red carpet to the music of "Pomp and Circumstance," draped in a fancy sequined robe as someone spreads rose petals at his feet—creating the kind of spectacle that pro wrestlers try to emulate today! Like now, wrestling then is staged, but everybody watches it. People have their favorite heroes and villains. It is carnival time!

I don't recall going to local matches. We watch it on TV.

Comically, pro wrestling later becomes an obstacle in my life when I date Lorraine. Her dad *loves* the sport and often has it playing on the TV at home. This is occasionally a problem when I am over at Lorraine's house. We are hoping her parents will go to sleep so we can make out. But her dad stays up to watch wrestling! I remember Lorraine's mom yelling out to him, "Come on, let's go to bed, Fivey!" (her nickname for him) She knows we are waiting for them to retire to their bedroom so we can . . . you know.

◆　◆　◆

CHAPTER 14

Hot Dogs and Arcade!

Never one to be stopped, my dad pivots to a new business after World War II shuts down his orange pulp trade. He opens a hot dog stand on Main in downtown Los Angeles between Fourth and Fifth Streets.

This is more than a makeshift "stand." It is a permanent structure, where you step up to the sidewalk window and buy your hot dog "to go." Or you walk inside and sit at the counter for a dog and soft drink.

We grill the hot dogs with onions on it. When I say "we"—I mean *we*. I am one of the cooks! On weekends and after school, I'm standing on a wooden box since I am only a little kid of ten, turning hot dogs and sautéing onions. I'm pretty sure this wouldn't be allowed today! But back then, there are no sanitation inspectors. At least none I ever see.

Making it all more interesting is that this is during the time of pachucos. Starting in late 1930s Los Angeles, pachuco is a movement by some Chicanos to wear distinctive clothing (zoot suits) along with developing their own music. They go from being an invisible portion of the Los Angeles population to making themselves known, parading around in their characteristic clothing and lowrider cars.

While interesting for me to be witness to this change, there is concern about tensions in the streets between pachucos and off-duty servicemen. It is a stressful time for everyone because of the war and sometimes that boils over into fights between the two groups.

71

Lots of servicemen hang out at our hot dog stand on Main Street. Leo places clubs at various spots underneath the counter so he can grab one if anybody gets out of hand. Fortunately, I never see any clashes.

Pennies Add Up

During this same period, my dad purchases an adjacent penny arcade—an indoor amusement center with coin-operated machines, whose wood exteriors are as tall as you. They are entirely mechanical—nothing electronic. Some are pinball type machines, or machines where you turn handles to manipulate a miniature crane inside it to grab a small stuffed animal. Or one where you squeeze a handle really hard to measure your hand strength—the result indicating if you are a "strongman" or ninety-pound weakling. I'm pretty sure there are machines that drop out little rolled pieces of paper with printed messages that supposedly tell your fortune. I know some arcades have "moving picture machines" where you peer into a visor while turning a crank to flick through small images—like a flip book—so it appears as a little movie (though I don't recall my dad having those).

The place is packed since it is on a street busy with pedestrians, especially off-duty servicemen. This is why Dad figures both the hot dog stand and arcade are good investments.

The arcade also has a tattoo parlor—popular with servicemen—and a big booth where somebody takes a picture of you posing behind bars as if you are in jail. The photographs are developed quickly enough to be done by the time a person is ready to leave the arcade. I remember the different pans of developers filled with smelly chemicals. This is way before Polaroid instant cameras (where developed pictures come right out of the camera) and *long* before modern digital cameras (with no photographs at all!).

I still have a picture of me and my buddies from Mandalay Drive in this jail, posing like we are a bunch of derelict kids.

Tiny's Restaurant

At the same time as all this, Leo has yet another business: a sit-down restaurant on North Broadway. Leo is a big guy (nearly 6 feet and 250 pounds!), so the "joke" is they name it Tiny's. I'm sure customers got a kick out of it whenever the "tiny" owner showed up to stroll through the room and say hello. It is a fairly small place with a simple menu. But restaurants are tough businesses to make successful, even

The "Mandalay Drive Gang," me second from left.

if you have a lot of experience running them. Leo doesn't and the restaurant doesn't last.

But Leo continues making good money with the penny arcade and hot dog stand. They endure until the end of the war, after which the area is no longer busy. That's when my father fully shifts his business focus to something completely different.

Horse racing.

♦　♦　♦

CHAPTER 15

Off to the Races!

Always on the lookout for new opportunities, my father is not satisfied with simply owning a penny arcade, hot dog stand, and Tiny's Restaurant. Even with running all those businesses, he finds time to start something new.

Leo meets a real character who becomes important in his life. Despite having the colorful name "Rocky," this street-smart man isn't some boxer with a bent nose and cauliflower ears. He is actually a good-looking guy married to a glamorous blonde, Georgia. Leo partners with Rocky and a number of others to purchase racehorses! One of those people is Leo's distant cousin, Benny Canter, the man who owns Canter's Deli.

What does Leo know about horses—let alone *racehorses*? Of course, not knowing about some new business venture never stopped Leo. That, and how he juggled extremely different businesses at the same time is beyond me. Especially as owning racehorses was a wealthy man's pursuit. That is not how I would describe Leo.

This is definitely a new world for him—and he is successful at it!

Leo makes money with horses in three ways: when his horse wins, when he bets on winning horses, and by buying and later selling horses for a profit.

Leo and Georgia and Rocky (with a trainer)

In racing, there is something called a "claiming race" where the horses are all for sale during the course of a race. You might have purchased a horse for $7,000 and if that horse runs well, someone may "claim" that horse and purchase it at your selling price of $12,000.

This is different than the normal stake races (like the famous Kentucky Derby). Those horses belong to the owners and you cannot claim them. The horses run only for their share of "the purse"—the total sum of money paid out to the top finishers. A certain percentage of that money is paid to the horse that finishes in first place, with lessor amounts to second, third, fourth, and so on. Jockeys get paid per race, and also a percentage of the purse if they win. Leo's horses win a lot.

My mom, Leo, Maxine, and I all go to the track. Again, everyone dresses up.

Leo, Maxine, Mom, and me at Caliente Racetrack in Mexico.

Running South of the Border

As popular as horse racing is in California, it all comes to a sudden stop during the war, as racetracks are assigned a *different* purpose.

After Pearl Harbor is bombed, President Roosevelt orders Japanese Americans to be placed in internment camps. While "more permanent" relocation camps are being constructed, Japanese Americans stay for months at different "assembly centers" in California, as well as in Arizona, Oregon, and Washington.

Santa Anita racetrack is the largest and longest occupied of these temporary WCCA (Wartime Civil Control Administration) camps. Starting in March of 1942, over 19,000 Japanese Americans from both Southern and Northern California live at Santa Anita racetrack in converted horse stalls or in rows of hurriedly built barracks covering its huge parking lot. This is a big operation with the encampment divided into seven districts that includes mess halls, stores, a hospital, post office, and classrooms, as well as improvised churches on the track's grandstand.

During 1942, the racetrack at Tanforan (where Leo's horses also race) in Northern California becomes an internment camp for 8,000 Bay Area Japanese Americans. From 1942 through 1944, Southern California's Del Mar racing grounds are used for military training, and later as a manufacturing site for B-17 bombers.

While there is no racing in the United States, horses continued running at Agua Caliente Racetrack in Tijuana, Mexico. So Leo developed this business in another country, stabling horses there and traveling down for races. Many times, I go with him, staying in San Diego or Tijuana. This is my first time out of the United States. Tijuana seems festive. It doesn't turn into a rundown border town until later.

Betting Basics are Very Basic

Racetracks in the United States have "totalizator boards" (or tote boards). This large display board on the infield lists how much money is bet on each horse in a race and if its odds of winning are twenty-five to one, five to one, even money, etc. This is how most people decide what to bet. Eventually those boards get electronic displays, but when Leo is first racing horses, the numbers are changed manually.

But in Agua Caliente, there are no such boards.

What they have are little stalls—small booths—each with a person updating their own board telling you the odds and what they're paying out. A bettor walks up to these individuals and places wagers with them. The bettor receives a ticket showing the amount of their wager and the odds.

If I bet on some horse and that horse wins, I go back to this person to collect my winnings. Very different from modern times in the United States, where you go to a window and tell the person what horse you want to bet . . . with all windows and bets controlled by the track.

Back then in Caliente, you are not betting with the track. You bet with an individual in a booth, and trust they will be there after the race!

I have this vivid memory of going up to one of these stands after a horse owned by Leo won. In those days, U.S. two-dollar bills and silver dollars were popular currency for making bets, especially as most of the people betting were from the United States. I don't remember how much we won, but I recall my father stuffing my pockets with silver dollars and $2 bills.

And me yelling, "We're rich, we're rich!"

Leo immediately "gags" me, explaining, "There are people around us. Who knows who might want to pop you over the head and grab the money?" He shushes me and we march out of there, my pockets bulging.

He slips a lot of our winnings in my jacket because nobody looking for a likely target will focus on a little kid. Plus, there are more winnings than Leo can cram in his own coat. Even just a few hundred dollars in silver dollars and $2 bills are quite a lot. With all that silver, I am carrying some serious weight!

Though having no previous experience, Leo is dealing with the trainers, the jockeys, the veterinarians. I enjoy listening as he talks with them. Maybe Dad is secretly a Jewish cowboy.

Speaking of which. . . .

Mel the Rootin'-Tootin' Cowboy?

During the time he owns horses, my father buys me a pony. This would be the dream of many young boys!

Yet despite my being given an elaborate cowboy costume when I am younger, being a cowboy is never my dream. And now I have my own horse! What am I going to do with it?

Leo has access to the best of the best riders: professional jockeys who would love to teach the boss's son how to ride. At some point, Leo gets me up on a small saddle. But truthfully, it is not a lot of fun. There I am, this little kid with his own pony and I could care less. I mean, it is almost embarrassing to admit this happened!

Me in cowboy outfit

Racing Back in the USA

When the war ends, the moratorium against racing in the United States ends as well.

Leo is now racing horses at Santa Anita, Hollywood Park, and Del Mar in Southern California. Plus Bay Meadows and Tanforan racetracks up in Northern California. He doesn't race outside of California.

He moves his horses between stables at these various tracks because different venues hold races at different times of the year. You might have racing at Santa Anita from November through December. Hollywood Park might be January through March. Tanforan might be in the summertime.

Mary Asha

Many of my horse memories are well-documented. When one of Leo's horses won, a framed picture of it in the Winner's Circle went up on the wall in our Mandalay home. These included the horse, jockey, trainer, and owner. Whenever I was at these winning races, I posed in these pictures with my mom and dad. This was a big thrill!

79

But our biggest thrill is a particularly special race.

Leo buys a horse—a one-year-old he names "Mary Asha" after his mother.

They race the horse for the first time when I am in eighth grade. I remember because it is the last day of school. I've been in a drafting class and need to clean up and get out of there so my parents can pick me up. The horse is running a big race at Santa Anita racetrack. I can't wait!

There is also a horse entered belonging to CS Howard. He is a multimillionaire Buick dealership magnate, with a 16,000-acre ranch that serves as a breeding and training center for premier thoroughbred horses, including the world famous Seabiscuit.

I have the privilege to go in the Santa Anita paddock when they are putting the jockeys on the horses as they prepare to parade out to the track for this race. A guy there tells me that the CS Howard horse is the big favorite. But I am not daunted. I counter, "Forget that. You should take a look at this horse called Mary Asha!"

Though this guy isn't acquainted with our horse, everybody in Boyle Heights knows of Leo's Mary Asha! There are high hopes riding on her—and a lot of money.

Uncle Sid and my dad bet $3,000 across—meaning $3,000 is bet on the horse to win, $3,000 is bet to place, and $3,000 is bet to show (first, second, third places). That means they've invested $9,000 on this horse. You need to realize that with inflation, $3,000 in 1946 would be worth over $45,000 today. This is a load of money!

We are all watching from my dad's box of great seats at Santa Anita right next to Harry James, the famous trumpet-playing band leader.

Everyone is so excited! Yelling, pointing, jumping up and down during the race! "*They're coming round the track. The final stretch . . . and it's Mary Asha first across the finish line!!*'

We can't believe it! We are screaming. Leo, Sid, and I literally run to the winner's circle.

Me, Leo, and Sid in Winner's Circle after Mary Asha win.

For just the wager to win, the odds are paying 14 to 1—that means for every dollar wagered, you get $14 back (times $3,000). That means we get $42,000—in 1946 dollars! And that is only the payout for the Win bet. We also get payouts for the place and show bets too!

Plus, Leo gets more money because he owns the winning horse too. This . . . is . . . huge.

Mary Asha ends up running only four times, winning just one other race. This first race is her big win. Somehow the horse breaks down. But that's the great story of Mary Asha. I still have pictures of all the wins and dates.

Flying the Friendly Skies!

In addition to our local tracks, Leo flies up for the Tanforan and Bay Meadows races in Northern California. I travel with him to Tanforan in the 1940s. It is my first time ever on an airplane and I get to do it with just my dad. A special moment for me.

Just getting onto the plane is far different from today. Now you move through an enclosed walkway from the airport gate directly to the airplane hatchway. But back then, you walk right onto the tarmac—the airplane runway—and then up a set of big portable stairs they roll up to the plane. Once everyone is inside, they close the door and roll the stairs away.

Flying is expensive and not a lot of children are on planes. The whole flying experience is so unlike what we have now. Everyone dresses up. Planes are smaller. They all use propellers. No jet engines. For me, stepping on that plane and watching out the window as *we leave the ground* for the first time is incredibly exciting!

This is my first time out of Southern California (and northern Mexico). After we land, we go directly to the track. Leo knows all the jockeys and the trainers in this new place just like he does in Los Angeles and Caliente. With only me tagging along as his son—it is a magical experience.

Limited Travels

We don't do much traveling aside from my trips to Tanforan or Caliente racetracks.

My family goes to a place called Murrieta Hot Springs about 82 miles southeast (with lodging and obviously, hot springs). We also stay at the Highland Springs Ranch & Inn, 100 miles east of Los Angeles—a summer "Catskills of the West for Jewish Families." There is entertainment, music and dancing, swimming, horseback riding, and other outdoor activities.

But we never journey very far. In fact, other than visits to Caliente, I don't leave California until I am a young adult in college—when I go to Nevada for a Las Vegas honeymoon.

Leo's Personality Traits

I often wonder what made Leo so successful as a businessman. He continually pursued ventures for which he had no training or background. Yet he usually flourished. It was most often other circumstances that caused his businesses to close (like World War II ending his orange pulp business or his gambling causing the demise of his horse racing).

He was certainly hardworking and passionate about whatever he did. Leo was very outgoing and could talk to *anybody*. He had lots of friends.

But he never revealed much to me about his outlook on life, except for one time . . . when there was something I wanted to do, but seemed unable to accomplish it.

Frustrated, I finally exclaim, "I can't do it."

I vividly remember Leo's response. He looks me straight in the eye and says, "There is no such word as 'can't.'"

And he means it. That resonates with me even as a kid. It certainly does when I take big chances in my own businesses later on.

It also helps explain Leo's success in arenas where he had no prior experience. I mean, talk about street smarts. His ability to risk-take in unusual new undertakings was astonishing to me.

Learn by Doing

Aside from spending time with my dad and enjoying his crazy enterprises, I am learning a lot along the way. Not that I know it at the time, but many of the traits that he demonstrates—*a willingness to try new things even as others caution "this hasn't been done before"* . . . *his unwillingness to ever accept the word "can't"*—lay the foundations for my own careers many years later.

But this isn't the only education I am receiving at the time.

While all of these escapades are occurring with my dad, while the country is suffering from the Great Depression and struggling through World War II . . . I am doing what most kids do both then and now.

I am going to school.

◆　◆　◆

CHAPTER 16

The (Formal) Schooling of Mel Baron

While I learn plenty from my father growing up—street smarts, selling yourself, understanding people, taking risks—my other education is more traditional.

When we live in a duplex on City View Street, I attend kindergarten at Sheridan Street Elementary school. While I don't recall my time there, the story goes that I had a "guardian angel" with me. My cousin Marilyn (who only recently passed away) is three or four years older. She is sort of my protector. Apparently, there is concern that Al might come looking to visit me there. Or maybe grab me up and take me away with him. This is a great fear of my mother's. Her hatred and distrust of this man is ever-present. But Al never shows up.

Not until some years later.

The rest of my early education includes Evergreen Elementary School, and then City Terrace Elementary for grades three through six when we live on Eastern Avenue.

At City Terrace, we live two doors from the school on the same side of the street. It is a pretty easy commute: go out my door, walk another forty feet, and I am on school grounds!

The principal's last name is Hill. When my sister and I are stuck attending some PTA meetings with my mother, we refer to the principal as "Old Lady Hill" a little too loudly. My mother cringes. My sister and I giggle.

Though my parents move a couple of times in City Terrace, I remain at City Terrace Elementary. Only my commute changes. After we move to Mandalay Drive, I walk half a mile to school with a pack of kids who live on our street. My parents are not very involved in my actual schooling as they have limited education themselves. But our mom is oddly fascinated by multiplication tables. She has those down pat and quizzes us all the time. It still fascinates me that she had this passion.

Giving Back

Even though I am not at Sheridan Street Elementary very long, the school comes back into my life much later. Or rather, I come back in its life.

I drive by the school every day when I teach at USC. This so strongly calls back nostalgic feelings that I decide to donate money to the school, and to provide fotonovelas that I create at USC to their library. It feels like a moving and fitting gesture.

Apparently, the school thinks so too. They make this huge deal out of it and hold a breakfast there in my honor with the whole community present! Frankly, I find it a bit embarrassing.

Scouting Party: My Shoeshine Box

During my elementary school years, I am in the Cub Scouts. At meetings, I get to wear a Cub Scout uniform while we do fun activities like weaving bracelets out of leather laces.

My biggest project comes when I am nine years old. I build a solid wooden shoeshine box. I use it to store supplies for keeping my shoes polished—an important task at that time.

Shoes then are different from today's. Now everybody wears some kind of a sports shoe: Nike, Adidas, Reebok. Back then, even if you were being athletic—boys and girls, men and women—all wore regular leather shoes. That's what we had on when we played in the street.

And in my family—you keep those shoes polished!

I remember putting taps on my shoes too—a small metal piece attached onto the heel so it doesn't quickly wear down. It saves on having to replace kid's heels so often, though the taps are a bit noisy.

If you are a very lucky kid, you might get a pair of PF Flyers. In 1944, PF Flyers comes out with kid's shoes and the slogan, "Run Faster, Jump Higher." Those are *the* canvas-top and rubber-soled shoes to own. I *know* I could run a lot faster if I had PF Flyers! Somehow I convince my parents.

Wannabe Entrepreneur

As a kid, I have a great idea: I ask my parents if I can take a streetcar with my shoeshine box and polish shoes downtown for money.

My parents give me a lot of freedom to go wherever I want, but even they say, "That may be a little too much." It would be different than me grilling at my father's hot dog stand. I'd be totally on my own while trying to hustle people to stop and buy a shine. Still, I am not worried. But my parents are.

Though I never earn money with my shoeshine box, I always keep my shoes polished, and continue shining my own shoes until years later when I have enough money for the local shoeshine parlor.

But I never give up my kit.

Today, my hand-built wooden shoeshine box *still* carries all the shoeshining equipment anyone needs! I'm not sure how good a carpenter I was back then, but my shoeshining box has lasted eight decades!

My 80-plus year-old shoeshine box!

Little Drummer Boy

We have a piano in our home, not that my family is musically inclined. People just had pianos back then. Kind of like many homes eventually have televisions. Ours is nothing fancy—an upright piano in the den. I take some lessons. But that is not where my passion lies.

When I am nine years old, I want to play the drums!

My folks buy me a blue drum set made by Ludwig.

I learn on my own by listening to records and playing along with the music. I play in our elementary school orchestra, and by the time I am in sixth grade, I am selected to play in the All-City Orchestra.

This is in 1944, during the war. The All-City Orchestra takes a few kids from each of the elementary schools throughout the city. I am among several percussionists in the orchestra (we use the word "percussionist" rather than "drummer")—all sixth graders. Though there is only one public performance, my mother takes me to multiple rehearsals.

It is here that I meet one of my most important and closest friends.

Here's . . . Johnny!

While we players rehearse, my mother chats with another mother. When practice is over, they introduce me to this other boy, John Shambra. Because I am at City Terrace and he is at Farmdale Elementary, I ask, "Where will you go to junior high?"

"I'm going to Wilson."

I happily report, "I'm going to Wilson too!"

That is the beginning of a wonderful friendship that carries through junior and senior high, college, and adulthood.

Finally the orchestra has their performance. This is a big deal as we are playing at Shrine Auditorium—a vast venue—and to a huge audience! It turns out one of those watching is Al.

But I don't learn this until much later.

✦　✦　✦

CHAPTER 17

Junior High Meets Anti-Semitism

Kids in City Terrace have a choice of where to go to junior high: Roosevelt (where most go) or Wilson. Wilson is newer and much smaller.

The better choice.

I will be on that campus for six years, since both the junior (grades seven to nine) and senior high (ten to twelve) are housed in the same facilities. The entire student population is about 1,600. The junior high student body is huge, but not all of them go on to the high school. There are 162 students in my graduating high school class. We are called The Vanguards (every class names itself) and we have our own class sweater.

It is an all-White, blue-collar school. The bulk of these kids who graduate will typically go into law enforcement or teaching.

First Encounter

The downside is that Wilson is some distance away. We take a bus to get there (until we are older and some students have cars).

Most of us taking the bus from City Terrace are Jewish. As soon as we arrive there for seventh grade, the bullies taunt us, calling our traditional yellow school bus "the Jew bus."

There is a lot of bullying in seventh and eighth grades—a totally new experience for me and my friends. Anti-Semitism is largely unfamiliar to us, but it is well-entrenched at Wilson by the time I am a student. In addition to name calling, bullies sometimes get rough with us during gym class and on the playground. This makes our transition to this school challenging.

But more and more Jewish kids are coming to this school. And some of those Jewish kids have been working out, getting big, and mean.

This upends the status quo.

By eighth and ninth grades, there are significant fights with serious bodily injury. I remember standing in line for a snack break with my buddy, Lazar (pronounced "laser"), when one of the bullies taunts us with anti-Semitic remarks. Lazar makes it clear he doesn't like it. The bully challenges, "Want me to stop? Meet me after school."

After school, the two face off. Everyone circles around, expecting this bully to prevail.

Lazar pulverizes this kid. Stuffs him into one of the large garbage cans! Then Lazar shouts to the crowd, "If any of the rest of you want to step into this, you'll be next."

Lazar is a tough and very angry kid.

Another incident occurs in a classroom. A Jewish girl is pitching a charitable drive for March of Dimes in front of the class when a boy makes a derisive comment about Jews and money. Another Jewish kid, Red Sternfield, gets up and cold-cocks him. Right there in class. The teacher doesn't say a single word.

Separately, a couple of brutal fights break out in bathrooms. Again, Jewish students thrash these other kids—one bully nearly getting beaten to the edge of life. Eventually, things settle down at Wilson. Jews are not disparaged or picked on anymore. Attitudes change and we Jewish kids sail through the rest of our time there without any trouble.

What's more, Jewish kids are getting very involved in the school: joining clubs, excelling in sports and academics, and running for office.

Mr. President

In ninth grade, I decide to run for president of the class. I give speeches and Leo prints up "business cards" for me to hand out with his idea for a campaign slogan. The cards have a picture of an owl with the motto: "Be wise. Open your eyes. Vote for Mel Baron for president."

Apparently, my oratory skills and sophisticated marketing campaign do the trick. I win.

As president, I conduct cabinet meetings along with other responsibilities having to do with student government, school policies, etc.

And I give more speeches.

✦　✦　✦

CHAPTER 18

Unexpected Visitor: Al Fink

One day while in eighth grade class, I am called to the principal's office. But I am not in trouble. The message is, "Your father is here."

I assume they mean Leo. "But why is he coming to school? What's wrong?" I am a little spooked.

And I am about to get *more* spooked.

I come to the office and Leo is not there. But this guy standing there is introduced to me as Al Fink. My father.

I'm speaking of my biological father, of course. Who had an affair while married to my mother who then divorced him when I was an infant. We never heard from him after that. For all intents and purposes, Al doesn't exist in our lives.

But now he is standing in front of me and wants to talk. We sit in his car. Al tells me that he is going overseas to fight in the war and wanted to see me before he ships out.

I barely hear his words. I'm kind of petrified sitting there with him. I am not worried for my safety. I'm struggling to process that he suddenly is here. Yet I manage to ask a pretty bold and confrontive question: "What have you ever done for me in my life?"

That takes him aback. But he tells me that when I was a sixth-grade drummer in the All-City Orchestra, he came to my concert. I have no idea how he even knew I'd be playing. He says that he has kept tabs on me from afar. I'm not sure what that really means, other than I suppose a relative or common acquaintance of his and my mother has been keeping him apprised.

He lets me out of the car and I go back into school. I don't know what to make of this. I can only figure he wants to see me before he ships out since it is possible he won't make it back if he dies overseas.

I don't tell my mother about this. In fact, I never tell her about Al showing up at my school.

Al never visits anymore and I never see him again. That is, until much later when I'm in my forties . . . and I make a decision to visit Al.

✦　✦　✦

CHAPTER 19

Enjoying High School

A lot of people speak of high school negatively. But I have a great time there.

My school life was very different from that of today. For one thing, where you lived and where you attended school pretty much *was* your life. Today you are in a world community: instant information, always available, you know everything! But we had no internet or social media. Students were not constantly checking (nonexistent) cell phones every few minutes. We were not comparing our media presence to that of others. We were not distracted by a thousand things.

It is a much simpler, slower, more relaxing time.

My friends and I avoid drugs. Though young people drink, that isn't the case with my buddies . . . my entourage . . . my posse. I don't try beer until college.

Only one of my friends smokes, though that is a far more popular pursuit at the time than today. Many adults smoke, including my parents. But it isn't something we find interesting. Plus, we all play sports and somehow understand that smoking can affect athletic performance.

Typical academic paths were different from today's too. Many of my classmates don't go beyond twelfth grade. But most of my Jewish friends are thinking about college even though none of their parents have formal education beyond high school, if they got that far. I am the first in my family to go to college. That's certainly different from my eight grandkids—six of whom are college graduates and some have advanced degrees, as do both of my kids.

College is not a given back then. There are no prep schools, private high schools, private preschools. Nobody is making sure their kids get into the "right kindergarten" to kick-start their elite academic careers and pay $40,000 a year for the privilege. You go to whatever school is local.

AZA Camp

Something else different back then are the community youth groups. At fourteen, I participate in AZA (Aleph Zadik Aleph)—an organization of Jewish high school fraternity-like chapters in various geographical areas. As a social athletic club, kids in my City Terrace AZA compete against other neighborhood AZA teams throughout the year in basketball, baseball, and swimming.

These competitions are serious stuff. We are playing in a gym! It is organized. We have uniforms. In fact, I *still have* my AZA team jersey!

It's in shockingly good shape. I must not have washed it very much! On the back is number 28. I put "28" on many athletic things as a kid. I'm not sure why I chose that number, though I do recall a famed USC football running back named Mickey McCardle who wore number 28. Perhaps I saw this guy play in 1946 and thought he was a big deal.

Another draw to being in AZA are the socials with the equivalent Jewish organization for girls called BBG (B'nai B'rith Girls). Yet perhaps most important, AZA provided a sense of community for its Jewish kids who feel out of place in a mostly gentile world.

Yet the truth for me is I never feel like an outsider in school, in organizations, or elsewhere. I actually feel like *an insider*, always part of wherever I am, one of the popular kids most involved. This is the case even during junior and senior high when I am in a non-Jewish environment for the first time. By the time I finish high school, I am just "one of the guys." This is because I know how to fit in, especially after the Jewish kids there earn the respect of others.

My City Terrace AZA camp buddies, with me in the first row, third from left.

My AZA group includes many of the same guys I grew up with during my junior high and high school years—seen posing here—and behind those fake bars in that "jailhouse photo" taken at my father's penny arcade.

(Of course, had I not kept on the straight and narrow as an adult, there might have been a very different picture of me behind bars.)

School Sports

In addition to AZA athletics, I play high school sports. Not being very tall, I play B basketball—which is like junior varsity—against other school teams.

But during football season, I am a Yell King! I wear white pants, a school sweater with a big "W" on it, and shout through a megaphone to lead cheers. To me, this is a huge deal. I am down on the field with the cheerleading squad as this (non-electric) cone-shaped horn amplifies my yelling to excite the crowd into a rooting frenzy for our team.

This adds to my popularity . . . and lets me hang out with cheerleaders.

Even though Woodrow Wilson High is named after our esteemed 28th president, our school is very "down home." Our yearbook is called *Hoof Prints*, with our sports teams nicknamed accordingly. Rather than typical mascots like the Wildcats or Lions or Panthers, we're called . . . the Mules. It's not like this intimidates or instills fear in our opposing teams. Everybody laughs at our name.

Still, the moniker sticks. Years later, you run into someone who realizes you graduated from Wilson and they'll invariably call you a mule. Basically, "Once a mule, always a mule." A stubborn concept, like the animal itself.

Jew and Non-Jew Camaraderie

I also get involved with school committees. I am a member of the Key Club, an organization whose activities, such as food drives and cleanup projects, benefit the community. It's something I enjoy doing . . . and perhaps a prelude to my later altruistic efforts.

I love the camaraderie these groups offer. It feels great to be part of something, and adds to my feeling comfortable with a wide range of school friends, male and female, Jews and non-Jews.

Johnny Shambra is my best non-Jewish friend. We know each other from when our mothers introduced us at the All-City Orchestra. He is from a large Italian family that widens my perspective.

The Shambras invite me over for dinner one night. As befitting true Italian custom, they serve salad at *the end* of the meal. I've never seen this before, so when I get home, I immediately tell my mom and dad.

Equally unworldly as I, my parents are equally bewildered. "What are you talking about? They serve a salad *after* everything else?"

I find this so interesting. When you are a kid, you assume everybody does what your family does. Not true, I find out, as John's is the first non-Jewish family with whom I spend a lot of time.

With Johnny Shambra, performing at our high school prom.

John's family is stereotypical in many ways. They are expressive and emotionally outgoing, especially his dad, who they call "The Chief." They are big huggers, and always generous of spirit and caring. They are fun to be around! I love their Italian cooking, which is mostly new to me! The few restaurants that my family visits are usually coffee shops or Jewish delis.

Religion is never an issue between John and me, though it does come up in an odd way. I am at his house when his grandmother is visiting. She doesn't speak much English and when she looks at a picture of John and me, she calls me "Jewey." But it is just how she identifies John's friend as someone Jewish. It is not anti-Semitic. I find it funny.

Johnny Shambra remains the closest of my high school friends, both in school and out, playing important roles throughout my life. One of our earliest and most important endeavors is the band we form in high school.

◆　◆　◆

CHAPTER 20

Boys of the Band

John Shambra has a lot of musical talent. He is a piano player. He plays the accordion (yes, the accordion!). I play the drums. We decide to put together a band.

Another student, Bert Smith, plays the saxophone. Ray Wurfl, who is older than us, plays the trumpet and bass. A guy I know on the Westside named Larry Wolff also plays the bass.

So what do we call ourselves? *Mel Baron and The Meltones.*

Rehearsals are at John's house since he has a nice piano. He puts everything together—he gets the music and acquires the arrangements. We practice until we are good enough to be paid to play at dances. I do advertising. We make business cards. My mother, God bless her, becomes my best press agent, passing out cards to everybody! Accompanied by boasts of how unbelievably talented we are.

As we become known, we get in that circuit of playing weddings and bar mitzvahs, and later, fraternity parties. People are calling my house. "Are you available on the second Sunday in September?" I am doing all of the bookings, making all the contract arrangements, paying the players, etc.

We play current popular songs and dance tunes. This is before rock and roll, so that is swing music like the jitterbug. At Jewish weddings and bar mitzvahs, we perform the hora and other Jewish songs. Those are always popular and everyone is excited to hear them.

In truth, we aren't really that good. We make it look better than it is.

Though a fair number of us are in the band, not everyone plays each time. How many of us perform depends on how much money we get for an event. If there is only a small budget, you get three of us. For a few bucks more, you get four or five of us. If there is a little more money, you also get our singer. It is all about economics.

When students at Wilson find out about these gigs, they say, *"You have your own band?!"* That is pretty impressive to a teen during this time.

For a couple of summers, two other musicians and I get jobs at a resort called Mont Vista Lodge near Ontario, California. My dad knows the owners: one of the Canter brothers (who owns Canter's Deli and is in partnership with my dad on racehorses.) Located at the base of the San Gabriel Mountains, the resort caters to Jewish family vacationers. There is expansive, green landscaping with winding stone pathways and Mt. Baldy looming in the background. They have swimming, hiking, volleyball, tennis, ping-pong . . . and entertainment. It calls itself "The Catskills of California."

We aren't the Meltones here, but just a trio: Dick and Marty Mitnick, and myself. Dick is on clarinet, Marty plays piano, and I am on drums.

We perform a couple nights a week and are busboys the balance of the time. We live and eat here, and make a few bucks (including tips as busboys). I'm thinking this is pretty cool! Our second summer there, we graduate to being waiters while still playing two nights a week. The money waiting tables is good.

I am kind of an independent young person. At sixteen, I have an income and a checking account at Bank of America. My parents are proud of me and our band's success.

Singers

We have a female singer for only a short time during high school. Then our singer is a boyhood friend from City Terrace, Marty Harwich.

But Harwich isn't a great name for a singer. One day we are hanging out at my house. I have a small megaphone from Desmond's Men's Clothing Store in the den, so I say, "How about Marty . . . Desmond?"

Marty Desmond remains our singer for many years. He actually becomes a professional singer later in life. Then he becomes an attorney.

We play many venues, but the highlight is when we perform at our prom! What a thrill to have our class see us up there! We look terrific. There are "stand fronts"—

Playing at our prom, which has a nautical theme.

boards of cardboard (or other material)—in front of every music stand like you see with big bands, each in matching blue and silver displaying our name, *The Meltones*. We wear white dinner jackets strutting around on our raised bandstand—as if we are Mel *Tormé* and The Meltones!

By a certain point, we nearly always wear matching outfits when we perform. This makes us look *very* professional. If you think about the big bands of the era, every player wears a "uniform" of matching jacket, tie, etc. Even later, when The Beatles and other British bands are popular—they all have matching outfits, usually "mod suits" with thin ties. Some of the Black singing groups wear identical attire as well.

Playing on stage gets us attention, including from girls. They come up to us between sets or after we finish, providing favorable opportunities to go out with someone new.

Mel The Musical Man

John Shambra is also responsible for my early "Off-Broadway" debut: I am cast in the high school musical.

Mel Baron. . . . *School musical?*

It helps to know the director and producer—Johnny Shambra. With minimal talent, I participated in a brief song and dance scene of *By The Sea, By The Sea, By The Beautiful Sea* with a female partner. We perform a couple of nights.

Of course, my parents come to see their son. *The star.*

♦ ♦ ♦

CHAPTER 21

Life as a Teenager

Aside from family, the most important people to me during high school are my cadre of close friends. All colorful characters. Many with names to match.

Dirty Eddie gets his nickname not because of what he says or even how he thinks—it is his wardrobe. Specifically, an old peacoat that he seems to live and sleep in! For his whole life, we know him as Dirty Eddie. It is also how my kids know him—Dirty Eddie—and he only recently passed away.

There is Klutz—a.k.a. Alan Shapiro—who is given his name

Me with Mom on Mandalay

because he is bigger and more ungainly than the rest of us. And, of course, there is Lazar. His real name *is* Lazar—likely derived (as is Lazarus) from the Hebrew name Eleazar. But everybody called him Lazar or just Laze for short.

We have the twins, Sam and Gene Danny. A couple of years older than me, we simply call each of them "Twin." They call each other "Twin."

Then we have Willie the Weasel (Willie Rosensweig). He earns his name because he always agitates Alan Shapiro. One day they get into a real scuff and Willie proclaims, "Watch out Alan. I'm gonna defeat you with words!"

Alan just smashes him.

Interestingly, Willie goes to USC, six months ahead of us. He joins ZBT (Zeta Beta Tau)—a big Jewish fraternity. *Now* Willie thinks he is a big-time guy and wants to show off. He invites us to a fraternity party.

We actually think that is pretty cool. A college party? College girls!

But he has a "requirement." He preps us ahead of time: "My name now is Bill. That is the only thing you can call me at the party."

"What're you talking about? You're Willie the Weasel!"

Willie insists: "Don't do that. If you say it, you will never ever come to another party here again."

College has changed Willie. At least his name.

Of course, you don't *need* a nickname to be a good friend. There is Harvey Shinerock, Marty Rashoff, and Bernie Cantos—all of whom live on my street.

Clothes Make the Man, Part Two

The snazzy look for guys during my high school years is a pair of corduroy pants or Levi's, white long sleeve shirt, and a cardigan sweater. If you have a letterman sweater, all the better. Also popular is the penny loafer, which has a little half-moon cut-out slot in a leather strip on top in which you place a penny.

Girls wear blouses and skirts. I don't remember any girls wearing slacks or pants. Of course, there are bobby socks and saddle shoes, though more commonly during college.

Modern Cars of Yesteryear

Of course, cars play a significant role in life back then too.

The old Model A Ford that my father won for me on a bet is soon gone. I then rely on a Chevy coupe for my transportation. Even though a coupe is a two-door, it is a big car and my drums fit in the trunk and back seat. This is before station wagons and certainly SUVs. It has a two-tone paint job—blue and gray. Pretty sharp.

Next to the two-tone coupe. Even years later, it is still important to flex!

Most cars then are pretty large and fairly primitive. There are no automatic transmissions. My gearshift stick is so tall you can rest your hand on it while driving. There is no power steering, which means turning the wheel requires serious effort! No air conditioning or heaters either. Music comes from AM radios playing out of one small tinny-sounding speaker.

No seat belts or airbags. No bucket seats. You have one long bench seat in the front and another in back. That means you can pile a bunch of people into the car—as many as you can squeeze in! People sit on each other's laps. No laws exist against any of this.

When I think about a luxury car today—Lexus, Mercedes, any nice car—you get a very smooth ride. Our rides were *bumpy*. Handling was loose. You didn't want to take a turn too fast, or your car might end up flipped on its side or in a ditch!

Yet some cars are a little different. After World War II, during the pachuco era, the Hispanic population in East LA around Boyle Heights customizes their cars into what we call hot rods. Body shops modify the vehicles. One kid might tell another: "Hey man, lower your car." The other driver then presses a button and his suspension relaxes to lower the car, often all the way to the ground. It is pretty cool.

There are practically no freeways or highways at the time. The Pasadena Freeway is the first freeway in the Western U.S. and opens in 1940. But that is pretty much it. This means long commute times in a city as spread out as Los Angeles. I remember my parents taking a ride to see some racehorses in Northridge. That was like a day's journey from East L.A.! Back then, the valley areas were farms, orange groves, and horse ranches.

Borrowed Wheels

Most families we know are one-car families. A few teenagers (mostly earning their own money) have cars. As a teenager, you try to get your hands on a car even if you don't own one.

A guy might call up and say, "Hey, can I use your car tonight?"

Your answer is typically yes. But then you ask, "Where are you going?"—because you figure it's for a date—and also, "With who?"

We are very nosy!

Or if somebody drives by a house and sees your car parked outside, the next day they pry: "Hey Mel, I saw your car at so-and-so's house, what were you doing there?" In these days long before social media, grilling friends is our way of keeping tabs on one another.

In general, friends pretty freely loan their cars. I'm not sure kids today would be quite so casual about it. But we loan out a lot of stuff.

Someone might come over to your house, look in your closet and say, "Can I borrow this?" People didn't have as much back then, so sharing was more commonplace. But that doesn't mean it always worked out well. One time, my friend Willie the Weasel asks, "Can I borrow your corduroy coat?"

It's a nice coat. I give it to him. But by the time Willie gets around to returning it, I have outgrown it!

Sharing car rides is also common. You ask your friend for a lift to school every day. He agrees to drive you, but wants you to chip in for gas. If somebody owns a car, that doesn't mean they are wealthy. Everyone we know has a tough life.

On the other hand, not *all* car adventures are "authorized." Or go that well. This same friend, Willie Rosensweig, takes his father's pickup truck without asking. A bunch of us are sitting on the truck bed in the back as he speeds through the neighborhood and hits a bump. That's when Alan Shapiro—who we have already labeled "Klutz"—goes flying and lands on the pavement! Thank God he doesn't get hurt . . . but it's a story that gets retold time and again among us.

(By the time I meet Lorraine, I am driving my mother's car. Nothing too impressive. But Lorraine has a Chevy convertible! Still no air conditioning or heating, but it's a *convertible*.)

Go West Young Man!

In our quest to find girls, my friends and I drive to the West Side of Los Angeles, around La Cienega and Pico.

That is where the clubs are for Jewish girls attending Fairfax High and LA High. These clubs meet one or two nights a week at some local drive-in restaurant. We find out where, pile in a car, and "happen" to show up at the same time.

Why go to all this trouble? Remember, the Jewish selection in East L.A. is very limited.

The girls stand around their cars, talking. We try to mingle (some might call it loitering). If we see a girl we like, we might tease her or do whatever we can to start a conversation. Willie the Weasel meets his future wife Marilyn at one of these drive-in gatherings.

I date a couple of girls in high school. Then, the equivalent for today's invitation of "Let's go out for coffee" is "Let's go to the malt shop." Meals at drive-in restaurants are popular too. Or we go to dances or movies. None of these are serious relationships, though I sometimes *think* I am deeply in love at the time!

Of course, once I am at college and meet Lorraine, then I know what it is really like to fall deeply in love.

Polio

Some people think nostalgically of the late 1940s and 1950s as a more innocent and easy time, but there are still many challenges. While most are different from those of today, some are unfortunately similar.

Like COVID now, polio is a huge concern. But nobody knows how it is transmitted and there is no cure. Even for those that survive, polio can cause paralysis. People have to use crutches or wheelchairs for the rest of their lives. It is the most feared disease of the 20th century.

The polio virus dominates every summer. Children are kept from playgrounds and birthday parties during the summer "polio season" out of concern they might catch it. Movie theaters close, along with city swimming pools. Public pools are popular then as few people can afford pools at their homes. People still go to the beach, as concerns there are not as great.

The March of Dimes is a fundraising organization aimed solely at conquering polio. It is founded by President Franklin D. Roosevelt in 1938, due to his polio. He wears braces on his legs, though they hide this from the public while he is in office. You never see him in a wheel-chair—he is always propped standing up.

Fortunately, a vaccine is discovered by Jonas Salk in 1955. By then, I am a pharmacist early in my career. I remember being at Birmingham High School, handing out polio vaccines on sugar cubes. These early "vaccines" are not injections, but rather, a liquid we pour over a sugar cube and hand to people. Believe me, nobody is protesting taking the polio vaccine! People eagerly line up to receive theirs. We hand them out to kids in school. Everyone thinks this is the miracle of miracles! Remember, we have already eradicated smallpox. This vaccine is considered another major milestone in healthcare. Jonas Salk becomes one of the most celebrated scientists in the world.

Lasting Legacy: Jews Shift the Culture

My high school years, coming right after World War II, are a time of great change in America. It is a time of great change in my high school too.

Long after I graduate from Wilson High, I run into our former basketball coach. He confides in me that life at the high school really transformed during and after my time there. When the Jewish students came in, everything shifted.

Kids started to get along as the reign of bullies came to an end. There was greater cohesiveness as Jewish kids got involved in all aspects of school life, including school clubs and politics. Burt Chortkoff, a semester ahead of me, became student body president. Jewish students took on other leadership roles as well, like when I was president of my ninth grade class. School sports programs improved as athletically inclined Jewish students joined them.

Importantly, academic performance shifted dramatically. Education is highly prized in the Jewish culture and most of my male friends went on to college. Admittedly, part of this was fueled by the belief that we needed to become some kind of professional. During this time, corporate America wasn't open to Jews. They couldn't join a company and move up the ladder. Jewish people weren't welcome there.

It was a time when many were changing their Jewish sounding names.

So you either went into business for yourself, or went to college to learn a profession—accountant, lawyer, doctor, pharmacist. You were not planning on working for anyone. As our Jewish graduates headed to college, higher education was seen as more obtainable to other students at Wilson too.

Of course, none of this was the case when we arrived at Wilson. The incoming Jewish population was treated as separate and strange. Some students there had never seen a Jew before and believed whatever myths they'd heard, like that Jews had horns. But the more we intermixed, the more those myths and prejudices dissolved.

Such preconceptions weren't limited only to my high school. When I taught much later in Japan for six weeks, I saw a lot of anti-Semitism. With very few Jews in Japan, the falsehoods about them continued uncorrected. People hated us and didn't even know us! I visited a synagogue in Tokyo—and it was almost a secret to find out how to get there. They had armed ex-Israeli soldiers guarding the door.

It was such craziness, much like our still being prejudiced against Black people. The Civil War ended 150 years ago and some people now are still trying to take votes away from Black people. They're frightened of anybody voting who isn't White.

A gentler but still illustrative story occurs more recently. While visiting our son Ross and his family in Utah, Lorraine and I go to Sunday services with them. Everybody there is extremely friendly, wanting to meet Ross's parents. Yet my teenage granddaughter Rebecca confides to us, "You know, the reason they're so friendly is they want to touch you to see what you are like. They've never seen a Jew before."

That really resonates. Until they meet you, a Jew is this weird mythical person, often viewed through the lens of stereotypes and even hatred. But once they get to know you, they see we are more alike than different.

Giving Back

Nine years ago, Lorraine and I were recruited to be part of a team called The Jewish Philanthropy Group that provides scholarships every year to Wilson High students starting college. I never lost my appreciation for my time at Wilson. I recently reopened my high school yearbook to remind me of all the people and the events that occurred there.

Today, the school facility that I had attended is known as El Sereno Middle School. The high school is a few miles away on top of a hill and continues to be called Wilson High. Most students presently attending Wilson are Hispanic, along with a few Asians.

In addition to providing scholarships, I've gone to the school a number of times to present career days. I tell them that I was once a student there and became the first person in my family to go to college. I speak at many career days at different minority high schools in LA.

I am motivated to do this because most students there have parents who are not educated. This is the student's chance to have a different life. I talk of my having been raised by noneducated immigrant parents, about the profession I entered, and what has happened over the course of my career. These students may be living during a different time with different circumstances. But they and I essentially have the same story.

I share mine in the hope it will help them.

✦ ✦ ✦

CHAPTER 22

The Rise and Fall of Leo Baron

While I enjoy my time in school and with friends, Leo continues his wild ventures to provide for our family. Though we don't have a lot, I never worry about money. If there are concerns, they are kept from me.

As it turns out, there are concerns.

People dealt with money differently back then. Some had lingering distrust of banks, since so many failed during the Great Depression and people lost their savings.

Colorful stories abounded about people, including some of our cousins, who kept their money buried in the backyard. According to my mother, when they needed funds, these cousins dug up the cash, washed and cleaned the bills, and hung them on a clothesline to dry. This surely gives a new meaning to the term "money laundering."

My dad isn't so distrustful. Our backyard is untouched by such buried treasures. He has an account at Farmers and Merchants Bank downtown. Between the arcade, hot dog stand, then horse racing and the occasional wisely placed wager, we are doing alright.

While they enjoy certain extravagances, my folks are not into what I would call cultural things. Our box seats are at the prizefights and the track, not at the opera, the ballet, or theater.

On the other hand, my mother does hire Ace Studios to design her bedroom. Even though we call City Terrace (where we live) "the Beverly Hills of Boyle Heights"—trust me—nobody ever hires a decorator. Mom adorns the bedroom in gray and maroon. It is the talk of the town.

What Goes Up . . . Can Come Down

Leo does well buying, selling, and racing horses. It is the gambling that brings about his demise.

His wagers are done at the racetrack, or on prize fights, or at cards with male friends and family members. The card games are not big stakes, but they show a consistency in Leo's pursuits, and point to what some would call a gambling addiction.

Most of us believe that when things are going great, they'll be great forever. So you take some additional risks. But then all of a sudden you have a crash. That happens to Leo on more than one occasion. It even occurs in a major way later in my own life.

Ideally, you pick up the pieces and see what you can do next. But for Leo, what he usually does next is more gambling.

One reason I remember my plane trip to Tanforan Racetrack is because of what happens after we returned to Los Angeles. While up there, my father bet big and loses $3,000. That was a ton of cash in 1948 (at that point, worth over $36,000 in today's currency). This occurs when my family is *not* so flush and my mom gets angry. They have a huge fight. One of their very few.

Clearly Dad made a lot of money on Mary Asha. It is also clear that most of it is gone by this time. That's the problem with those hooked on gambling: even if they lose big, they believe the next bet or next hand or next roll of the dice will be the big win that makes them financially whole again. They have to try as gambling becomes an addiction. A disease. Strangely, I'll learn years later that my biological father, Al, has the same affliction.

Baron the Bookie

Rocky becomes a bigger figure in our lives after Leo is on the downswing from gambling losses. Perhaps befitting his name, Rocky is connected with "the Syndicate." I don't know if that means mafia, but it's something close.

Leo reaches out to Rocky, who gets Leo involved in the Syndicate's bookmaking operation.

Bookmaking is illegal betting. Leo is doing the same thing the track does: giving odds, making payouts, receiving money from the losers. But the racetrack gets no percentage and no taxes are paid on winnings. Leo becomes a bookie taking bets with the Syndicate's backing. Of course, the Syndicate takes a percentage of his bookmaking operation when he is ahead.

Until this point, Leo has always been in charge. He's created his own businesses. But by this time in his life, due mostly to his gambling habit, he has no choice but to "get in bed" with these people. Leo needs to survive and provide for his family.

Leo deals with the customers, but he doesn't take any money from them before the race or sporting contest. He simply records their bets and passes that information along to the Syndicate. Then every morning around 3:00 a.m., a little brown envelope from the Syndicate arrives in our mailbox. Inside is a tally of the previous day's transactions, so Leo knows who he has to pay and from whom he has to collect.

Leo Gets Sick

At a certain point, Leo starts to feel unwell. He is diagnosed with a serious illness (more on this later). Leo can't make these cash runs anymore.

So Mel Baron becomes a bagman.

Even though my mother has a car, she is a terrible driver. The last thing we want is for her to get stopped or have an accident . . . and the cops find her with all this cash along with the Syndicate envelope and its incriminating evidence.

Some teenagers sell newspapers after school. Others work in a local soda fountain shop. I am out collecting bets for an illegal syndicate.

I'm driving to all these strangers' houses, taking their money or paying out cash. But I never fear that harm will come to me from these individuals. They never seem weird or shady. (They may also know I am "backed" by the Syndicate—not a group you want to mess with.) These are mostly small bets: ten or twenty bucks. Not every kid gets an opportunity to experience this part of life!

I have a checkered past.

Family Business

I am not the only family member to get involved.

Bookmaking on the scale that Leo is conducting isn't a one-man operation. You need people to answer phones and take bets all day long. Lots of people. You also need a place where these people can do this.

So who better to help in this than . . . my grandparents.

Leo and my cousin Millie arrange it. I'm not sure what they tell my mother's parents is going on, but they set up this whole answering service inside my grandparents' home. Multiple telephones lines are installed and people are hired to come in, answer calls, and take bets over the phone. There are no fax machines or computers at this time. Everything is strictly done by telephone. They are running a bookmaking operation out of my grandparents' house.

My mother is part of this too. In fact, when Leo gets sick, Mom takes over. The Syndicate assigns her the code name Broadway. Whenever someone from the Syndicate calls, they say, "Let me talk to Broadway." I presume this is so if the police get wind of the operation, or if any of the syndicate's phone calls to her are overheard (if our phones are tapped), the police won't know her real name and it will be harder to trace the operation back to her.

So the bet-taking phone banks continue running in my grandparents' house. My mother's primary role is to review the contents of those little brown envelopes that appear daily in our mailbox, and determine who I must collect cash from or pay off.

Owning and racing horses completely fades away during this time. While it has been successful, Leo's gambling forces him to sell his horses to pay off debts.

Eventually, there is only the bookmaking.

Trouble Comes A-Knocking

Fortunately, all is going well. Everything is working and money is flowing in. It is a smooth-running operation.

Until one day there is loud "knocking" on the door.

The police show up and raid the telephone bookmaking operation! At the home of my grandparents who barely speak English. The cops shut the whole thing down. Fortunately, I am not there.

Somehow, neither my grandparents nor my mother get arrested or go to prison. That's particularly fortunate since this operation becomes a focus of Senator Estes Kefauver from Tennessee, the great crime-buster. Heading a U.S. Senate committee clamping down on illegal gambling, he runs well-publicized investigations into organized crime in the early 1950s (perhaps to aid his political aspirations, since he twice runs for president and becomes a running mate to presidential nominee Adlai Stevenson).

Kefauver holds public hearings in fourteen cities that are televised live. He ends up reading both Rocky's and my father's names into the court records. But by the time all this occurs, my father will have passed away. Rocky goes to prison. I don't know for how long. But I never see him again.

◆　◆　◆

CHAPTER 23

Dreams of UCLA: "Going, Going, Gone"

As his bookmaking operation thrives, Leo opens an auction house in Baldwin Park. Maybe he sees it as a way to get out from under the Syndicate.

This begins around 1950, as I remember going to the original In-N-Out Burger across the street at Francisquito and Garvey. Barely ten square feet, this In-N-Out Burger is California's first drive-thru hamburger stand. I *really* like their burgers.

The auction house sells furniture along with smaller odds and ends. It is legit, though Leo has shills in the audience—people he employs to pose as customers and bid on items to drive up prices. It is the only business left after the bookmaking is shut down.

At the same time as all this is going on—I am graduating high school and hoping to go to college. I've long had a dream of going to UCLA.

I vividly remember my excitement at receiving a postcard from UCLA saying that I have been accepted to the university. I am ecstatic! Being able to enroll there as a freshman is the only upside in my life at this time. I look forward to living in a dorm on campus and becoming more independent.

But it is not meant to be.

With everything that's happening, my mom wants me to live at home rather than in a dorm in West Los Angeles, so I am closer to Baldwin Park to help her with the auction house. At this time, getting to UCLA from where we live is a long distance. There are still no freeways going there.

Mom says, "I know your heart was set for UCLA. But if you don't go there, the money we would have been paying to put you in the dorm . . . could maybe help with tuition at USC—if you could get in there."

USC is much closer to our home in East LA.

This is really disappointing. I do not want to do what she suggests. But circumstances are what they are.

Korean War Beckons

Once this new reality sets in for me, I suggest that I not attend school at all. I should work to help with finances for my mother and sister, who is only twelve at the time.

Mom won't hear of this. Partly because she wants a better life for me. But her main concern is that I might get drafted to serve in the Korean War that starts in June of 1950.

This worry about me going off to war and maybe never coming back is paramount in my mother's mind. The rule is that if you are a full-time college student and keep a certain grade point average, you are deferred from the draft. Unlike the patriotic and courageous spirit that people had during World War II, people respond to the Korean War much like they do later with Vietnam: "What are we over there fighting for?" It is a conflict between North Korea (supported by China) and South Korea (supported by United Nations forces of mostly U.S. troops).

I have my required military physical and am classified 1-A, which means I am in the top category of those most likely to be drafted. So at my mother's insistence, I apply to USC—and get in. My dream of attending UCLA is now officially over. I am going to USC.

. . . *Thank God.*

Though I don't know it yet, USC will have huge positive effects upon my entire life—none of which would have occurred if I had gone to UCLA.

(Later by the time I finish college, the war is over. By then, I am married to Lorraine and have a child, which places me into a lower draft tier. So I am never drafted for military service. Truth is, war is not glorious no matter what. You go if you have to and I would have done it. But I'm not unhappy that none of my children or grandchildren have served in the military.)

Our Gang Goes Separate Ways

Growing up, my friends and I have zero exposure to adults who've gone to college. Most of our parents are immigrants like my mom or first generation like my dad. All trying to figure out how to survive and make a living. Nobody has had higher education or private school or prep school. Nobody played tennis or golf.

The boys in our neighborhood are almost like an *Our Gang* comedy or the *Bowery Boys* movies. You have this pack of guys roaming streets, all close to the same age, getting into mischief, doing goofy things. We grow up together. We are in school together. In Hebrew school together. A whole cadre of remarkable friends living in homes all on one street.

Yet there comes a time when many of us move on—to college, to jobs, to other neighborhoods. While we all look forward to becoming adults and whatever is next, there is also a sadness as we realize what we have will soon come to an end.

I have stayed in touch with these friends over the years. Most of them did pretty well, whether they went to college or not. Many have been passing away in recent times, which brings a new sense of sorrow. Yet I don't hear of this same kind of growing-up experience from my children or anyone else I know. People don't have this kind of life anymore. It is fraternal, brotherly.

These close bonds created a joyful childhood for me.

✦   ✦   ✦

CHAPTER 24

Leo's Passing & Life Transitions

As I enter my freshman year at USC, Leo's health deteriorates. He has cancer and treatments are limited. There is no chemo or radiation. My mother tries a bunch of medications from the pharmacists at Barbanell's corner drugstore, including early steroid drugs. But it is to no avail. Leo eventually has a heart attack as well. He lives at home, but is very ill.

It's odd the things you recall during difficult times. Steve Allen is popular on the radio and I remember Leo listening to him in the bedroom. But Leo worsens and returns to the hospital. I visit him there during his last days. My mom is with Leo when he dies. Only 42, he passes away on March 11, 1951. Though his death is not unexpected, I feel the loss intensely. I have lost my dad. I will never see or talk with him again. My sister is devastated as well.

For some reason, they don't let my sister go to the funeral. She is thirteen, so maybe they think it is too much for her or she'll cause a distraction. But many years later, my sister still talks about not getting to say goodbye to her father.

Leo is buried at the Home of Peace Cemetery in Boyle Heights. The oldest Jewish cemetery in Los Angeles, it is still around today.

After the service, we sit shiva at our house. Though we are not particularly religious, my mother covers all the mirrors with cloth, trying to honor the tradition of an orthodox shiva house. Food is brought by family and neighbors. We sit shiva for seven days. Lacking sufficient furniture, most everyone sits on boxes as we honor Leo's life.

Leo's death is a huge loss for my mother. The flamboyant sparkle that had been such a part of my mother's life with Leo vanishes. She becomes the much more subdued person known to Lorraine and my children. Perhaps one cause for this is that our own lives now demand a different focus. Leo leaves us with many debts.

When I start at USC, I am helping at the auction house, taking my mom back and forth there every day since she doesn't really drive. Unfortunately, the auction house is but a short-lived, last-ditch effort by Leo. We can't make it successful and it closes sometime after Leo dies. Essentially, we are penniless. My mother has to sell our house to pay for funeral expenses and other debts. My mom, sister, and I move into a rented duplex at 1650 Stearns Drive near Pico and La Cienega on the Westside in a predominantly Jewish area.

One unexpected treat for me: Willie the Weasel, who lived at the other end of our block on Mandalay Drive when we were there, has also moved with his family to Stearns Drive—at the other end of the block. He is going to USC too and living at home, and is once again my neighbor. So we drive to USC together and hang out again as well.

Finders Keepers

Part of the challenge of moving includes sorting through possessions to decide what is worth keeping. It is especially difficult going through Leo's things. And sometimes surprising.

I find an LAPD lieutenant's badge.

We have no idea how Leo got this, or even more worrisome, *how he may have used it.* The badge is now long gone and I've no idea where it is. But the mystery remains to this day.

The Boarding Barons

To bring in extra income, my mother takes in boarders at our Stearns Drive duplex, renting them rooms and cooking them meals.

It is a lot of work for my mother, but everybody is congenial and gets along harmoniously. I find some of the characters living there fascinating.

Though the duplex is in a Jewish area near Fairfax, our boarder Wayne Hoff is not Jewish. He works for UPS while pursuing a singing career. Even then, people come to Los Angeles hoping to break into the entertainment business. Wayne is in a group called The Jones Boys that is minimally successful. Though I never hear him singing in the house, he is a real nice guy and a pleasure to have around. We get other musicians too.

We have Joe Levy, a fraternity brother of mine at the Sigma Alpha Mu Fraternity at USC. Joe first tries living at the fraternity house. But Joe is a little rich boy (his family owns the Gottschalks Department Store chain in Northern California). Given his upbringing, Joe feels the fraternity house is a noisy, unclean . . . dump. With less than satisfactory cuisine.

Since we are fraternity brothers, I tell him, "Joe, my mom has a boarding house. It's quiet. It's clean. She's a good cook. How about you live with us?"

Joe leaps at the chance.

It is great to have a friend stay with us. Joe also intrigues me because I have never known anybody rich. He has a fancy car, and during our first year, we drive up to Berkeley where USC is playing a football game. Along the way, we stop at his family house in Fresno. To me, it is a mansion. I am a 19-year-old kid and have never been in such a place! Joe has an entire room just for his train sets mounted on a big platform. There is live-in help that constantly tends to the house.

I'm like, *"Who the hell lives like this?"*

To bring in additional income, my mom works with my Aunt Katie at her shoeshine stand on Alvarado Street, and at someone else's restaurant on the same street. No careers. Just survival jobs.

Even with the money I get from my band playing on weekends, we are just scraping by as a family. Yet whenever I might say to my mom— "Have you got a twenty somewhere?"—she will pull out $20 and give it to me. How she does this, I do not know. Mom was an amazing lady.

My New Crossroads

When Leo dies, my whole world changes. I've lost my father. Our family faces financial difficulties. The country is at war.

I don't know where I am headed or what to do with my life. I can no longer get by simply being "The Second Coming." I am forced into some degree of adulthood.

It is time to grow up.

✦ ✦ ✦

CHAPTER 25

College Boy

My sister cruises through high school. Grades are not that important to her. She is more interested in doing things with the other girls and in how she dresses. Mom is fine with that. There is no academic pressure on her whatsoever. That's how it is for girls during this era. What's important for a young Jewish girl is to marry a nice Jewish guy with money and buy a house and have kids and live happily ever after.

On the other hand, *I do* feel pressure to attend college and succeed. Unlike today's focus to find a career that you love, the goal then is to find some line of work that will earn a living so you can get married, buy a house, have kids—and live happily ever after.

Going Straight

Most of my peers are planning to learn professions at college. As I've said, Jews aren't welcome in the corporate world. So the best options for us are to start our own businesses or learn a profession.

We hope to have better lives for ourselves than those of our parents—who are mostly entrepreneurial, on their own, and all too often just making ends meet. I am part of a new generation with a different plan . . . which is interesting since I am raised by a man who never had one.

Leo's plan might be called, "What's next?" A man whose endeavors aren't always what you call entirely legitimate.

Something I marvel about my own life is that I end up "going straight." Growing up, I was surrounded by somewhat shady characters, like Rocky and Uncle Sid. My father kind of lived on the edge, and the police badge may hint at other dubious parts of his life that I was not privy to. I know he was in partnership with the Syndicate. He had shills artificially driving up bidding at his auction house. He was a gambling addict.

I don't know if there is a conscious effort on my part to "go legit." Lorraine claims I'm a big gambler too, though I think a better term is "risk-taker." I don't gamble with money in terms of wagering. But I certainly take chances in business and other ventures.

Some are super successful. A couple are major disasters.

My New Band of Brothers: Fraternity Life

Having grown up with my community of close friends, it's natural that I seek the same at college.

As a young adult, I am not religious. But I culturally feel close to Judaism. I participate in Hillel, a national organization that serves as a Jewish community center on various college campuses. The Hillel hosts Shabbat and high holiday services and is a place for young Jews to congregate and feel part of something.

I also look to join a Jewish fraternity. There are a number of Jewish fraternities at USC. Willie the Weasel is already in ZBT (Zeta Beta Tau). But they are mostly wealthy kids and I don't feel comfortable there. So I join Sigma Alpha Mu, commonly known as "Sammies," another Jewish fraternity.

There is an initiation period when you join a fraternity. For a pledge (someone who just joined) at the Sammies house, they have *hell week*. Today, we hear horror stories about kids sometimes dying after being forced to do crazy pranks or excessive drinking as part of their fraternity initiation. At Sigma Alpha Mu, there is nothing exceedingly dangerous. . . . Just exceedingly unpleasant.

Like having to keep a fresh piece of raw squishy liver in your underpants as you go about your day and attend classes during the week. Worse, if one of your fraternity brothers sees you during that week, he'll say, "Mel, present liver." You have to put your hand down your pants and pull out this quivering piece of liver. Can you imagine stuffing a liver in your jockey shorts for a week and having to pull it out? Especially if girls are around?

The liver thing is a main feature of hell week initiation at the Sammies house. I don't think you can do this anymore with pledges. But at least we aren't risking our lives. Only our dignity.

I join Sammies to have camaraderie through college. Yet some of these guys will go on to play roles in my life. Howard Press is a well-read, intellectual guy, who speaks very proper English. His parents live in a lovely home in Cheviot Hills. His mother drives a foreign car. I don't know anybody whose parents own a foreign car.

But more important, it will be at Howard's family house where Lorraine and I will have our first date (more on that later!).

Howard is a different kind of guy than those I've grown up with. He fascinates me and we remain friends throughout our lives. At USC, he plans to become a college professor, but after taking a biology class, he falls in love with the biological sciences and ends up being a physician. It is extraordinary how certain things, like a single class, can affect one's entire life. Howard eventually marries Phyllis Coates—the first actress to play Lois Lane in the *Adventures of Superman* TV series in the 1950s.

A little older than myself, Jerry Wish is in military service before coming to USC and joining the Sammies. He lives with his parents, but by himself in a house in the back. His place is kind of a hangout. After Lorraine enters my life, she comes with me many times to listen to music and have late-night discussions about all kinds of things. Jerry is an early music intellect and interested in some really cool jazz stuff. He knows a lot of people in that music world and introduces us to a new culture.

This is a time period when many small jazz clubs pop up around LA, like The Haig across from the Ambassador Hotel and Shelly's Manne Hole in Hollywood (Shelly Manne is the owner and a drummer). We also drive down to Howard Rumsey's Lighthouse in Redondo Beach where he leads a band called the Lighthouse All-Stars. Many famous jazz musicians cycle through there.

These are super popular places at the time, with local people like Stan Kenton (pianist, composer, and leader of an innovative jazz orchestra) and Shorty Rogers (a principal creator of West Coast jazz that relies more on composition than improvising). It is cutting-edge stuff in the jazz world, and Lorraine and I are really into it.

Gil Schy is another Sammies character and funny as hell. Though attending USC, Gil is not a serious student—just a crazy young kid. A trait that Gil never entirely outgrows.

After graduation, Gil becomes an executive with Seagram's, the whiskey conglomerate. When he and his wife are living in LA, they are close friends during our early marriage. At this time, there are a lot of TV commercials for Bandini—a fertilizer whose primary ingredient is manure. The commercials are intentionally silly and make us laugh, and we tease one another by calling the other "Bandini." One day at our first apartment on Colfax, Lorraine and I find a 50-pound bag of Bandini manure dropped off at our door. That's Gil Schy.

There are many others in my fraternity—a whole cadre of young men totally different from my high school buddies. Some quite wealthy, some very intellectual—they all have an impact on me. Exposing me to different ways that people live and view the world. This provides me pictures of what success can look like *and* that it is attainable. Eye-opening.

Of course, just being at college is an awakening. Far different from City Terrace where most parents are immigrants and no one attends concerts. Nobody is at the ballet. There is no conversation about such things.

USC nurtures and molds me in many ways. I am so grateful for these classmates, many of whom remain close friends throughout my life.

Boys of the Band Continue

My high school band keeps playing all through college. John Shambra is at USC too and remains in our group. But not all our band members matriculate to USC. We take on new players in college, with band members changing at times when they are no longer available. But it is still Mel and The Meltones. We play the same kinds of events—bar mitzvahs, weddings, dances—and still wear matching "trendy" outfits. We are just a little older now. No longer a high school band.

Playing in our band is a major piece of my high school and college life with an appealing side benefit of making me kind of popular. Yet after a while, I find it somewhat tedious. But it is good money and most of the time we are paid in cash, so for me and everyone else, it remains cool.

Though a full-time student, I help family finances in other ways too. During my early days at USC, I work as a salesperson at Brown's Clothing—a downtown men's store on Broadway owned by a Jewish guy named Charlie Brown (yes, just like the kid in the *Peanuts* comic strip). Though I am happy for the job, it is not the best setup. The store has an open-air setting that gets a lot of pedestrian traffic. So much so, that from time to time, the manager yells out, "Hey Mr. Aoygn"—which is code for us salespeople to keep an eye on some "suspicious-looking customer" to make sure they are not stealing. "Aoygn" is actually Yiddish for "eyes." All the salespeople are Jewish. None of the customers are.

Fortunately, I get promoted to their Wilshire Miracle Mile Store—a better and classier location. This is big-time and I do very well there. I have an eye for what looks good and how to match different articles of clothing. I am also a good salesman, which proves valuable throughout my life. You're always selling in some way. Even if not pushing a product, you are often selling yourself. Convincing someone to hire you or that you have a great idea that you can succeed with.

I'm sure I get both of these traits from my dad. Leo often dresses up with a nice hat—which is the look of the time. Nobody wears jeans and or even khakis. For men, it's shirts and ties, slacks and suit jacket. Of course, Leo is also the ultimate salesman. I'm sure all of this rubs off on me.

For one thing, I like clothes. While I need to look nice as a salesman, I also get a discount there and buy myself a *really* nice $95 suit for personal use. That is expensive—the equivalent of $900 today!

College Classes

Classes at USC are a world away from those in high school. I am placed in dumbbell English and dumbbell math as I am not well prepared coming out of Wilson High. But I am able to survive and get through it. Sometimes with help from my fraternity brothers.

Bud Fishman is a genius. On the day of his statistics class final exam, he arrives late with only twenty minutes left for the one-hour exam. Surprised, the teacher says, "Are you sure you want to take this exam or would you prefer to take an incomplete?"

Bud insists, "The exam."

He takes the test and aces it. Bud becomes a TA for the statistics class and is very helpful to me. And tries to be to others . . . though not always successfully. Irwin Freeze of our fraternity enrolls in the statistics class knowing that Bud is the TA. Bud assures him, "I'll get to grade your five-week exam, so don't worry. I'll take care of it and you'll pass fine."

So Irwin takes the first test—and flunks it—because Bud *doesn't* get to grade it. Irwin's test goes to another TA for evaluation.

Next is the midterm exam. Again, Bud doesn't get to grade his paper, and Irwin does not excel.

Now comes time for finals. Irwin pleads, "Bud, you've *got* to get my exam to grade or I'm going to flunk this class!"

Bud says, "Don't worry. I'll take care of it."

This time, Bud *does* get to grade Irwin's test. Of course, Bud doctors the answers and Irwin aces the exam!

But after results are all tallied, the professor says to Bud, "This latest exam—this is from *Dummy Freeze?*"

The professor knows that Irwin Freeze bombed his first two exams. Bud thinks quickly on his feet. "I guess he wasn't paying much attention to his studies when he took the earlier tests. Isn't it great that you turned him into a more serious student?"

So Irwin Freeze passes statistics. However, Dummy Freeze becomes Irwin's nickname forever after Bud shares the story with friends.

Bud eventually marries a girl from Chattanooga, Tennessee. I don't know *anybody* from Chattanooga, but apparently at least one Jewish girl is from there. Bud becomes an attorney and later successfully defends Gil Schy (of our fraternity) in a big lawsuit. Like I said, the bonds formed as fraternity brothers carry through long after graduation.

Unfortunately, Bud passes away at a very young age. His widow, Paula, remarries and lives near us. We've been friends with them ever since. So, in a way, my dear friend Bud "remains" in my life.

◆　◆　◆

CHAPTER 26

Lorraine Ross

As a single young man in college, I date a few girls during the first couple of years. Nothing serious. Not until a summer fraternity party in 1952.

Oddly, I am at this event with my mother for reasons I no longer recall. A girl there sees me and tells a friend of mine that she thinks I'm cute and hands him her phone number to give to me.

I have no idea who this girl is. But I figure, "Well, if somebody thinks I'm cute . . . I might as well give her a call."

I phone up this young woman named Lorraine Ross.

We talk. Not a long call, but there is enough interest that I tell her my band has a gig at my fraternity's barbecue party at a private residence in Cheviot Hills on July 4th. "I'll be playing the drums. If you don't mind, you can come there with me and afterward we can go out for a dinner?" She agrees.

I am living on Stearns Drive in West LA and she lives up Beverly Glen in Sherman Oaks. It is a long commute and I'll be in my mother's sedan. I am thinking, "Mr. Wonderful doesn't even have his own car."

But soon that isn't my biggest concern.

July 4th arrives and on my way over, I am having second thoughts. "Why in the world am I doing this? I don't even know what she looks like. This could be a disaster!" I am thinking of all kinds of excuses to use if she opens the door and is unattractive. I rehearse different options in my mind:

"Oh, sorry. I got the wrong address. I'm looking for my buddy."

"Oh, is your sister home? I'm supposed to meet 'Margie.'"

Obviously, I am not thinking this through. Lorraine will recognize me from the party. I'm kinda stuck.

However, when she opens the door, I am immediately smitten. I forget all of my rehearsals. Lorraine is gorgeous. I can still tell you what she was wearing: an aqua dress with spaghetti straps.

Now I am excited.

We drive to the fraternity barbecue party. As my band plays, I make a decision: I am not going to try to kiss Lorraine on date one. I don't want to move too fast. This is too important to risk messing up.

As we go out that night, everything is so easy. I feel like I've known Lorraine forever. She just has this way about her. I return her home after our date and thank her for the evening.

I want to see her again. But at this time, I am in summer school taking *two* physics classes as I want to finish the needed prerequisites for entering any of the USC science-related graduate programs (which for me is to be dental school). I am also working as a clothes salesman at Browns and playing in the band. I don't have time to start dating anyone. Yet. . .

"Lorraine, what are you doing tomorrow night?"

Rather than being impressed that I am putting my priorities aside for her, Lorraine tells me that she is pretty popular and isn't sure how much time she has for me. Yet. . .

We go out for the next six nights in a row. I never date another girl. I am nineteen. Lorraine is one day younger than me.

Fate (and Lorraine's Mother) Intervenes

The only reason Lorraine is even at the fraternity party where she first sees me is because her mother makes her go. Lorraine agreed to be some guy's date but then decides she doesn't want to go with him. But her mother tells her, "You made that date. You're not calling him up at the last minute with some fake excuse."

So Lorraine goes to the party. Of course, since she isn't happy being there with that guy, she is looking around for someone better. . . . . Me.

She makes a good choice, in my opinion. I am forever grateful to her mother.

Lorraine and I keep dating, often repeating the same scenario as on our first date because I am so busy: she accompanies me as I play a weekend wedding or bar mitzvah or other event. She sits there two or three hours while the band performs, then she and I go out.

Unfortunately, Lorraine isn't *always* sitting.

I'm playing this one event and a guy notices Lorraine just sitting there and asks her to dance. I kind of recognize him because people refer to him as "the pastrami king" (don't ask me why).

They start dancing.

I am up on stage watching them and don't like how he is dancing with her. My drumming gets louder and louder as I get madder and madder. We finally finish the song and I rush off the bandstand—my bandmates wondering, "*What is going on?*" I break the two of them up. I am not a nice person in that moment. I am furious: "What do you think you're doing? That's my girl. Get away from her!"

Things fortunately do not escalate into a fight as Lorraine assures me that nothing is going on between them. She sends the pastrami king walking and it's over. This is the only time that ever happens. Not my best moment. But at least Lorraine knows I really like her!

Despite this incident, we continue dating. And Lorraine continues to help me pile all my drums into the car and set up when we get to my next show. Afterward, usually late at night, we go somewhere to eat. A place called Googie's on the Sunset Strip part of Sunset Boulevard. Or the nearby Cyrano's. Or the original Hamburger Hamlet with a piano player in the back. It is quite a hangout. The strip is a very cool place.

Probably not your typical courtship. But it still brings us closer.

◆　◆　◆

CHAPTER 27

Change of Course: Pharmacy

Though my father led this wild and crazy life, it was pretty successful. Yet he (and my mom) push me to go to college and become a dentist. What's more conservative than being a dentist?

It is a respectable and stable vocation. People will always need dentists. I can't say I am all that excited about the prospect, but at this time, people are looking less for their "life's calling" than for a dependable source of income. Dentistry makes sense.

Once the summer of '52 is over, I have one semester left of undergrad before I would start my dental school studies. So I take the dental aptitude exam at USC. The test is both written and verbal, plus physical carving. They actually have you carve material as you might do when shaping a tooth. An unusual exam.

Yet my heart is truly not in it. Plus, I have the world's worst manual dexterity. I struggle through the testing.

I go to learn my results at the dental school. Someone from the school sits down to meet with me, carrying a folder. He looks at me. He looks in the folder. He looks at me again. After a long pause, he says:

"You don't look this stupid."

I am stunned. I figure I hadn't done great. But hearing that, I don't know if I should cry or punch the guy's face. I choose neither and barely manage to walk out of there. Rejected from dental school.

In somewhat of a daze, I go over to the psychology building. I am enrolled in an abnormal psych class and I find the professor. I have no idea what instinct guides me there, but lo and behold, he's in his office. He can tell that I have something weighing on my mind and invites me in.

After listening to my story, he says, "You know, only the top ten percent of students even get to take that test."

Then he asks, "What else do you want to do?"

"I . . . have no idea."

"Well, what are your friends studying?"

"Some are in optometry school. A couple of buddies are going to pharmacy school." That's all I come up with.

So he inquires, "If you have to make a choice right now this minute, what would you say?"

I answer, "Pharmacy."

"Okay then. Pharmacy school is at the other end of campus. How about you go down there, pick up an application and fill it out."

Like a robot, I leave his office and go to the pharmacy school and get an application. Then I do something unexpected.

Though we're only dating at this point, I call Lorraine on a pay phone. I tell her what happened and ask what she thinks of my new choice. Lorraine is supportive and encouraging.

"If you think pharmacy is a good idea, go ahead and do it. I'm there with you."

Encouraged, I fill out the application. Several months later, I get my reply—I've been accepted. *Thank God.*

And thank God I never become a dentist. I would have killed more people than I cured. With my lack of manual dexterity, I could have set the profession back two hundred years!

My Pharmacy Education

I begin pharmacy school in January of 1953. On the very first day, I am standing at an orientation with my other incoming classmates, predominantly men. There are only five or six women students in the

PHONE RICHMOND 2311

UNIVERSITY OF SOUTHERN CALIFORNIA
3518 UNIVERSITY AVENUE
LOS ANGELES 7

OFFICE OF ADMISSIONS
PLEASE ADDRESS COMMUNICATIONS
TO THE DIRECTOR OF ADMISSIONS

January 9, 1953

Mr. Melvin F. Baron
1650 South Stearns Drive
Los Angeles 35, California

Dear Mr. Baron:

We are pleased to report that you have been selected for admission to the School of Pharmacy, University of Southern California, for the class which begins on February 9, 1953.

If you accept this appointment, please send us notice to that effect within 10 days after receipt of this letter. Your notice of acceptance must be accompanied by the required fee of $25.00 which is not refundable, but which may be applied on your tuition for the coming semester only.

A Permit to Register will be issued when your notice of acceptance has been received.

(Signed) H.J. Sheffield
Director of Admissions
and Registration

HJS:ht

An important life-changing event, I still have my
pharmacy school acceptance letter after 70 years!

entire student body (in stark contrast to today where 70 percent of our pharmacy students are female).

As we all stand there listening to some guy drone on endlessly about labs and supplies and a variety of other trivial topics, another student leans over to me to whisper, "Do you have any clue what this guy is going on and on talking about?"

I answer, "I have absolutely no idea."

This is the beginning of a beautiful friendship.

"Hi, I'm Herb Weinberg," he says.

At pharmacy school, we study together. Or rather, we *try* to study together. I meet with him and two other close friends to group study, which normally can be very helpful as we quiz each other, etc. Except it becomes clear to three of us that Herb's mind is in a league of its own. He is a genius. Herb is a super-great guy, but there is no way we can study with him. I end up studying with just these two other guys while Herb . . . well I don't know if Herb ever needs to study.

But he is fun. Sometimes too much fun.

Lorraine and I are out to dinner with Herb and his wife and another couple. I am wearing my super expensive suit that I bought when I was working at Brown's Clothing. We are all having a great time and even though we leave the restaurant late at night, they want to go walk on the beach.

I object, "Are you guys crazy? I'm wearing my $95 suit. I'm not going anywhere near the sand!"

We end up on the beach.

They are sitting on the sand, making jokes and talking—while I carry on, "How can you guys make me do this? It's a $95 suit!"

It's all I talk about. What a fun guy I am!

Herb and I go through pharmacy school together and enter the same profession. He works at different places, buys his own pharmacy and is quite successful. We are at each other's weddings, and Lorraine and I socialize with Herb and his wife, Leah. Our kids are near the same age and are social in their ways. He and I do some business together—knowing each other now for nearly seventy years and counting!

He's a really interesting guy, great storyteller—and also funny as hell. Recently, I get a call from Herb: "Hey Mel, I saw the picture that USC took of you in a suit, standing at the corner of Brooklyn and Soto in your old neighborhood. Nice photo. *So Mel—is that still your $95 suit?*"

Rho Pi Phi

I make quite a few friends at pharmacy school. I join a Jewish pharmacy fraternity, Rho Pi Phi, that is important to my time there. Jews are a minority at the school.

Pharmacy school is very competitive. The other main fraternity—Phi Delta Chi—produces most of the teaching assistants. That gives the rest of Phi's fraternity members an advantage in classes. Partly to counter this, members in my fraternity develop a true family camaraderie—sharing information, studying together—becoming a close-knit united group.

But competition isn't limited to inside the classroom. Pharmacy school has an annual picnic—along with a touch football game every year—where it is largely Phi Delta Chi fraternity against my Rho's. This is pretty much a bloodbath—mean and angry and violent. Both because of our rivalry, and because Phi Delta Chi knows we are Jewish.

The close bonds we form in Rho Pi Phi help us through school and carry over after graduation. We are all going to be professionals in the same field, and these connections and friendships will be invaluable to our careers.

◆　◆　◆

CHAPTER 28

Blossoming Romance

I meet Lorraine's family soon after we start dating. Phil and Rebecca Ross have a beautifully furnished home. I am surprised to learn that her mother goes by the name of Bert rather than Rebecca, having never liked her given name nor its traditional shortened version, Becky.

Not surprisingly (given who Lorraine is), her parents are lovely people. Lorraine has a sister, Sharon, nine years younger. Lorraine at times is kind of a mother figure to her. They have a wonderful relationship too.

Though both parents are from England, Lorraine's father came to the States early enough that he has no accent. Her mother, however,

Lorraine's parents

has this really interesting English accent. It fits her—as she is quite proper—especially in how she sets the table and dresses.

However, I will discover that away from "properly" setting tables and serving meals—her mother can be playful with a great sense of humor! She is a big personality who can really let loose, dance, and have lots of fun. That matches perfectly with Lorraine's father who is not "proper

English" at all. Americanized and larger than life, he is outgoing and funny. Both of them are upbeat and extremely social with plenty of friends.

It is also apparent to me that her mother really loves Lorraine even though she isn't particularly demonstrative, while her father's love is more overt. Lorraine's father has a retail furniture store near Van Nuys Boulevard and Sherman Way called The Hitching Post. It is a big, barn-like building in which they sell cheaper furniture lines bought by people who pay in installments over time.

Her parents have a fabulous marriage. Yet as they see Lorraine and I spend more and more time together, they have concerns. *About Mel.* They know my family is just my mom, my sister, and me. They know I don't have any money.

What kind of future is there for Lorraine with Mel? Where is this guy going in his life? When I first meet them, I have not even begun pharmacy school. I am not the typical dream guy.

Yet we continue going out and six months after our first date, I give Lorraine a cashmere sweater and put my Sammies pin on it. For young people then, this is almost an engagement. It is a *pre-engagement*.

I am serious about Lorraine.

In January of 1953, I begin pharmacy school. Though Lorraine's parents now have less reason to worry since I am in a professional school . . . now *my* mother has concerns about my getting married. She likes Lorraine, but since my mother has fairly recently lost her husband

and I'm kind of a stable force in the household, my mother feels, "Why don't you wait a while longer?"

Lorraine is aware of this pressure my mother is placing on me to put off getting married. Lorraine, however, feels we've waited long enough.

"Mel, it's either now or never. Are we going to do this or not?"

She understands my moving out creates a void for my mother, but feels we need to go forward with marriage or it might never happen.

Soon after, Lorraine and I are at the home of some of her relatives—the Waxes. It is the start of summer and we are sitting by the swimming pool. I look tenderly at her and say, "Lorraine, if I ask you to marry me, will you say yes?" She smiles broadly and indicates she will.

Yet this is not an official proposal. More like a *pre-proposal*.

The Real Proposal

About six months after I give Lorraine my Sammies pin, we are going to dinner at the Plymouth House, a fancy restaurant up on the Sunset Strip. I am planning to pop the question.

Though I haven't written about him here after my dad's passing, Uncle Sid actively stays in my life, giving me emotional support. And if I sometimes need money, he helps there too.

Knowing that I am planning to propose at the restaurant, Uncle Sid grins and hands me the keys to his new Caddy. "You know what, Mel? Take my Cadillac tonight."

I so appreciate this! It is a big deal to travel to the restaurant in style.

At the restaurant, we order cocktails. When she isn't looking, I slip an engagement ring into Lorraine's drink. I saw this in a movie and thought it was pretty cool. We continue talking while I watch to make sure she doesn't drink from her glass without looking and accidentally swallow or choke on the ring. That would spoil the mood for sure.

Finally, Lorraine picks up her glass to drink—and spots the ring. She is totally surprised—and I pop the question.

As promised, she answers, "Yes."

Wedding Bells

Six months after I propose, we are to be married at the Sportsman Lodge in the Valley on December 20th, 1953. The Sportsman's Lodge is "the fancy wedding place" at the time. Both Lorraine and I are just 21 years old.

As per tradition, the bride's family is to pay for the wedding. Yet her dad asks us straight out: "Would you rather have the money or the wedding?"

Given our situation and me being just a student, I am thinking money is the practical answer. Lorraine is of the same mind. But she is also thinking her parents will be crushed if we don't have a proper wedding. (She also doesn't believe they'd go through with just giving us the cash anyway.)

Lorraine and me at our wedding

So we have the wedding. A big wedding. A *huge* wedding. Maybe two hundred people. Everyone is very dressed up. Lorraine's wedding party consists of her girlfriends of many years. John Shambra is my best man. Howard Press is there (especially since our first date was at his home). Gil Schy. Other fraternity brothers. Herb Weinberg, of course.

Despite her earlier concerns, my mom has a great night. She is very festive and enjoys herself. She loves Lorraine and feels super comfortable with her. My mother also has a great relationship with Lorraine's parents, who know my mom is a widow and are always kind and caring toward her.

It also happens to be my sister's fifteenth birthday. So December 20th now celebrates her birthday *and* our wedding anniversary.

Lorraine pretends to be horrified as I consult
a *Honeymoon Hints* book, illustrated.

Mr. Right Goes Very Very Wrong

For our wedding night, I make a reservation at the Santa Inez Inn in Santa Monica (located where the marvelous Self-Realization Lake Shrine near Sunset and PCH is now).

One obstacle to our romantic getaway is getting away from some overly enthusiastic wedding guests who follow us in their cars while honking endlessly. I finally lose them and we arrive at the inn. Smooth sailing from here on.

Or so I think.

At the front desk, I announce that Mr. and Mrs. Mel and Lorraine Baron are here for our night in the bridal suite.

The man at the desk says, "I'm sorry, but the bridal suite is occupied."

What?

Well now I'm going to show Lorraine that she married the right guy who can handle any situation. I get belligerent and tell the desk clerk in no uncertain terms that I made this reservation weeks ago.

This desk clerk tries to be helpful. "If you'd like, I can make some phone calls to other hotels in the area to see if I can get you one of their honeymoon suites. All we have available is a normal room—with two twin beds."

I carry on about this is a terrible mistake on their part, tell them they need to honor *our* reservation at *their* hotel.

He says to give him a moment as he checks their records and finds my letter of correspondence. He shows it to me.

There it is in black and white that I have indeed made our reservation . . . *for the next night.*

I am horrified.

But Lorraine is kind enough not to say anything about my error. Together, we decide to stay at this place rather than start looking for new accommodations. We go to our room with the twin beds. Somehow, we are not bright enough to pull out the little nightstand between the two beds and move them together. We end up in one small bed together.

This is the first night that Lorraine and I are physically intimate and we don't waste it. Unfortunately, that small bed is pretty light and it keeps banging against the wall!

It's Vegas, Baby!

After our memorable wedding night, we set out to Las Vegas for our honeymoon. This is my first trip out of California as an adult.

We drive in Lorraine's car—a yellow Chevy convertible with the canvas top down. The car has no air conditioning and no heater (it has a radio!). Going to Vegas, riding down the Strip in a yellow convertible—this is a dream to us twenty-one-year-olds.

Vegas at the time is a big honeymoon destination. Classy and hip. We stay at

Enroute to Vegas, we stop at Hoover Dam.

the Sahara, which opened in 1952 and is only the sixth resort on the Strip. The length of our stay is dependent on how much cash we get at the wedding. We receive a total of $300. A good sum then, but we can't spend it all on our honeymoon. It also has to help us get started as a couple. We've already rented an apartment in a brand-new building on Colfax in North Hollywood. A nice place though unfortunately more than we wanted to spend. Rent for the month: $81.50.

But now, we are in Vegas and having a great time! The Vegas Strip is quite glamorous. Everyone dresses up. We gamble only a little. Instead, we eat wonderful dinners, hear terrific music, and go to shows—including one with comedian/actor Dick Shawn who is very funny and goes on to appear in thirty movies, including *It's a Mad, Mad, Mad, Mad World* and Mel Brooks' *The Producers.*

We are having a fantastic time, but leave earlier than expected as we are running out of funds, and are eager to get to our new apartment!

Loving Life Living with Lorraine

It is a year and a half from our first date until we marry and move in together. No odd personality traits or habits surface. Lorraine and I have been upfront with each other from the start of our courtship. There are no charades or putting on a different face. It's not like today where everyone is trying to put on a show. Who we are is who we are.

Until we move into our first apartment, neither Lorraine nor I have lived outside our parents' homes or with anyone besides our families (except for a few boarders for me).

There are a few "adjustments."

My mother always cared a lot about how I look and the appearance of my clothes. Lorraine is aware that my mother ironed my T-shirts and socks. So Lorraine announces, "Let me tell you something right from the beginning—I will not be ironing your underwear or your socks."

Aside from such small "changes," living together comes pretty easy.

Partnership with Lorraine

Though classes are nearly all male, there is one woman extremely important to my success at pharmacy school.

Lorraine.

Pharmacy school is highly competitive and not easy. I am really a B-student so I have to study super hard. To me, college is more a test of persistence than intelligence.

Lorraine quizzes me constantly with three-by-five cards filled with facts and information. As much as she wants to spend social time with me, she is very supportive of my studies at night. Plus, I am interning at Major Drug (I'll speak more of this) and working weekend gigs with the band, so the limited time we have together is special. In fact, she continues going with me to my band performances, so we have that time together. She even still helps load my drums in the car and schlep them at the venue. The most beautiful roadie in the world!

So our "date nights" are usually late in the evening after the band finishes. We still go to places like Googies Coffee Shop on Sunset Boulevard next to famous Schwab's Pharmacy (a popular hangout for movie actors and others in the film industry, though neither of us get "discovered" there). Our typical "romantic dinner" at that hour is eggs and coffee. Or we stop at the Hollywood Ranch Market close to midnight and do our shopping before heading home. It is the only time we have to shop together.

She is protective of my time. Her folks say, "Come over for dinner. We haven't seen you both in so long!" But Lorraine explains that I need to have dinner at home and study.

Working Woman

While I go to pharmacy school, Lorraine works. Though she doesn't have any significant secretarial skills like shorthand or typing, Lorraine is charming and people are easily taken with her.

In fact, she is hired for a sophisticated office job with Steinway pianos and is in way over her head! She spends most of her day crumpling papers on which she keeps making mistakes, stuffing them into her purse so no one sees. She is there only a short period before they figure this out and must dismiss her.

So Lorraine goes to business school, and becomes an escrow officer doing second mortgages at Benton Mortgage on Ventura Boulevard. The bulk of her clientele is Jewish. She is in heaven there as her charisma can come out in full force. Everyone loves her and she flourishes.

Her job is another way that she supports my studies since it brings in a major portion of our income. Plus, I use our one car to get to school while she takes the bus to work. We live in North Hollywood and USC is quite far, while her job on Ventura Boulevard is close to our apartment. Still, this is generous on her part.

✦　✦　✦

CHAPTER 29

Mel Out in the World of Pharmacy

All freshmen in pharmacy school are required to get an internship at some point, but I look for a paid internship right from the get-go because I need the money. When living with my mother and sister on Stearns Drive (before I marry and move in with Lorraine), I notice a drug store on Pico Boulevard within walking distance to our house. They have an opening. Pay is only a buck-and-a-quarter per hour, but money is money. I apply and get my first job. Great!

But not so great.

I'm there for two weeks, observing how this pharmacist deals with customers and patients and conducts his business. I'm not liking what I see.

"If this is pharmacy, I think I've made a bad choice of professions."

I am having sudden doubts. I tell Lorraine. I tell my mom.

Mom says, "You know, Cousin Millie is a regular customer at Major Drug over on Fairfax. That's still close. Maybe she can help you get a job there."

Sure enough, Cousin Millie puts in a good word and I get hired at Major Drug. A great place with great people.

Owned and run by Joe Rosslaw (along with Joe Finkelstein, the second pharmacist), there is an entirely different feeling to it—homey and friendly. It is like the 1980s TV show *Cheers*, where everybody knows your name (but without the booze). Joe is familiar with pretty much everyone who walks in since they're from the surrounding neighborhood. In fact, pretty much everybody who goes there knows everybody else who goes there!

I learn about patient care, medications, how to treat people and run a pharmacy business—and even *compounding*. Back then, it is common for pharmacists to make up a lot of the medications ourselves. For example, a doctor may prescribe an antihistamine together with another type of drug. We grind up the different manufactured medications and mix them together into capsules. Or we might get a prescription for mixing two to four different ingredients to make up a cough syrup or lotion.

Secundum Artem

Sometimes when a physician prescribes a medication to be compounded, they'll write the ingredients to be included and then say, "secundum artem"—meaning *take the ingredients and make it according to the art*. They leave it up to the pharmacist to determine how to best blend those ingredients so they're the most effective. In the case of oral remedies like a cough syrup, or a topical lotion, the idea is to make it the most palatable. I may flavor it or mix it with something that in my judgment will make it the most agreeable to a patient. For me, it has always resonated that while pharmacy is a science, it is also an art form.

As students of pharmacy, we are trained to do compounding as most community pharmacies compound at the time. This has since gone out of favor as most prescriptions today come preformulated from manufacturers. However, there are still specialty pharmacies that we call compounding pharmacies.

This is all legit at the time. Yet some things we do when I am at Major Drug would get us arrested today! There are no computers. We create our labels on a special Smith Corona portable typewriter. Believe it or not: We are not allowed to put the name of the drug on the prescription label! The label can only list the patient's and doctor's names, date it was filled, expiration date, and instructions like "one capsule, three times a day." That is it.

While this industry-wide restriction is intended to preserve confidentiality, it is absolutely crazy. Not being able to label the drug *or* what it is used for can lead to serious mistakes by patients at home—especially if they have more than one medication.

Working at Major Drug is a great experience for me. In many respects, I learn more in that internship than in my classes so far. However, the Doctor of Pharmacy degree that I am working toward (called PharmD) is a new concept and pretty advanced. USC is one of the few universities to offer a doctorate degree in the field.

Joe Rosslaw, who has less pharmacy education than I will go on to have, likes to tease me about this, calling me "College Boy."

Focus on People's Needs

Pharmacies back then look quite different from those of today. We have a soda fountain, plus ice cream (used most often for making ice cream sodas: drinks made of ice cream in either a soft drink or a mix of flavored syrup and carbonated water), and even a lunch counter. People come in for coffee and breakfast and lunch. There is a cigar counter with cigarettes and cigars, and a cosmetics counter.

Still, not all products are out in the open. A certain propriety dominates the culture. If someone wants sanitary napkins like Kotex and Tampax, we wrap them in green paper so they are "hidden." The necessity for such items is something people don't talk about. If a person wants condoms, they have to ask the pharmacist for them (not a counterperson) as those are kept behind the prescription counter.

Major Drug is a fun place to be. My sister even gets a job behind the soda fountain for a while, packing ice cream. This is all before the common use of credit cards. People pay cash or have it tallied on their in-store charge accounts and pay what is owed at the end of each month.

We know each of the customer-patients personally and treat them well. If Joe hears that one of our patients is sick in the hospital, he might stop by on his way home and visit them. We also have "delivery boys" who deliver prescriptions . . . and more. A customer has no qualms calling to ask, "Mel, can you go next door and pick up a rye bread from Nate's Butter Churn, along with a pound of fresh churned butter and a quarter pound of American cheese and put those into the delivery too?"

Ah, those were the days.

Uncle Sid Becomes Ill

Uncle Sid is hospitalized in 1954 while I am at Major Drug. His hospital is around the corner and one day he calls me: "Mel, I need you to bring me a corned beef sandwich."

Sid has had a heart attack, so I respond, "Are you crazy? You're in a hospital. I can't bring you a corned beef sandwich."

Sid replies, "If you don't bring me the sandwich, I will never speak to you again."

I'm freaked. I call my mother. "Uncle Sid wants me to sneak him a corned beef sandwich in the hospital. He threatens that if I don't, he'll never talk to me again! I don't know what to do."

My mom's answer: "It's simple. Get the corned beef sandwich."

So I sneak into the hospital, past nurses and staff, up the steps, through the corridors—and bring Sid the forbidden sandwich.

By this time, Sid and Aunt Pebe have been living what I would call a nice lifestyle in Cheviot Hills on the Westside, an upscale neighborhood. They have done quite well. But sadly, Sid dies in 1960, when he is only 45. A short life, like my dad. Pebe passes away only four years later at 51.

Hospital Pharmacy

Though my pharmacy schooling lasts four years, I work at Major Drug for just three. During my senior year, I need to get a job at a hospital pharmacy. I don't actually want to take a hospital job, but feel I must.

I worry, "What happens if I can't get a job at a community pharmacy and need to be employed in a hospital but don't have that experience?" It is a genuine concern. There are no big drug store chains at the time. They're all independent pharmacies. Small mama-and-papa shops.

I start work at West Valley Hospital. I do not realize it at first, but my time there will be life changing.

The pharmacy is run by Bill Behrns. My experience here is very different from my time at Major Drug. We just fill orders that come from the doctors and nurses. Medications, but also preparing injectables (the small glass vials of drugs that nurses draw into syringes to inject patients), and IV solutions (bottles of IV saline solution, along with the medications to be added and the equipment needed to infuse patients). We bring them to nurses' stations, ready for the patients.

This is no longer about basic medications or over-the-counter products that would typically be in a community pharmacy. I am learning about different drug categories and how to work in a hospital setting. We have no interaction with the patients. These jobs aren't easy to come by. I feel lucky to get this experience.

When I need another car, my father-in-law gives me an old one so I can get to the hospital. I can't remember the make of this car, but it is a junker of the highest order. It uses more oil than gas. I have to put in oil every day! Fortunately, a gas station near the hospital sells cheap "reclaimed oil" (used oil drained during car oil changes that gets filtered).

I soon realize hospital pharmacies are not where I want to spend my career. A place like Major Drug is a much better fit to my personality and far more fun.

The Band Plays On . . . Until It Doesn't

After I marry and am in pharmacy school, our band continues to book as many gigs as we can for three more years. It is good income for us.

I stay in the group until I am about to graduate from pharmacy school. My last gig is New Year's Eve 1956. Even though I'll miss this musical chapter of my life, I am ready to move on. My skill is limited and I will never be a professional musician. Talented as he is, John Shambra stops playing professional gigs as well. He becomes a teacher and elementary school principal, and works in education his whole life.

As my band days come to an end, I look back and see that what I enjoyed most was meeting wonderful people. And making some money.

It is now time to look forward to a new life.

But what will that life be?

Highly Trained Graduate

The USC School of Pharmacy graduates the first Doctor of Pharmacy class in the United States and the world in 1954. The course load is two years of pre-pharmacy (undergrad) plus four years in the College of Pharmacy. Up until this time, pharmacy degrees are only bachelor's degrees, requiring just two years of pharmacy education—and in the past it is even less. My Major Drug boss Joe Rosslaw likely only has six months of pharmacy school training.

When I will graduate in January of 1957, there may only be a total of 200 PharmD degree graduates in the world.

(Today's USC pharmacy degree is a total of *eight* years: four years of pre-pharmacy and four in the College of Pharmacy.)

Many changes are happening in my life during this time: Lynn is born during my last semester. My final gig in the Meltones. Once I graduate in January and pass my state boards in February, I officially become a pharmacist.

Yet there is one more incredible change *already* in motion. . . .

✦ ✦ ✦

CHAPTER 30

Shield Pharmacy

About halfway through my senior year of pharmacy school, my life takes another huge turn as my boss, Bill Behrns, makes me an offer I can't refuse.

"Mel, you've done a great job here. You are a wonderful hard worker, and I'm going to suggest something to you. There's this doctor constructing a medical building in Van Nuys who wants me to put a pharmacy in there. Mel . . . do you want to be my partner?"

I am floored. But I don't hesitate a moment.

"Are you kidding me?? Of course! How much money do I need to invest?"

"Five grand."

I assure him, "I can do that. I'll get it. I'm going in this with you!"

The truth is I don't have anywhere near that kind of money ($5,000 back in 1957 would be equal to around $50,000 today). Yet I know this is a great opportunity for me and that I have to find a way. I can't even remember everybody that I borrow from, but somehow I collect $5,000.

So I graduate in January 1957 with my PharmD degree . . . and on August 1st, 1957, we open our new pharmacy.

Taking Aim at a Name

First things first—we need a name for our pharmacy.

I remember being advised in college: "Never title a pharmacy with your own name because it'll be hard to sell later." So we aren't going to call it Behrns Pharmacy or Baron Pharmacy or Mel's Pharmacy.

Lorraine and I are flipping through the phone book for ideas, saying them out loud to see how they sound. We aren't coming up with anything.

Then I recall that my partner has another pharmacy called Medallion Pharmacy. So I come up with our new name: Shield. I then sketch a shield, draw a line across it, and put "RX" and a Caduceus on it.

I think I'm a marketing genius!

That becomes our name. A good sounding, generic name.

So what happens during the years I am there? Customers assume "Shield" is my last name!

"Hi Mel. How's the Shield family doing?" Or "Mel, how are all the little Shield kids?" I am known as Mr. Shield. Lorraine is Mrs. Shield. And our kids are the Shield children.

Our original Shield Pharmacy

The pharmacy is at 7301 Sepulveda Boulevard in Van Nuys, one block north of Sherman Way. It is in a small medical building with offices for a couple of general practitioners, a dentist, and later an ophthalmologist. This is a small group of people on which to build our business. But they have huge practices and I gamble that these guys can keep us busy.

Our ongoing mission is to maintain good relations with these physicians since they are the source of all our prescriptions. I use all of my charm to constantly assure, "We'll take great care of your patients!"

When we start, we rely on prescriptions generated by these doctors. This is different from Major Drug, where we mainly serve residents in surrounding neighborhoods. Most people who see a doctor in a medical building don't live down the block. We aren't on a street with a lot of foot traffic.

Though there mainly to service the doctors' offices, we want to continue servicing any patients who fill a prescription with us. We make extra efforts to be personable and caring, and get to know all the patients. Even though in a medical building rather than a community pharmacy, I create a homey and friendly environment.

ANNOUNCEMENT

*We are pleased to announce the opening of
our new prescription pharmacy. The store is modern in
every detail and is stocked with a wide assortment
of fine-quality pharmaceuticals. To you and your patients, we
pledge unexcelled service—prompt,
courteous, and efficient. You are invited to stop in
and inspect our facilities at your convenience.
Your consideration is invited.*

SHIELD PRESCRIPTION PHARMACY
Melvin Baron, Ph.D.
7301 SEPULVEDA BLVD. • VAN NUYS, CALIFORNIA
Phone: STate 61935

Original announcement sent out to neighborhood residences.
Interesting to see how telephone numbers are written.

We also deliver, so our location does not have to be an obstacle. Whatever prescription refills these people may need, we can serve them.

Also mailed to area residences. Notice the graphic style popular at the time.

With this patient-centric approach, we build a pretty good business.

Mel in Charge

I pretty much run our new business, and Bill teaches me how to do it. He is a wonderful mentor and guides this young, recent grad well. Bill educates me about bookkeeping, dealing with banks, how to order from the wholesaler, what medicines to stock, etc. I probably know more about meds and prescriptions than he does, but not how to run a business. I am there all the time, filling prescriptions and dealing with patients. Bill pops in and out to talk about business, how things are going, and different approaches we are trying.

Bill starts the pharmacy with me primarily as an investment. He isn't interested in running it. After four years, I am confident I can run it entirely on my own. This feels like time to make another bold move.

I say to him, "Bill, can I buy you out?"

Fortunately, he is quite amenable to the idea. He comes up with a number to which I agree.

Mel Baron is now the owner of Shield Pharmacy.

Thinking Long-Term

Business is going well. We have successfully been serving both sets of clients: our building's doctors, along with their patients and families.

But I am always thinking about how to grow even more.

One day, I realize that long-term care facilities—those that house and provide medical and personal support care to patients who no longer can live independently—must have prescription needs too.

There are a number of these nursing care facilities in our area and nearby Canoga Park. I visit to convince those in charge that Shield can better provide for their needs than whoever is doing that job currently. The fact that Shield is located in a medical building adds to our cachet. Plus, I am a good salesman.

I start getting their business for Shield. This is big! And demanding. We take orders for whatever they require and deliver it directly to them. I quickly learn that once you get involved with skilled nursing facilities, you are basically on call 24/7. New patients may be admitted in late afternoons and can get sick at any time of night. After hours, the facility phones our answering service that in turn reaches us. "Us" means me—since I can't afford to always keep someone else on standby. This is sort of being on call like a doctor. It can be in the middle of the night or you might be in the middle of a restaurant dinner: If you get called, you respond.

Back then, pharmacies are typically open Monday through Saturday. But many weekends, I go in and open my pharmacy on a Sunday to prepare what is needed, and even take the kids with me in the car as I deliver the meds. It isn't that there is no one else at home to be with them; they *want* to go along: "Can we go for the ride with you?"

Speaking of kids and family. . . .

✦ ✦ ✦

CHAPTER 31

Family: Baby Barons

There is never any doubt that we want children. We are excited when we first learn that Lorraine is pregnant. She is still working and I am still in school, finishing up classes, preparing for finals, and studying for the state board exams. An intense time for us both. She is due just before I graduate.

But not all goes smoothly. In her ninth month, Lorraine gets into a car accident. She is okay, but we're freaking out and praying that nothing has happened to the baby.

New Life Comes into Our World

One day in October, I am walking to class when the school secretary spots me and rushes up with a message: "Your wife is in labor."

"Excuse me?"

My two buddies with me urge, "We'll take notes for you in class— you go. Go now!"

I jump in the car and speed down streets to the old Cedars of Lebanon Hospital (today the Scientology building!). I skid into a parking space and race upstairs—and there is Lorraine with her big belly.

Without thinking, I exclaim, "Did you already have the baby?"

She looks at me weirdly.

I clearly am new at this sort of thing.

They move her into the delivery room, and I stay behind. Fathers are not allowed in delivery rooms then. Lorraine gives birth without me (though I did have something to do with the whole thing).

I vividly remember seeing our baby for the first time. It is truly the miracle of life. A breathtaking beautiful thing!

And my first profound words upon seeing her? "She's got really curly hair!"

Lorraine stays in the hospital for five days. It is a normal delivery and the baby is fine. The car accident has not caused any issues.

In fact, another happy surprise comes after our baby is born: we collect a $900 insurance settlement from the car accident. When I graduate a few months later, I still owe a total of $1,000 for my education. We find another hundred bucks to come up with the thousand.

Today, students can graduate college owing $250,000 or more. These are huge numbers! I am fortunate to be able to pay my debt off soon after graduation. A big deal for us to be relieved of that burden.

Especially as we have something (*someone*) else to focus on.

Beautiful Bouncing Baby Baron

Lynn is named after Leo. Obviously not an exact match; we simply use the letter L. We give her the middle name of Susan, though I can't recall any particular reason for that. It doesn't matter. Turns out that Lynn doesn't like her middle name and never uses it.

Lynn brings us absolute joy from the moment she is born. It is magical to have a child in our lives. Turns out she is full of energy and interested in everything! I also notice early on that she has lots of opinions, especially about how she wants to look and be dressed.

Second Baby is Born

Ross's birth happens a bit differently from Lynn's.

Early on a September morning, three years after Lynn is born, a pregnant Lorraine casually turns to me and indicates she'd like a heating pad since she is having some kind of cramps.

I say, "Lorraine, I don't think those are just cramps. I think you're getting ready to have our second baby. We need to go!"

Her parents hurry over to be with Lynn as we race to Encino Hospital. Lorraine will never let me forget what I say next: "Lorraine, think you could deliver the baby pretty soon so I can get to work and open the pharmacy by nine o'clock?"

The look she gives is enough to scare a grown man. 'Cause it does.

I'll never live that one down . . . though, in truth, she does deliver pretty quickly and I open the pharmacy by nine.

We name this baby boy Ross, after Lorraine's maiden name. His middle name is David, though frankly, I don't remember how we came up with that one either.

But he is Ross David Baron.

Two and Done

Now we have a pair of children. Do we want more?

This is an important question because both of us have Rh negative type blood. Pretty rare (only 15 percent of the people in the U.S. have this). It is yet another way that Lorraine and I are "a match."

But this blood type can make it dangerous to have a third child. Firstborn babies usually aren't as affected by this, but it can cause harm in later pregnancies. Today, they are able to test if you can safely have more children, but not then.

We decide, "We have a boy and a girl. Okay then, that's it."

This is around the time that birth control pills come out. In fact, they are so new that I have concerns about long-term use. We are really young; Lorraine is not even 30. I think, "What might be the consequences of birth control pills over a long time period?"

I don't want to risk her health in any way. I tell Lorraine, "I'm going to get a vasectomy. Then you won't have to worry about birth control."

This is a pretty significant decision for a couple, because what if, God forbid, something happens to one of your kids? What if you then want to have another child? We discuss that too and decide that if something were to happen, we will deal with it. We don't want to base our life on what-ifs.

New Family

The Baron Family

Our kids have it much easier than I did growing up. I'm sure we occasionally spoil them, though maybe not as much as they want. Nobody gets a pony (though I suppose I did!).

We play with them. We read to them. We transform our home into kid-friendly zones, like putting a swing set in the backyard that includes a teeter-totter (seesaw) that Lynn and Ross love.

Lynn also has lots of dolls that she adores. *Lots* of dolls.

She has so many dolls that I build a set of shelves with a frame around it to hold them. This looks like a giant picture frame hanging on the wall except with Lynn's dolls sitting in it. It comes out pretty well, though I have to say that this and the shoeshine box I make in Cub Scouts are the full extent of my carpentry accomplishments.

When she is young, Lynn romps around the neighborhood with the local kids, playing games and riding bikes. We decide to create a little stage in a breezeway between our house and the garage where the kids put on plays. They are a joy to watch.

Time for the latest hairdo and a manicure.

Me giving Ross an early pharmacy lesson in the hope he follows in his father's footsteps. But no matter how hard I tried—he wasn't having it.

We also learn a valuable lesson about simplicity: After something is delivered in a giant cardboard box, Lynn and her friends play more in that damn empty box than with all Lynn's toys!

When Ross is born, Lynn takes to the role of big sister. If he drools, she takes care of it. Now *that* is being a big sister all the way!

An easy child, Ross is very attached to his mother. His sister teases him about this as well as his tendency to worry (believe me, he outgrows this). He frets, "Does the school bus driver know how to get me home?" When it is time to attend camp, he doesn't want to go and wear a swimsuit. At one Halloween, he gets dressed up and then doesn't want to go out.

Yet in these early days, he is also running around the neighborhood with the local children.

Kids, Kids . . . and Kitties

When we're in our first house on Whitaker in Van Nuys, the street has loads of children! Ours are out all the time playing with neighbors—much like when I grew up. The same thing happens when we move to Julie Lane in the Woodland Hills area. We are fortunate our kids can live where there are so many neighborhood children.

And more than a few cats.

Our family never has a dog. But we certainly have cats. A very young Ross gets to see our cat Boggy deliver kittens in the closet in our bedroom. Quite an educational experience about life. Later we have another cat, Buttons, and one day Ross announces, "Buttons is having kittens too." Sure enough, the Baron household is once again awash with kitty-cats!

Mel, Medicine Man

Ross really gets into sports. In that way, he and I share a lot—following football, knowing the teams. We review the sports pages, go to games.

My dad takes me to "sporting events" too—but those are horse races and the fights. Also different from my dad . . . I play catch with Ross.

When Ross plays on the Pop Warner football team, I go to practices and games. When he joins Indian Guides (similar to Boy Scouts but with a Native American influence), I participate along with other fathers. Being a pharmacist, they declare me their "medicine man."

School!

Though we can afford to send our kids to private school, there is never any conversation between Lorraine and myself about doing so. Both she and I went to public school, and unless we encounter some reason to do otherwise, that's what our children will do.

Public school better reflects the real world. That is very different from the current emphasis in Los Angeles where people do whatever it takes to enroll their children in the "right" private schools. Both our children go to Round Meadow Elementary School in Hidden Hills. Later they attend AE Wright Middle School in Calabasas, and then Agoura High School. All public.

They are getting good educations. Los Angeles public schools at this time are of a higher caliber than most today.

Not a Morning Person

It takes me what seems like forever to realize: "I don't think Lorraine likes getting up in the morning." It is a revelation to accept that Lorraine is a night person and I'm a morning person.

So I get up with our two kids when they are in elementary school and make their breakfast. I pack their lunch in little brown bags, folding them crisply, and put a little note inside each bag every day. Some simple saying like, "Have a great day" or "Hope you learn wonderful things!"

At lunch one day, Ross's buddy says, "Your mom makes the best lunches I have ever seen!"

Ross looks at the kid and says, "My mom doesn't make my lunch. My dad does."

Puzzled, the kid asks, "Is your mom dead?"

But Ross clarifies. "No, she's sleeping."

Religion

When our children are growing up, we belong to Temple Judea along with another temple in the Valley. We are always members of some synagogue with our kids.

Though I don't feel particularly religious, being connected to a group of people who have survived thousands of years, even with all the persecution they faced, is something amazing to me. I want to be a part of that. Whenever I am at temple, I feel a sense of community, a sense of belonging, a sense of continuing the tradition. A sense that there is some higher power. I like that for my own children. Both our kids go to Sunday school, and Ross is bar mitzvahed.

Our family with Ross
for his Bar Mitzvah

Parenting Generations

Turns out, Sadie and Leo's parenting style is similar to mine and Lorraine's in some ways.

I am at work a lot when the children are young. I leave early and come back late. So the parenting is pretty much done by Lorraine, much as was the case with my dad and mom. My mother was the disciplinarian and Lorraine takes on that role more than I do. Of course, when one of the kids doesn't behave, she employs that time-honored threat: "Wait till your father comes home"—much like my mother did with my sister and me. This too is an empty warning. But it takes our kids a while to catch on to that.

One major difference between my upbringing and that of our children is that Lorraine and I strive to provide a stable environment for them. I have steady, dependable work. We don't have the financial ups and downs that plagued my family.

Leo was a gambler. I am a risk-taker in business, but mine are different kinds of risks. The result is that I predictably work nine to five (or six)—six days a week. I am easy to reach. Later, as a faculty member, I have an even more predictable lifestyle, meeting responsibilities for students and deadlines. Interestingly, both my kids are organized, disciplined, and hardworking.

Reflecting back, I realize that even with all the uncertainties of Leo's careers and lifestyle, my homelife growing up had stability in some other ways. I always felt loved. I hardly remember my parents fighting or yelling or using foul language. It was not part of their household just as it isn't part of Lorraine's and mine. I, and our children, grow up in a better environment than many kids.

Times were also different. My parents—like many others—were scrambling to make it through the hardships brought on by the Great Depression, lack of work opportunities, World War II, etc. Even with all that, my parents found ways to be involved in my life. They attended my All-City Orchestra performance, and every one of the three nights that I performed in my high school musical. I went on all kinds of "adventures" with my father (orange pulp business, penny arcade and hot dog stand; horse racing in LA, northern California, and Tijuana).

Lorraine and I prioritize attending our kids' events: On Friday nights, we go to high school football games to watch Lynn perform with the drill team. Then Saturday morning, we watch Ross play Pop Warner Football. Plus there is my participation as "Medicine Man" in Ross's Indian Guides. We go to USC games. There is a lot of time with the kids growing up even though I work a lot of hours.

One big difference between ours and my parents' household is that we do not believe in the old adage that "children should be seen but not heard." We always have conversations with our children at the dinner table. We *want* to know what is going on in their lives.

What We Don't Do Also Makes a Difference

One of the things that Lorraine and I decide *not* to do for our children is lecture them. We feel you learn best from what you witness, not from what someone tells you. That is our philosophy.

We each model different types of behavior. I demonstrate a strong work ethic and problem-solving. Lorraine models deep caring and understanding about people. But we don't demonstrate these traits simply as lessons for our kids. It is how we live our lives. It is who we still are. Even today, we do not give our children advice.

Another thing we don't do as parents is help our kids with their homework. This is a conscious choice. (As it turns out, they are smart enough that our help isn't needed.) My parents never helped me with my homework either. But that was because they didn't have the skills. I also don't think my parents were aware of being role models for me, or of guiding me. That's not to say they weren't loving. But as I said, they were a little preoccupied in those early years dealing with the difficult times.

Drive-Ins

Among the fun things that Lorraine and I do with the kids are drive-ins. Though few exist anymore, there are two types that we enjoy.

Drive-in movie theaters become popular starting in the 50s and 60s. For those who may not know, instead of watching a film in a movie theater—the "theater" is outside—essentially a big parking lot with a huge screen at the front and a post by each parking spot with a wired speaker that can be placed in the car so occupants can hear the movie. Sound quality isn't great, though it later becomes possible to play the movie's sound through a car's FM radio. Lorraine and I take the children when they are small because they fall asleep in the back seat and we can watch the movie uninterrupted.

Drive-in restaurants like Bob's Big Boy are also fun. You park on the lot outside the restaurant, and carhops (waiters) prop metal serving trays up on your window from which you grab your food to eat in the car. The kids get burgers and fries and a junior hot fudge sundae. It is a real treat our kids still talk about! Some drive-ins even have carhops on roller skates delivering food to your vehicle!

I am nostalgic for drive-ins, especially for Dolores on the west side of LA. Years later, for our 25th wedding anniversary, Lorraine and I hire a school bus and invite friends to dress in 1950s style clothes. Guests board the bus and we drive to Dolores hamburger stand and have their special curly Q French fries and hamburgers and milkshakes. Everybody eats on the bus and has a great time! Then we all return to our home to enjoy cake and the period music playing on a jukebox we rented!

Grandparents

Sadly, with Leo having passed away so early, my kids never get a chance to spend time with their grandfather like I am able to with mine. Fortunately, my mother treasures being a grandmother. She comes up with special names for both our kids. She calls Lynn "genius" for reasons that become obvious. Her nickname for Ross is "Mazel" because it is a Jewish tradition to believe that a boy child brings luck. She adores the kids.

Our visits to see her are always pleasant and always end with a poignant moment. Whenever we say goodbye, she stands at the window waving as we drive off. Our kids still remember this.

Because my mother lives some distance away and there are no freeways, it is quite a schlep to get her over to our house just to babysit for part of the day or evening since she doesn't drive. Instead, we occasionally pick her up and bring her back to our home to spend a few days with us and the kids.

Lorraine's parents live in the Valley, much closer to us, so the kids see them more often and they occasionally babysit. It is great fun for everyone. But when Lynn is kindergarten age and Ross only one or two years old, that perfect world changes dramatically.

I am working at the pharmacy when I get an urgent phone call: Lorraine's father is dying. I drive as fast as I can but by the time I arrive, Phil is lying on the floor, gone. All I can do is console Lorraine.

Phil's passing is terribly sad for everyone. Phil has been another father figure in my life. I strongly feel his loss.

Because they are young, our kids don't remember Phil very well. But they remember Grandma Bert. They loved being pampered at her place. It was still all very "proper" since Grandma Bert was still very English.

(Lorraine, and now Lynn, continue to follow some examples set by Lorraine's mom that come right out of English society—how the house is kept and how a table is set formally with spoons, forks, and knives. And you *never* place a soda can on the table. It is always in a glass. Plus, Lorraine and Lynn enjoy serving tea.)

Lorraine's mother adapts to life without Phil—and soon to a new man. David Solomon has long been Phil's best friend and a devoted friend to both of Lorraine's parents. Frequently visiting from Liverpool, England, David becomes such a part of our family that our kids refer to him affectionately as "Uncle David." In fact, he is around so much that I half-joke to Lorraine, "David is waiting for your dad to die so he can marry your mother." Sure enough, fifteen months after Phil passes, that is exactly what happens. I am happy for her. David is a really nice guy and I like him.

David is wealthy, so together they live quite a posh life. This is amusing for the kids who get a big kick out of all their fancy stuff. Lynn and Ross sometimes sleep over, spending a couple of days there. Super fun for them—and for us—especially when the visit is over a weekend and Lorraine and I can go off to enjoy ourselves.

Still, life does not always go smoothly.

Years later, the four of us are traveling together with our children to England. Lorraine's mom and David then go to Scotland for a wedding. On their train trip back, David gets off at a stop to grab some coffee, trips, and falls beneath the train. He is run over.

Lorraine and I and the kids have been home a week when we get the awful news. Lorraine's mother flies the body back, and settles into yet another stage of life, alone again, in an apartment. She does not live very long after this. David's loss, on top of losing Phil, is a tragic experience and perhaps too much for her.

Both of Lorraine's parents, and David, are buried at Eden, a Jewish Cemetery in the Valley.

◆　◆　◆

CHAPTER 32

Civil Rights

After the children are in school, Lorraine takes classes at Everywoman's Village on Sepulveda Boulevard in Van Nuys. It is a series of adjacent buildings that looks like an old motel. As a nonprofit community adult school, it offers classes especially for women whose educational paths or careers are "interrupted" by getting married or having children, or who may be intimidated back then by the thought of going to college.

Lorraine thinks about a woman's role in society. This is during the early days of women's lib and big changes are brewing . . . *throughout* our culture.

It is around this time that Lorraine and I watch the Watts riots unfold on television. These erupt after police stop a Black motorist and residents accuse the officers of using excessive force. But this is just the trigger. It is really the joblessness, poverty, and segregated schools that sends South L.A. residents into the streets. For six days in August, they set fires and battle police. There are 34 deaths, 1,000 injured, and over $40 million of property damage. The riots bring massive attention to the hopelessness of society's race problems, and spur African Americans across the country to take action. Numerous organizations form.

Having witnessed this initial event, Lorraine poses a significant question: "What are we going to tell our children when they ask, 'Where were you, Mom and Dad, when all of this was going on?'"

I am also prompted by what happened to Jews during the Holocaust, and that my mother escaped Russia because of persecution of the Jewish people. It gets me thinking: "What *are* we going to do? Do we just sit here and say, 'Oh gee, what a shame.'"

We decide we can't just sit there.

Friends of Operation Bootstrap

At Everywoman's Village, Lorraine discusses this with a man named Donald Freed who agrees, "You know, you're right. We need to get together. We need to organize. There's a meeting tonight we should attend."

Lorraine gets a babysitter, and we drive to a meeting for Operation Bootstrap, where a group of Black people gather in South Central Los Angeles—an area that Lorraine and I have never come close to frequenting.

Yet here we are, at this meeting. There are three African American principals: Lou Smith, Bob Bailey, and Robert Hall. They want to educate young Black people about entrepreneurship and creating their own businesses—opening a dress shop, maybe purchasing a gas station. They want to put community members to work and experience economic empowerment. This is the late sixties.

After our meeting, Lorraine and I and others form an organization called Friends of Operation Bootstrap. I am its president (a role I play for ten years). It is a support group to Operation Bootstrap, with Lorraine as heavily involved as I.

We are doing this together.

Brave New World

One night a week, we meet down at Jones' Garage on 42nd and Central to have a dialogue. Actually, I'm not sure I'd call it a dialogue, but rather, an opportunity for Black residents to vent. We listen. And learn. And I see the fear that many Blacks have of Whites, and the anger.

I admit, the first few times we go down to south central, Lorraine and I look at each other: "Are we sure this is a good idea?"

Everybody there notices us—a White couple—as we drive through. They naturally wonder, "Who are these White people and what are they doing here? Maybe they're spies for the police?" Plus, down the block from Operation Bootstrap is the office for the Black Panthers, a militant group recognizable on the street by their uniform of black leather jackets, black pants, black berets and dark sunglasses.

This is a bit scary.

It only adds to our apprehension to learn that most of the Black males carry guns. One of the guys from our group, Cornell, calls me and asks, "Mel, do you want a piece?"

"No, Cornell, I do not want a piece. I don't even know how to use one. No pieces for me."

But he insists, "You got to have it. I'm going to bring you one. You keep it in your glove box so it's always handy."

I insist: "Cornell, *do not* bring me any guns."

Clearly the people meeting with us have a different world view. Yet it is through our discourse that everybody is becoming acquainted. None of us have met before. We certainly have never been social. We have never been to each other's homes or "broken bread" together. But we begin to do just that.

Including at our home.

Hovering Helicopters

People gather at our house on Friday nights. We meet to figure out how to best be supportive. We work to develop new businesses for people in the Black community, as well as deal with various other situations, such as making sure that people in Black neighborhoods are fed on Thanksgiving.

We have as many as thirty people, many of them Black, at our house in an all-White Woodland Hills neighborhood.

Apparently, not everyone around us is comfortable with this.

A helicopter hovers above our home on these meeting nights. I have no idea who is alerting the police about our guests. No one in the neighborhood ever asks us who these people are. The police never come to our door. They just hover.

Meanwhile, inside our home, we hear more four-letter words than we ever have in our lives! "You MFing this" or "Those MFing that." The word is as common in Black lingo as our saying, "Yeah." It's street talk and it is real. It certainly isn't part of Lorraine's or my normal speech, but our kids are at home during these meetings and hear everything. We meet at other people's houses too so everyone gets to know one another and see how each other lives. Sometimes we picnic in a park, Whites and Blacks together.

Through Operation Bootstrap, we end up with some wonderfully authentic friendships. As a Jew, you kind of have an antenna up—you can be in a group and get a vibe that others are uncomfortable with you. Our new Black friends had big antennas too. They knew who was real and who wasn't and who was at ease with them. We were different from one another, but we had more in common than it might seem.

Raw Realities

We come to better understand the ongoing plights of Black people.

Bob Hubbard, one of my new African American friends, assists me at our house when I need to take an extra television set to someone's home. Bob helps me load it in the car and as we get in to drive, he says, "Mel, we will be stopped within five minutes of leaving the house." He's a Black man in a car, with a big TV. I think he is being ridiculous.

Within five minutes, red lights and sirens pull us over.

"What are you guys doing?"

The officers demand to see our IDs. We are compliant and cautious. We explain what we are doing while they look us over suspiciously. Finally, they let us go.

On another occasion, a lovely woman by the name of Eleanor Childs is at our home. She is a good friend and the kids love her. Suddenly, we are alerted of a fire in our area and asked to evacuate. We have to quickly decide what to take. Pictures? Papers? Valuables? We scurry around, grabbing items.

Lorraine asks Eleanor to take our sterling silver in her car.

Eleanor looks at us and says, "Are you nuts? A Black woman leaving an evacuation area with a box of silver? I'll get arrested for sure!"

We never even thought of this. But she is *very* conscious of who she is and the neighborhood she is in. She has to be.

Mel in a Riot

One day, I receive a call from people at Operation Bootstrap—*who desperately need help.*

The police are belligerent: clearing streets, threatening residents. Our friends are afraid it will escalate since the police are not listening to them at all. They need people in our group to come down to South Central LA—White people dressed up in shirts and ties and jackets—to see if we can calm the temperatures down there.

I call four friends in Friends of Operation Bootstrap. The five of us dress up and hurry to 42nd and Central. Sure enough, the cops are out in full force, roughly clearing streets. We try to cool things down, but it doesn't work. The cops start beating people.

Now we're thinking, "We need to get out of here!"

But it is impossible to leave. Streets are crowded or blocked. I dive in through the open door of a small house, ending up in a group of people finding shelter there. Among them is Angela Davis, the famous Black activist.

Outside, people are being beaten and bleeding. Essentially, it is the police who are rioting. Angela Davis and I, along with others, administer first aid the best we can. The havoc continues all around us.

It is a terrifying night. I am not sure we will survive. We wait a long time until things calm down enough for us to get back to our cars and I can return to Woodland Hills.

Prominent Activists

At many of the "normal" events we attend, we meet a variety of well-known participants in the civil rights movement. Stokely Carmichael is a leading organizer. At another party, we fundraise for James Baldwin, the Black novelist, playwright, poet, and activist, whose essays explore racial, sexual, and class distinctions in the U.S.

William Kunstler is at another event. He famously defends the Chicago Seven, as well as Blacks and other oppressed peoples in a variety of cases, and is a director of the ACLU from midsixties to early seventies. We meet Diane Nash, civil rights activist and cofounder of the Student Nonviolent Coordinating Committee (SNCC) that focuses on student involvement in the civil rights movement in the 1960s.

It is a wide variety of fascinating and committed people trying to improve our society. Lorraine and I are proud to be part of that.

Awakened

All of this is a rude awakening for Lorraine and me. Not everybody lives the life that we do. We see the pain, poverty, and discrimination. We aren't even that wealthy, yet I see how privileged we really are. When we first get involved and hear stories about police brutality and prejudices, it is hard for us to fully grasp it.

Unfortunately, many of these same conditions continue today. That same fear and hatred. When you talk to Black families now who have a son driving a car, the fear that police will pull them over and do who knows what to them is extremely present. It is a justified fear.

There are Successes

Friends of Operation Bootstrap provides connections, advice, and funding to help start businesses.

One of our biggest achievements is helping start a doll company called Shindana Toys. This toy factory produces black dolls, not white dolls that are simply painted black, but dolls with Black features. One critical piece of this is Ron Loeb, a brilliant attorney and sweet guy who is also cousin to Elliot and Ruth Handler—two of Mattel's founders. Mattel helps us get this company off the ground. (Interesting to me, Ron Loeb is a classmate of Ruth Bader Ginsburg.)

New Direction: Public Administration

Operation Bootstrap and everything we learn from it alters our lives—changing our perspective of who we are and what we are doing. Though I stay involved for ten years, by the late 1960s, I wonder how I can be more impactful in this social movement.

I see everything going on: breaking windows and burning buildings—all kinds of large protests. It brings attention to the issues, but long-term, it isn't working. You really need to think about how to change our principles and policies—how to create change from within the system.

I consider going back to school. Maybe I should become a lawyer. Or maybe run for Congress. I visit USC to inquire what might be available in terms of classes and meet with Professor Bill Williams in the School of Public Administration. He advises against becoming a lawyer or congressman. He says, "There is another route that I think will fit better for you, Mel."

He tells me about their programs in public administration.

I am interested in working with nonprofit organizations to create social impact—and what Bill describes sounds appealing. The USC curriculum teaches organizational theory and leadership, and how to motivate and move groups of people to help others. There are courses about practical things like finance as well.

I make a decision that Lorraine supports, and in 1970, I enroll in a master's program at USC in the School of Public Administration. My course of studies takes me three years (rather than two) because I am still working at the pharmacy.

I hire Fred Bray to help with the pharmacy to better free up my time. While I don't know it yet, hiring him will be key to Shield evolving and growing—with Fred carrying the workload at the beginning—and eventually moving us toward adding entirely new arenas to our Shield business (more on this later).

Bill Williams is an interesting and brilliant person. An African American professor, his fields are speech, linguistics, and epistemics (study of human information-processing using logic, philosophy, and psychology). His specialty is communication. Bill is my mentor in navigating what roles I might take in guiding others.

In truth, what I learn from the USC program and Bill gives me abilities and tools that positively affect the rest of my life. Even much of my success in building the pharmacy and in the corporate world has been the result of my communication skills.

Bill continues to be a friend to this day. Though he's retired, we still visit and even after all this time, he continues to be a mentor.

New "College Graduate" is Put to Work

In 1973, I earn my master's in public administration while also continuing to work as a pharmacist.

The university knows I am this weird dude with these two degrees. When they want to put on a summer seminar session on substance abuse, someone recommends me to play a major role in creating it.

I think, "Who the hell am I to be doing this?"

But upon reflection, earning my master's degree is a self-acknowledgement that I can step into new areas to help others. The degree validates those capabilities and gives me confidence. I dive in to help produce this summer session and quickly become excited about the opportunity, which also gets me out of the routine of being in the pharmacy. I've never done anything remotely like this. It is a fresh challenge. I am like a kid in the candy store of a whole new world.

UNIVERSITY OF SOUTHERN CALIFORNIA CONFERENCE ON **ALCOHOL AND DRUG ABUSE**

June 1973

Honestly, we do a hell of a job putting the event together. Bill Williams even joins our team to create a superb couple of weeks for those attending our sessions of classes and speakers. I even create a striking image of a martini glass of booze and ice cubes with a syringe in the glass, which we use as the cover of our booklet.

Our event is attended by people from all around the country who treat substance abuse: counselors, psychologists, caregivers for alcoholics, even people in politics developing policies around substance abuse and alcoholism. In a profound way, we are educating the educators.

One Leads to Another: California Alcoholism Foundation

A woman attending our seminar named Romana Edwards seeks me out during the event. "Mr. Baron. We have an opening for the Associate

Director of the California Alcoholism Foundation. I would very much like you to take that post."

Again, I say to myself: "What the hell do I know about doing that?"

And again, I say "yes" and take the job.

It is heady stuff to be considered for these positions. My master's in public administration plays a role in my taking this on. The foundation may not be about civil rights, but it is about *health rights*. People have a right to be well cared for.

Soon I am traveling all around California, helping organizations develop training programs for alcoholic caregivers. One of the groups we work with is the United Airlines' mechanics union. Why them? I learn that 10 percent of any workforce is likely alcoholic. Their members are mechanics working on airplanes. Helping them is critically important to the safety of anyone who flies.

But the Foundation benefits all kinds of people and often those in very challenging situations whose circumstances have made it difficult or impossible for them to have a good job at this time in their lives.

Sadly, health care today continues to be a challenge for many in our country. Look at how difficult it was to pass and preserve the Affordable Care Act. Yet all of this is so basic to life and liberty. Why don't we have universal health care? It's nonsense.

Home Alone: The Foot Comes Down

I am traveling all over California, gone for lengthy periods at a time, developing programs with these people. I am doing great work!

But I am not at home.

Lorraine is frustrated. Especially as Ross, now a teen, has started sleeping on the floor at Lorraine's bedside at night, worrying that something is going to happen to his mom while I am away.

After about a year of my traveling, Lorraine puts her foot down. "Mel, you need to stop this. Get out of the California Alcoholism Foundation and come back home and back to the pharmacy." She stresses the alternative: "Or are we getting divorced?"

She is serious.

Once I realize my being away is causing pain at home, there is not even a choice for me. I immediately turn in my resignation to the California Alcoholism Foundation.

Home Again

I return home full-time. Lorraine is happy. Fred is happy. I am at the store. It is really busy.

So I am back . . . but I am not the same Mel.

Working on civil rights and then for the California Alcoholism Foundation—seeing people suffering and the plight of what it really means to be an alcoholic, and the sadness of addiction and substance abuse—changes my whole idea about patient care. An eye-opener that transforms the rest of my life.

I think differently now, am less judgmental and more compassionate. More caring. There's a different feeling when working with underserved populations. I realize how privileged I am compared to those either uneducated or who just haven't had opportunities. It also shifts "my comfort zone." I am at ease talking to anybody, from any walk of life.

I realize there must be deeper compassion and caring for those in need. By intimately seeing people suffer from alcohol or other addictions, people feeling the effects of discrimination and poverty, I develop a different view of what the world really is. Sometimes you live in a bit of a bubble and that's all you see. But this is no longer the case for me.

These experiences make significant and lasting changes to how I see life now, and the choices I will make in the future.

✦ ✦ ✦

CHAPTER 33

Growing Up Baron: Finding Their Way

Aside from our being a loving family, I think the most significant thing our children witness is when Lorraine and I become involved in the civil rights movement.

We don't lecture the kids about what we are doing or say much about it at all. We don't have to. They can see that we are totally immersed in it. They get to experience a different culture. They attend social events attended by African Americans and Whites. Many people who aren't Jewish (as well as many who are) are part of everything going on.

Lynn

Though she plays with friends in the neighborhood while growing up, I cannot say Lynn has the same freedom to explore as when I was young. I had more independence. Like many parents of my generation, Lorraine and I are a bit more cautious (I believe generations of parents that follow us are even more cautious). However, when Lynn is around sixteen, we allow her to go to Hawaii with a girlfriend. So by a certain point, we let her exercise greater freedom.

Lynn is a studious kid. She is neat. Organized. She does her homework. She does well in school. She is on the high school drill team. They dance at games much like cheerleaders except they don't do cheers, but march along with the band during football halftime. Lorraine and I attend those games just to see her.

As a teenager, Lynn is relatively easy. She is not rebellious. She's not into drugs. She doesn't hang out with "the wrong crowd." In fact, I'm not even an overprotective father with regard to boys, since Lynn doesn't really date a lot in junior high and high school. Though she has a lot of girlfriends, there isn't a lot of boy-crazy stuff. Just endless phone calls and kids in and out of the house all the time. Lynn focuses on her hair and her clothes and all of the typical teenage girl stuff. She can be in the shower for hours.

I am like, "How can anyone stay in there and do their hair for so long? This is crazy!"

Lynn is nearly always late for the school bus because she tries on three different outfits every morning before the bus arrives. We have a

On her 15th birthday, Lynn's latest fashion accessory: a new bracelet.

two-story house and she comes down for breakfast and then races back up to change her clothes again. (This becomes so frenetic that she actually falls down the stairs one morning doing this.)

Ross and I will already be sitting at the breakfast table. We know the morning drill. Whatever Lynn is wearing when we first see her is probably not what she will have on when she leaves the house. She finally chooses and then runs to the bus at the last second.

On some other occasions, however, Lynn is more relaxed about her appearance. "Too relaxed" in the view of some people. One day, Lynn and I are picking up her proper English grandmother and David from the airport. Lynn's hair is rolled up in curlers under a bandana. Her grandmother takes one look at Lynn and exclaims, "How can you do that? How can you possibly be out in society with your hair in rollers?" For Grandma, this is beyond humiliating. For Lynn, it is one of those things you never live down. I don't think Lynn has ever forgotten that moment.

I certainly know the rest of the family hasn't!

Ross

Ross doesn't excel in elementary and secondary school in the same manner that Lynn does. Yet, at the same time, even from a young age, Ross shows passion in his pursuits. When he decides he wants to know something, he takes it on with intensity. He becomes fascinated by dinosaurs and soon knows all their names and facts about them. When he gets interested in presidents, he memorizes specific details about each one.

Although not always academically focused, Ross does not tend to get into trouble like some teen boys. That's not to say he *never* gets into mischief. During his early teens, Ross and his buddy throw rocks next door and break a bunch of windows. We confront him and he claims total innocence. Unfortunately, his bleeding hands and Band-Aids don't make for a convincing denial. A budding lawyer he is not.

Lorraine and I both make him apologize to the neighbors and make amends. Still, I am more permissive than Lorraine overall. As I've said, she is more the disciplinarian. Especially with Ross. I think that's because in my heart of hearts, I want him to love me so much, unlike my relationship with Al, who left and didn't seem to care.

Ross is a bit more challenging as a teenager. His hair is way out there beyond an Afro. He is skateboarding. Surfing. One time, I go away with

Ross at 15 with hair. Lots and lots of hair.

him and some of his buddies to go surfing—as their chaperone—and am very pleased to see he is really good at it!

Lorraine and I are lucky to have pretty good kids. Sure, they can be mischievous. But nothing with dire consequences . . . though we later find out that could've been otherwise. Years later, we learn that when Ross was a teenager, he jumped off the roof of our house on Julie Lane into the pool. If we had known this at the time, we would've been beside ourselves: "What if you missed the pool and landed on the cement?"

The thought of this boggles us. But we never know of it at the time.

Boys of the Band—Next Generation

Ross plays the drums as a teenager, much like I did when I was young. Combining some parts of my old Meltones drum set along with his own drums, Ross practices in the garage and plays in different rock bands. They even have a few paid gigs. Ross is more musically inclined and a much better performer than his dad ever was.

At this time, rock bands wear all kinds of bizarre costumes. Unlike the matching outfits worn by me and my bandmembers, in rock groups, everyone tries to be more outlandish than the next. I go with Lorraine to a couple of events where his band is playing. When they go out on stage, Lorraine says, "I think he's wearing one of my robes." Or maybe it is one of her belts. But his drummer's garb includes some of Lorraine's clothing. Some way-out outfits!

At the time, as far as we know, Ross isn't heavy into drugs. Lorraine thinks he is probably smoking some pot. But I don't want to admit that could be true. In hindsight, I believe it probably was the case. (It certainly fits with being a surfer *and* a drummer.) Yet I denied it to myself at the time so I didn't have to confront him about it. That's how much I want to keep our relationship intact.

Mobile Mabel

Though Ross isn't really rebellious, he is an independent kid. When he is in high school, Lorraine gets on my case that we never see books at home. And that he is so often out surfing. He never appears to do any homework. But he always seems to do okay in school. He doesn't flunk anything. We don't get calls from the office.

Yet a bigger disagreement occurs after "Uncle David" (who married Lorraine's mother after Phil died) leaves both Lynn and Ross a few bucks. Ross wants to buy a car. Actually, a truck, so it can carry his surfboard and his drums. Lorraine doesn't think he is responsible enough to have the truck and is very concerned about him driving at sixteen. I think it is fine. This becomes a significant issue between Lorraine and myself. We seldom fight, but it's something that she is really against.

Somehow, I "win" this argument. Ross gets a brand-new truck that he names Mabel. Why? I have no idea. But seriously, how much trouble can a boy get into when he calls his truck *Mabel*?

When Ross first gets his truck, Lorraine and my mom follow him in a car to see if he's driving okay. He seems to "pass" that test. But periodically, Ross runs out of gas. We can almost count on it. He doesn't put enough in the tank or just doesn't pay attention to the gauge—and he's stuck, in the truck, out of luck.

One day, Lorraine is driving home on Valley Circle and sees Ross stopped over to the side by the curb. She waves at him and just drives on by. She knows he's out of gas again, but she doesn't stop. She figures he'll have to figure out some way to get money and the gas. A teaching moment.

Exploring the Bigger World

As our kids mature, we want to expose them to more of the world. When they are in their teens, we begin taking them to Europe.

Since Lorraine's parents are from England, we make a number of visits to see their families. On one such trip, the kids are staying together in their own room when Ross calls down to our room, hysterical. "You have to come up right now! Lynn's going to kill herself. Over her hair!"

We race run up there. "What in the world is going on?"

At this point, Lynn is a young teen and hair is one of life's most crucial challenges . . . and she is having a major hairdo catastrophe!

Hair calamities aside, we also travel with the kids to France and Italy. In Italy, we meet two guys buying a bunch of flashy jewelry and necklaces. Both we and our kids think they must be drug dealers! Turns out, they are two of the nicest Jewish guys from New York—one a school principal and the other a vice principal. Every time we go to New York or they come to LA, we get together. After many visits, they whisper to us, "Do you know that we're gay?" This is back when people were not so open about it. But we know right from the get-go. It certainly makes no difference to us. We are just happy they aren't drug dealers.

In addition to Europe, we take the kids to Mexico, Alaska, and Hawaii, plus most of the continental United States.

(Many years later, we venture to Washington, DC, with our grandson Joshua and meet Senator Orrin Hatch from Utah. Because of Ross and his connection to the Church of Jesus Christ of Latter-day Saints in Utah, we are able to go to the senator's office and meet his staff. Like they say, "It's all about who you know." I know Ross.)

I'm happy we could expose our kids to the wider world. That was not something I got to do when I was young. Leo and Sadie were not traveling around Europe. Most of my most distant travels as a kid were to racetracks.

✦　✦　✦

CHAPTER 34

Al Fink: Closing the Past

Life is going great. Business, Lorraine, the kids. I couldn't be happier. But something is gnawing at me. Something I feel I must do.

Believing my cousin Millie may have been the conduit giving Al information about me when I was young, I call her to ask if she knows where Al, my biological father, is living.

Millie tells me where to find him.

Viva Las Vegas

So why this desire to meet Al again after all these years?

Perhaps because he abandoned me and my mother when I was so young, I've long yearned for a father figure. I certainly have one with Leo and different male mentors throughout my life. Yet this longing hasn't entirely gone away.

Plus, my mother always spoke so bitterly about Al. I need to know if this guy is really a monster.

By this time, I am fairly successful with business. I'm happily married with two children. Maybe this is my chance to let him know I've done well.

I phone him up. At first, he has no idea who I am. He has never heard my voice as an adult. After I reveal who is calling him, we agree on a date for me to visit where he lives, in Las Vegas.

As my plane lands, I have second thoughts. "Why am I doing this?" I'm suddenly skeptical of my whole plan. This is folly. But here I am, standing in front of the Vegas airport waiting for Al to pick me up . . . and I realize neither of us has any idea what the other looks like! This is long before cell phones so we can't call each other.

How is this even going to work?

Then I see this old Cadillac driving by with a man who has my face. As he pulls over . . . I also see he is wearing the exact same eyeglass frames as me. This is mindboggling.

Then as I get in the car, he says, "Hi, son."

That is even more startling! I don't even know what that means to him. I am immediately uncomfortable. We drive to his home. I have no idea where it is, but in my nightmare imagination, he lives in a trailer park.

Finally he pulls into the Tropicana Mobile Home Trailer Park.

"Oh my God," I say to myself. Even better—Mae is there. The woman he cheated on my mom with.

Mae opens the door to their trailer and welcomes me in. The only thing I recall about the interior is an entire countertop on which sits a slew of mannequin heads—a wig on each one. I have no idea why. Mae is too heavy, and by now, certainly too old, to be a showgirl. She is a waitress as far as I know.

Long-Awaited Time Together

Al introduces me to quite a few of his neighbors. I just keep saying, "Hi. Good to meet you." I don't know what else I *can* say. This is all so weird.

And is about to get weirder

It's morning before noon and Al asks, "Would you like a drink?"

I decline, saying it's a little early. We spend most of the day talking about our lives. I tell him about school and my family. I'm kind of giving him my report card, what I've done with my life. He shows me pictures of my mom and him that I've never seen before. I am stunned at how handsome a couple they were.

Al drove a laundry truck for most of his life. He is retired, but still works at the casinos as a runner carrying chips and cash between the cage where money is kept and the gaming tables.

It is an emotional visit for both of us. At one point, he says, "Do you remember what you said to me in the car when I visited you at school?"

I answer, "Yes, I do," and repeat, "What have you ever done for me?" But Al says nothing more about it.

I have on a sweater rather than shirt and tie, and am wearing a beard at this point, since that is kind of the look of the era. Yet Al questions this: "So why do you look that way, with a beard?"

Lorraine and me during my "beard period"

I think, "Al hasn't seen me in thirty years. Is questioning why I'm wearing a beard and how I dress really most important right now?"

As the afternoon progresses, he finally asks, "What would you like to do for dinner? How about Chuck Wagon?"

Chuck Wagon is an open buffet, all-you-can-eat restaurant. I answer, "Truthfully, I'm not a Chuck Wagon buffet kind of guy."

So where do we go?

Chuck Wagon buffet. Downtown Vegas (not the Strip).

Dinner Break

Mae, Al, and I are finishing up our dinner at Chuck Wagon when Al gets up and leaves without explanation. I don't know where he goes. But he doesn't come back. Finally I say, "Mae, I have to get to the airport for my flight."

We go look for Al and find him next door at the craps table. He knows we're there since I am standing behind him while he plays. I am immobilized. I feel like a little boy who doesn't know what to do. I haven't seen him since the eighth grade and have been overwhelmed all day. And now this.

After a period of time, I finally say, "Mae, I've got to go."

As I leave to find a cab, I hear Mae yelling at Al. "What are you doing? You haven't seen your son for all these years! He needs to get to the airport." She drags Al away from the table and we get into his car and drive to the airport. Will I even make it in time?

When I finally get on the plane, I say to myself, "Wow, that was one gigantic disaster."

I don't know what I expected. But I don't have any feeling that Al thinks I turned out to be this pretty cool and successful man. Nor is anything said about his having regrets that he missed my growing up.

I leave there thinking this Al is pretty weird. I mean, I spend all this time there and he has to pull himself away from the dice table just to get me back to the airport. It is all very painful to me.

I do not tell my mom that I visited him. I never tell her.

Guess Who's Coming to Brunch

Some time later, I hear from Al. He's going to be in Los Angeles and wants to see me. I don't know why Lorraine and I say okay to this, but we do. Again, my mom never knows of it.

Al comes over to our house for brunch without Mae. He's wearing white pants and white shoes. A real Las Vegas outfit. His hair is white by now and he is shorter than I am. But he still has my face in a sense.

Our kids are there. To this day, my daughter has not forgiven me for telling her to kiss Al. She says it traumatized her. But I wanted my kids there since they never saw Leo, as he died before I even met Lorraine.

We have our meal. We spend time together. But nothing memorable comes up in conversation. After he leaves, Lorraine and I look at each other. "Wow, what was that all about?"

A couple of months later, a letter arrives from Al. As I open it, I wonder if it will be some sentimental or heartwarming communication, saying all those things he might not have been able to say in person?

Nope. He's asking for supplies.

Knowing that I own a pharmacy, Al asks for a back brace and other items. I ship him what he wants and naturally don't charge him.

Viva Las Vegas, Part Two

After a few more months pass, I reach out again to Al.

"I have to visit Las Vegas for business, but afterward, we all can go out to dinner. But instead of Chuck Wagon, why don't I take you both to the Sands Hotel on the Strip for a really nice meal? Then I'll fly home."

By now, he and I have had more contact with each other. We know each other better. I hope this time together will be different.

The three of us meet at the Sands. We are not into dinner very long . . . before Al gets up, leaves the table, and doesn't come back. Again. I end up having the whole meal with Mae.

I finally say, "Mae, I need to catch my flight back to Los Angeles." We go out to find Al. Sure enough, he is at the dice table. A replay of my first visit.

"Al, I have to get to the airport." He ignores me.

By this point, I am more angry than hurt. This is totally unacceptable. I emphatically state, "Al, if you're not taking me, then let me have your keys since I left my briefcase in the car."

Al finally turns around to face me—and hands over his car keys.

I shake my head, walk to the parking lot, open the car, take my briefcase and drop the keys on the floor by the front seat. I get a cab to the airport.

No Regrets

Lorraine feels for me. She knows I am trying to discover my past. She has been totally supportive of my going to visit him: "If you need to do this, you should do it."

When I return after my second disastrous visit to Vegas, she says, "Why torture yourself? You now know what this guy is. There's nothing there for you."

God only knows the fantasies I may have harbored about Al, about what it might have been like had he stayed in my life. That perhaps my mom made a mistake. But my experiences with Al only validate her decision to leave him. He is a creep and I thank God my mother got rid of him. God only knows what it would have been like for me had they remained together. Fortunately, I got Leo instead and my life was much better. My mom made a good decision. It makes me appreciate her courage even more.

I'm glad I found Al. I have no regrets. I come to recognize that Al most likely has a gambling addiction, like Leo. But it doesn't matter. I have closed this chapter of my life.

Sometime later, Mae writes me a letter apologizing for Al. He is having a hard time. He's been fired from his job at the casino after some suspicion about missing money.

I send back a note saying, "Dear Mae. Al has abandoned me more than once. At this point, I have my own life. You have your life. Goodbye."

I never see or hear again from Al or Mae.

✦ ✦ ✦

CHAPTER 35

Back to Business: Growing the Pharmacy

After Lorraine wisely lays down the ultimatum for me to give up traveling for the California Alcoholism Foundation and return home, I am back full-time at the pharmacy.

Cutting cake to celebrate Shield's "Bar Mitzvah,"
our 13th anniversary.

As I mention earlier, I hired Fred Bray to run the pharmacy while I earned my public administration degree and worked for the Foundation. Now that I've returned, Fred says to me, "Maybe we should think about carrying some medical supplies. I have a background from my work at the hospital in surgical supplies, elastic stockings, corsets, collars to wear after neck injuries, and similar products. Why don't we see if there's something we can do with those?"

Though this is not an area that most pharmacies are into at this time, I am open to it. But I'm not interested in handling the day-to-day tasks of this. I tell Fred, "You know what, go ahead and you do it. And I'll give you fifty percent of anything we make on those types of items."

We put together a little brochure for "convalescent aids" (a term we'd never use today) and start making a few bucks. Soon a sales representative from the company providing us this equipment visits us and says, "You know, there is a bit of a market in ostomy care—colostomies, ileostomies, and urostomies." He encourages us to try selling products for those as well.

This would involve us in a whole different set of medical issues facing patients and their health-care professionals. Fred's interested, but I say, "Fred, we don't know a thing about this. If we are to give it a try, we need help." We hire Bernice Rosen as a consultant. She's an enterostomal therapist nurse who works with ostomy and incontinence patients. She explains these conditions, who the market is, and where we can buy the products wholesale.

I learn we are talking about three different though related medical issues: colostomies, ileostomies, and urostomies. Which of these approaches is needed depends on what surgical procedure the patient has.

For example, most colostomy patients are those who have cancer, where surgery bypasses a damaged part of the colon so bowel contents exit through a hole surgically created in the patient's abdominal wall. Ileostomy patients are usually those with Crohn's disease, where surgery connects the last part of the small intestine to an opening in the abdominal wall. Both types of patients are fitted with bags to collect intestinal waste.

I quickly realize, "Fred, we've got to keep Bernice Rosen around as our consultant. If anybody asks us questions on this, we don't know enough." So we hire Bernice and begin offering products for this type of care. It is yet another area we don't know anything about, but we do it anyway.

Helping Patients Find Us

As we expand into this new arena, we learn the decision-makers for which supplies a patient needs and where to get them are not the doctors who do the surgeries. It is these enterostomal therapist nurses.

We decide to romance this group.

Fortunately, they have an organization and we start going to their meetings, getting to know the therapists and convincing them that we can provide for their patients. Our approach is successful and soon more and more patients are coming to us for supplies.

We discover this world is controlled by the Hollister company. They are the market leaders in the manufacture of all these ostomy products. Like many companies, they have tiered pricing for their products. For example, if you buy one to five pieces, you get a certain price for each. If you buy six to ten, you get a better price, and so on. The most you can buy is two hundred boxes and that's how you get their best price. This is true not only for us, but also for the hospitals that purchase their merchandise.

This gives me an idea.

Mel the Middleman

I visit the purchasing agents at hospitals, show them my Shield Pharmacy business card and ask, "Do you buy ostomy equipment?"

They do, but may only get a limited number of boxes at any time given their demand isn't that high.

I suggest, "What if I can offer you the same products, but at better prices than you are getting now?"

My thinking is if I buy two hundred boxes and get a very good price from Hollister, I can sell the products to hospitals for less than they are presently paying, and still mark up my pricing to make a profit. After a few of these "exploratory visits," I can see there's interest. But I also realize I must change how I present myself to these potential clients. I return to the pharmacy and say, "Fred, we have to change the name of our business. Let's print a separate business card that says, "Shield Ostomy."

So for $7.50, we print new cards. Now I call on hospitals representing myself as Shield Ostomy—a company that specializes in supplying their needs in this area. As I do this, I notice some of these hospitals have old ostomy products on their shelves that are looking pretty shabby. So I add to my sales pitch: "If you buy from me, not only will I give you a better price. I'll even take back all of your old outdated products and give you a credit for them."

They love this.

So I collect their old product and send them a credit for some number I make up on the spot. I then either donate their old boxes to the American Cancer Society, or try sending them back to Hollister for credit.

We are now buying two hundred boxes at a time that we, in turn, sell to all these hospitals. Well, two hundred boxes take up a lot of space! But we're still in our original Shield Pharmacy of only 750 square feet. We get permission from the landlord to expand the store out another ten feet to have more room.

Everything is going great. But as I continue visiting purchasing agents at hospitals, I am asked, "Do you have a catalog?"

Of course, we don't. But I don't say that. Instead, I claim, "Oh, we're working on our new catalog right now."

I go back to Fred. "We need a catalog!"

Problem is, we don't have enough money to produce a sophisticated, custom-printed catalog. We decide instead to get a three-ring binder and design it to look much like a Hollister binder.

But Fred's wondering, "What are we going to fill it with?"

I think a moment and say, "Let's write to every ostomy company that produces this type of equipment and ask them for their literature."

So now we get boxes of literature describing products, and I explain, "Fred, all we need now is a three-hole punch. We'll put all these product pages in our catalog and on the outside of the binder, we'll say we represent these companies."

We fill up our binders with product pages from two dozen companies that we list on the outside as if we represent their product lines. In reality, we don't have all these products, but we don't care. We have a catalog! I go to purchasing agents in hospitals with a new introduction, "We're Shield Ostomy. I've got our catalog right here."

Of course, I push the products that we carry. But sometimes, they ask us for a particular item I know we don't have.

I say, "You know, let me call the warehouse and see if we have it."

Remember, this is still in the days before cell phones. So I rush out to a pay phone in the hospital lobby and call Fred.

"Fred, can you see if we can get hold of this certain product and how much it would be and call me back. Here's the number for my pay phone."

Fred calls me back in ten minutes after having located someplace we can get this product. I go back into the purchasing agent's office and report, "Yes, we have them in a warehouse. I can have them for you tomorrow." Then I make up some price above what we are paying for it so we can still turn a profit.

The purchasing agent is satisfied and becomes a steady customer. We are now fully in the business of selling medical supplies.

As this side of our business grows, we are soon running out of room for storage again! Fortunately, there is an ophthalmologist and optometrist office backing up to our pharmacy in this little medical building—and they're leaving. We get permission from the landlord to take over their suite of offices.

That gives us more space to stock products as our business expands like crazy.

Private Rooms

In addition to buying wholesale product and reselling it to hospitals, we also sell directly to patients in our store. It isn't long before Fred realizes the way pharmacies are designed is all wrong for this. You can't do what we're doing in a typical pharmacy. A person who needs an ostomy bag or someone who is incontinent (lacking sufficient control over their bowels or their urination), won't want to have that conversation at the register with four other people standing around them.

"Fred, you're right. We need some private space."

Fortunately, the doctor's office suite has the kinds of rooms we need to have these conversations and go over the equipment behind closed doors. While we don't actually fit patients for ostomy bags, we have a staff of people who have had colostomies or ileostomies themselves. They know what these patients are going through and the kinds of care needed. They relate to the psychological and emotional concerns firsthand.

We utilize these staff members both for phone consultation as well as in-person discussions when patients come into the pharmacy. This is in addition to the enterostomal therapist who acts as our consultant to teach us about the equipment.

Patients coming to us are referred by their own enterostomal therapist to buy the needed equipment. The ostomy fitting must be perfect, so we have to make sure they get the right equipment. The surrounding skin also needs to be treated. There are a lot of issues facing these patients.

We really train on customer service. I see this as a paramount concept for us.

Homing in on More Storage

Using these office rooms for private consultations means we need to find alternative additional space to store our ostomy equipment and supplies. Right behind our medical building is a residential district. I say to Fred, "Let's see if we can buy one of these houses. I happen to know one is owned by Stewart Stampterfer, a patient of ours."

I approach Stewart at his home and say, "Hello Stewart, I would like to buy your house."

He looks at me. "What? Really?"

I say, "Yes, really. If you're interested. How much would you want for your house?"

"$30,000."

I think I'm a smart guy so I start to negotiate. But Stewart stops me. "You said you wanted to buy the house. It's $30,000. Do you want it or not?"

We buy the house for $30,000.

There is just one little problem. Some of this ostomy equipment is made with a substance called Karaya, which is heat sensitive. The Valley is so hot that it will melt the stuff! So we air condition the garage and move all the product in there, while we make the bedrooms into offices. We turn the living room into a shipping department—because now we are shipping product all over!

So we expand into this new space and before too long, I realize we *still* don't have enough room. We are warehousing, hiring more medical staff, more clerks, more shipping people. So I buy the house next to that house. Now we have two houses.

Of course, none of this is entirely legal since we're running this business in houses in a residential area—Zoned R1—which means homes only. No commercial businesses. So we are mowing the lawns neatly and making sure the shades are down so as not to raise suspicion.

Everything is going great and soon we buy *a third* house up the street on the other side. At times, especially when it's raining, it's like a comedy scene. Employees with umbrellas scurrying from house to house to the pharmacy and back carrying boxes and equipment. Luckily, none of the neighbors are the wiser. Or just don't care. No complaints are ever made.

That is, until a semitruck delivering supplies for us, slams into some lamp posts and knocks out all the lights in the neighborhood! It's chaos.

I say, "Fred, this is crazy! A pharmacy. Three houses. Trucks coming in and out. This is all Mickey Mouse. We need to find a better location."

But Fred is bugging me about something else that we need to settle. Our business has really grown and he no longer wants to be my employee. He wants to be my partner. For everything.

I think about it. Fifty percent of our business is more than I'll ever be able to do on my own—and I need Fred to do it. Fred is doing most of the ostomy stuff while I am doing the pharmacy portion.

I make Fred my 50–50 partner.

✦　✦　✦

CHAPTER 36

Going Big in a Bigger Space

Having made Fred my partner in Shield, we now must together make a big decision.

Our problems with inadequate space can no longer be ignored (including the craziness of a running pharmacy and three neighborhood houses for storage and shipping and delivery trucks bashing residential streetlamps and knocking out power). *We have to move.*

We look at a place at 6705 Valjean Avenue. *A big place*: a 15,000-square-foot industrial warehouse.

Remember, we started at just 750 square feet.

This expansion would be a major investment. Of course, I consult with Lorraine before we decide. Fortunately, she is supportive of me on this. She knows my excitement for it. Ross and Lynn sense the thrill too. Even early on, they love hearing about the business, asking when I come home, "So Dad, how many prescriptions you do today?" Plus, by this time, Lynn has worked in the pharmacy—cleaning and organizing shelves—so she has been in the midst of everything.

In the beginning days of Shield, it's fun growing the business on a small scale. I always arrive early, excited for the day and to meet our customer-patients. It is kind of like *Cheers* where everyone is hanging out and everybody knows everybody. But by 1980, we are pretty sophisticated. We are in a new era of ostomy and incontinence care, thinking about spinal cord injury patients, all kinds of stuff. So we take the money we get selling the three houses . . .

Fred's mother loans us some additional money . . . and we purchase the warehouse.

It is about two-and-a-half miles from our current location. We know we are going to lose a lot of local prescription patients since we'll be in a different area. But the rest of our business is really rolling—our ostomy business and wholesaling supplies are far bigger than anything else.

There are extremely few pharmacies doing this ostomy care. In fact, a lot of patients are now coming in through referrals from pharmacy chains because those places never deal with any of it. But we are careful not to overstep those opportunities. By that, I mean if someone comes to buy ostomy equipment, we don't try to get their prescription business. We feel that will be counterproductive. Why would a pharmacy send us a patient for ostomy care if we then try to steal their prescription business? In fact, if a patient says, "Well, do you want to do my prescriptions too?" We reply, "You know, you are doing very well at your own pharmacy for that. We'll just take care of your ostomy needs."

Landmark Moment

Our move is a big turning point for us.

In some ways, Fred and I are opposites. He's frugal and thinking practical, while I'm out here dreaming big. It's why this whole thing between us works. I'm exploring new and bigger ways to do more business, and he's making sure we have what we need in stock, that we're billing and collecting from clients and patients, that we're delivering on time.

While the building we move into is 15,000 square feet, it will be divided in half. We'll occupy 7500 square feet, while a company that makes specialized cameras will rent the other half of our building.

In the case of our new pharmacy, I want to design the interior from the ground up and not to look like any other pharmacy. But Fred wants to build and furnish it on the cheap. In this instance, I insist: "Fred, let's do this right. Let's hire a designer—and have it be a designer who's never done anything in health care or medical before. We'll let them create this space."

I explain my thinking to Fred: "Every pharmacy out there looks the same. Go to Rite Aid or Walgreens or CVS—and tell me the difference except for the signage on the door? There isn't any. That's the way pharmacies have been for years. We can create a space that nobody has ever seen before. Let's not do it in sterile white. Let's use color. Let's install skylights and bring in natural light. Let's put in plants—real plants. Besides, a typical pharmacy design doesn't really work for us and the people who will come here, given what we are offering."

Fred . . . agrees.

"Designer Pharmacy"

A lot of considerations go into our plans, by both the designer and us. I encourage, "Let's really think about this. We'll have many people coming here in wheelchairs. Let's put the shelving low enough that they can reach it while sitting in their chairs. In our consulting areas, let's make sure the tables have a pedestal base, not legs, because people in wheelchairs bump into legs."

To further help us, we hire the person in charge of disabled students at UCLA to do in-service trainings with our staff about various sensitive issues that patients could have. He trains our employees on how to deal with people in wheelchairs. We create the store so if one of our staff helps someone in a wheelchair, we can sit with them at eye level. We put chairs in different places of our facility so those patients don't have to look up to us. It changes the dynamics. Our bathrooms are wheelchair accessible, long before the Americans with Disabilities Act makes that a standard. We spend a lot of time thinking about how to make this experience work for everyone. I mean, if you think about most pharmacies, they are not comfortable. CVS or Rite Aid—from their point of view, they can't get people in and out fast enough!

That's their goal. You can't even find a comfortable place to sit. It's not designed for you.

Ours will have a whole different approach to how people are treated.

As I describe earlier, ostomy and incontinence conditions are difficult for patients, both physically and emotionally, and challenging for doctors and enterostomal therapists assisting their care. Ostomy devices must be properly fitted along with other considerations. Our store design will include private rooms and consulting areas.

Incontinence for when someone is not able to control their urine can have various causes, including prostate cancer or spinal cord injuries in which patients have no control over parts of their body (and may urinate without knowing it). For patients with less severe conditions, we offer underpads. In fact, we only use the word "underpads"—we never call them diapers or adult diapers. "Diapers" are for babies. I consciously make these choices to help provide some dignity. It is why we don't put incontinent devices in the diaper section. Psychologically, it is totally wrong.

The Dream Takes Form

So we change the interior dynamics to best accommodate and care for the patients who will come in as we make everything more visually inviting. All plants are alive—no fakes—including a fifteen-foot ficus tree in the middle of our space! We put in skylights. Instead of a sterile white decor, we use color.

Some people have called my doing this "visionary." But I believe it simply reflects wanting a space that provides ease and dignity to those people already dealing with challenges. My desire to help in this way comes in part from my involvement in civil rights and seeing the heartbreak of poverty and discrimination, as well as working with the California Alcoholism Foundation where I witness the suffering of those addicted to alcohol *and* the pain experienced by loved ones—since entire families can be in misery around this too.

The knowledge that not everyone lives an easy life shapes how we design our facility and care for our patients. I cannot solve everything, but I can certainly support those who come to us.

These considerations will inform my USC teaching later on as well. It will be my mantra to the students: "Think about the needs of the people who come in. Have staff on the floor to help them. Have the pharmacist talk to patients to make sure they know how to take what they are given and ask what other medications they may have (that could interact), etc."

Today, unfortunately, the service level stinks in most pharmacies—certainly in the large chains. It's often hard to find anyone to help you.

The Mezzanine

In addition to our main floor, we build a mezzanine—a kind of partial low level second floor between our main floor and the ceiling. That's where we put our office. Yes, Fred and I decide to share one office. That's because we start a conversation on Monday morning and it'll go back and forth for the whole week nonstop. Easier to do in one office.

The mezzanine also has desk areas for staff to be on phones, a conference room, and space to do a lunch meeting or continuing education programs.

I tell Fred that we should also have a really nice bathroom upstairs for employees. With real towels (not paper). And a shower.

Fred goes, "And a what? Shower?"

I explain, "We're here for many hours, yet sometimes we have to go to outside meetings. We can take a shower here, change clothes, and look presentable."

"That's crazy," Fred counters.

Anyway, Fred lets me do it.

The bathroom turns out great. In fact, Lorraine has me put some potpourri on the sink to make it super nice. Potpourri is a mixture of dried flower petals mixed with spices, placed in a bowl or small cloth sack to add fragrance to a room.

Yet we discover that not everyone is familiar with the concept of potpourri. Fred goes in there and because of the delectable smell, figures it must be a kind of flavored crackers. So he puts some of the potpourri in his mouth. It is not the mouthwatering flavor he is expecting!

Befitting our new larger location and that we're creating something beyond what a normal pharmacy offers, we decide to change our name. We leave behind Shield Pharmacy . . . and become *Shield HealthCare*.

We also change the logo. It now looks like a family: a simple cartoon-like silhouette of a man, a woman, and two kids.

Naturally, Lynn and Ross think the kids are them. They're really not, but we tell them: "Of course it's you two!"

Grand Opening

Finally, our new store is finished. I'm ecstatic about all we've done!

Lorraine still remembers her response upon seeing it: "This is so creative and beautiful. Not like any other pharmacy, it is big and in such good taste. Anyone walking in would say, "Wow, I have never seen this before!"

It is now time for people to walk in.

Our grand opening is an open house for invited friends, family, professional and USC colleagues, the nurses and therapists we work with, and of course, current patients. It is a big party and we have it catered.

Colorful hanging fabric throughout lowers people's eyelines so it doesn't feel like a warehouse with high ceilings. Lighting is soft (not harsh). This area's chairs and tables are convenient and comfortable anytime a staffer speaks to a patient or shows equipment. Tables are on pedestals so wheelchairs won't bang into legs.

Another area. Again low-hanging fabric. Trees and plants—all real.

Extra wide aisles allow wheelchairs to easily navigate and turn. Note merchandise on low shelves is reachable by someone in a wheelchair.

Close friends of ours, Deanne and Allen Lange, come early to help us prepare for the open house. They take it upon themselves to wash the floor at the entrance to make sure it shines for everyone's arrival! That's incredibly touching. Finally, the doors open. . . .

People love the place!!

It is huge: 7,500 square feet of floor space plus another 3,000 square feet on the mezzanine—and so unlike other pharmacies.

Shipping and storage area in the back.

John Biles, the dean at the USC School of Pharmacy, an innovator himself and a mentor, comes to tour the place. When Lorraine and I see him walking down from the mezzanine level, he has tears in his eyes.

Tears! He embraces us and says, "This is unbelievable. Just unbelievable!" It is a great moment.

But it isn't just the "professionals" who are impressed. My mother is there and thinks it is incredible too! In fact, my mom's a bit of a "neat person." So after we are open for business, I instruct the staff that whenever my mother will be visiting: "Please make sure the place is super clean, neat, organized—and dusted. Knowing my mother, she'll likely run her finger along the counters to make sure!"

No News is Good News

One group of people we *don't* have at our grand opening are reporters. That's because Fred wants to stay low-key and out of the spotlight.

Of course, I'm a show guy. I want everybody to know! But Fred isn't interested in getting into local papers, or having pharmacy magazines come and take pictures. In fact, he is adamantly against it.

He feels, "We really got something special here. We don't need to tell everybody." Fred doesn't want publicity because he doesn't want other pharmacies to steal our concept and recreate what we have. I listen to him and we don't seek that kind of attention.

But we do need to attract the attention of *another group.*

"If you build it, they will come"

So we build it. But we can't simply open our doors and expect people to rush in. For ostomy and incontinent patients in particular, we get the bulk of our referrals from special nurses, and from other pharmacies that don't carry this kind of equipment or provide these services. But to get more of those referrals, we have to convince people—a lot of people—that we know what we are doing and provide a high level of care.

Fred and I travel the country to meetings and conventions to inform people about our facilities and the equipment that we offer. We even set up booths so convention-goers can talk with us at length.

It works. Our business really builds.

✦   ✦   ✦

CHAPTER 37

Professor Mel

I never plan to be a teacher. I am never educated to be a teacher. I am a pharmacist. An entrepreneur. An innovator.

Yet that life takes a new turn after I write a letter.

Pharmacists have long been trained to primarily be chemists—basically technicians filling prescriptions and dispensing medicines. That is how I am taught when I attend USC in the 1950s.

Then sometime in the early 1970s, a couple of colleagues at USC begin to visit patients in long-term care facilities, reviewing their charts and writing comments like, "This is a duplicate medicine . . . Suggest discontinuing this medication . . . Patient has been on this medicine longer than necessary . . . This is a subtherapeutic dose," etc. Those are not put on the medical charts themselves because those become legal documents. But these pharmacists create notes regarding this. That becomes known as clinical pharmacy, practiced in long-term care facilities and institutions like hospitals.

This also becomes the focus of student education. But after working in the field for so many years, I believe the way pharmacy is being taught is a mistake. I write to the dean at the USC Pharmacy School, John Biles.

"Why can't you teach students to perform clinical pharmacy in the outpatient setting as well—not just in long-term care and hospital facilities? Community pharmacies are where the majority of graduates' working lives will be, so clinical pharmacy should also be taught for this setting. In the real world, ambulatory care (care provided outside of hospitals) is where most pharmacy work is performed."

The Committee

I hear back from John, who reports they agree with my suggestions! In fact, they are forming a group to look into revising the school's approach. "Mel, would you join our new committee?"

John is the dean who is so moved when attending the grand opening of our Valjean Avenue facility for Shield HealthCare. He believes I will be the perfect person to help develop this course and judge who is qualified to teach it. I go on the committee.

I lead our team in rethinking the curriculum for training our pharmacy students. We restructure it from teaching only in hospital settings to also include an outpatient focus.

The committee begins a search to find somebody to teach this new class. But we look and look and continue to come up empty. Most professors do not have extensive experience with building or running a pharmacy. John finally says, "Mel, we can't find anybody to teach this. *Why don't you teach it?*"

I answer, "What the hell are you talking about? I'm busy running my company."

"We know. We just would like you to teach two days a week for just a couple hours."

By this time, readers of this book probably realize I'm a person who tends to say "yes." I agree to John's offer and am given a part-time position at the school of pharmacy. I am now *Assistant Professor Mel Baron.*

As I continue developing this new curriculum, I make another radical suggestion to John Biles:

"Pharmacy students should be placed out in a community pharmacy (similar to an internship) during their first year of pharmacy school, not wait until their third or fourth year. Let them get a feel of what a pharmacy looks like, feels like, smells like. They won't become pharmacists after a four- or six-week rotation there, but it will give them some sense of it and allow the pharmacist working there to be a mentor to them. This approach will provide more clarity and depth to everything the student then learns over their four years of schooling." John and the school agree this makes sense and it becomes part of the new program.

Yet my changing the status quo doesn't stop here.

First Class

In 1981, I start teaching my first class, which is now mandatory for all freshmen. But I stipulate to John Biles that I don't want to teach all 180 freshmen at the same time in some large lecture hall. "Let me do smaller seminars of thirty students each for six weeks apiece, and spread these groups throughout the first year."

John is agreeable to this.

Yet there's more. I also don't want students sitting in class behind each other, staring at the back of somebody's head while I talk up at the front. I want to conduct my class in the round with everyone sitting in a circle, interacting with me and each other.

So that's how I design my class called "Introduction to Community Pharmacy." In addition to teaching how to run and build a pharmacy business, one of its core concerns is how we deal with our patients.

It also includes the *externship* that I mentioned above. For the duration of each seminar, every student has an outside job at a pharmacy. It is much like an internship, except those are typically done during summers. The externship occurs in the academic year and is part of my class.

USC places students in different area pharmacies where they spend two days each week from 1:00 to 6:00 p.m. Then we meet a couple times during the week in the classroom for two hours and go over what happened at their pharmacy.

The pharmacy department already has externships, but until I start teaching, they are never in the first year. In addition to their externships, I give them assignments and required readings that we discuss. My classes introduce subjects not previously part of the curriculum, such as legal issues, because there are many regulations in terms of how you store, control, and dispense medications.

I also talk a lot about communication skills. I even tell students: "I know some of you are having trouble dating, partly because your communication skills suck. In this class, not only do I teach you pharmacy, but I'm also giving you some life lessons—so pay attention."

When I mention dating, they *really* pay attention.

Discussion is in the round and very interactive. By having classes in a circle, we are already breaking the old model of the technician pharmacist who doesn't know how to talk to people. I'm requiring them to socialize in a professional-like setting. At the same time, I'm hearing about their experiences in pharmacies and giving them feedback and advice.

By the end of the six-week class, they are interacting much more effectively at their pharmacies.

And maybe in their dating lives as well.

(Nowadays, students in their first year at pharmacy school learn even more: CPR, giving injections, doing physical assessments like taking blood pressures. When I am in school, God forbid if you touch anybody! You would never give an injection or take blood pressure.)

Later on, I add a separate freshman class on Introduction to Hospital Pharmacy during which each student does an externship in a hospital. These remain the core classes I teach.

In addition, I guest lecture in other professors' classes, speaking about pharmacy over the counter, as well as lecture on ostomy equipment and incontinence.

I am forever grateful to John Biles, who not only gives me the opportunity to be in academia, but also allows me the freedom to do it *my* way.

Leadership

In my classes, I challenge students about their own career plans and expected paths, and how they can do things differently than they are presently imagining.

Later on, I add a leadership piece to the classroom discussions. In my mind, most of the students we enroll in pharmacy school are basically going to be managers, not true leaders. Leaders are a different group of people, a different culture.

But there is a small core group of students who *are* leaders. Leaders will be the ones who innovate and advance future pharmacy practices. I encourage these people to think differently than how a manager thinks, while discussing the core values that leaders share. There is a lot of literature in this area that I introduce to students.

Yet most all of this is from my own experiences, which is pretty unique among the faculty. Others may have worked in pharmacies and may have great clinical and research skills far beyond my own. My focus has been in the worlds of management and leadership and building a large business. Later, that will include working in corporate America. I am trying to bring some of my awareness to the school.

And the response to my teaching? The students love it! They eat it up because I present important pieces of the puzzle.

Faculty Comes Around to the Round

After teaching at the school a while, I say to Dean Biles, "John, the faculty meetings are *boring*. They're tedious. Why are we all sitting as if we are in a typical classroom? Let's seat the faculty in the round. Plus, bring in some wine. It'll transform the whole atmosphere."

They do and it all changes for the better.

Some people believe I simply cannot help but think outside the box. Yet some of these things seem so basic to me that it's beyond comprehension that we haven't already changed them.

"Secret" Dress Code

From my very first class, I'm always dressed up in a shirt, tie, and jacket or suit.

Some professors do this, some don't. But no one really cares. To me, I'm a professional and this is how one should dress. I'm trying to impress upon students that how you appear at a pharmacy is important. Are you showing up looking professional?

Over the years, it is never written in my syllabus or mandated anywhere that everyone coming to my class should dress up—guys in shirts and ties, and women equivalently attired. Yet somehow, students begin to realize this is how Professor Baron wants them in his class. I never speak about it, but soon everyone showing up to my classes is dressed like a professional.

Believe me, that is not typical student attire on campus! In fact, if someone walking on campus or at the cafeteria is well-dressed, other students comment, "They must be in Dr. Baron's class."

Busy Busy Baron

Right from the get-go, USC gives me an office where I hold office hours like all professors, so students can meet with me and ask questions to clarify what we are learning, an assignment, or an upcoming test or final.

But most of the students really come to me for career advice. They want to talk about their future and often grand plans to open a business. In response, I talk generally about career paths, along with this stock answer: "You've been a starving student for all these years. Get a job, get a paycheck, and get some experience. Then think about the bigger plans. No matter where you take a job, it's not forever and you can change it. But first acquire some experience and then think about where your passion is."

In addition to office hours and classroom teaching hours, I am prepping for my classes and grading papers. This is all at the same time as I'm running and growing my own business. Fortunately, I'm pretty good at time management and organizing.

It is a talent that comes in handy repeatedly.

Sheer Pleasure of Teaching

If anyone had asked when I am in pharmacy school, "Mel, would you ever be interested in academia?"—I would have replied, "That would be the *last* thing I would ever entertain!"

So when I return to the university to start as a part-time professor—while I'm still full-time at Shield (and later Bard Corporation)—no one is more surprised than me that I find teaching fun and enjoyable!

When you are a professor, you have a stage. To me, it is almost like giving a performance. It is my soapbox and a chance to talk about my thoughts and theories about the profession and share my ideas. I vividly remember walking to class even at the beginning, centering myself to be ready to perform as I enter the room.

Mel Baron is "on."

Over my thirty years in pharmacy, I amass this vast knowledge. Yet there is no opportunity or venue to share that with anyone until I become a professor. The students are my captive audience. I have authority over what they hear from me. I hope the information is meaningful to them—and judging by their attention, questions, and feedback—it appears to be just that.

◆　◆　◆

CHAPTER 38

Lynn and Ross Leave the Nest

We live in the Valley, in a big two-story house with a yard and swimming pool. As our kids get older and leave home, Lorraine and I wonder, "Why are we still here?"

"Where would we love to live? How about Santa Monica?"

We tell this to a friend of ours, who responds, "Well, there's a condo being built right around the corner on Fourth and San Vicente."

This is a Sunday and I ask, "Can we go look at it?"

We see it that day. It is a brand-new condo in a sophisticated, beautiful area just a short walk from Ocean Avenue and the cliffs overlooking the Pacific Ocean. What's not to like?

I say, "Lorraine, this is it." She totally agrees, "I know!"

Monday morning, we buy it.

We still have to sell our house. I contact a real estate agent and a "for sale" sign goes up in our front yard the next Thursday. We are advised that selling a house can take a while and to be prepared for that.

By the time I return home from work that Thursday, the doorbell rings. I answer the door to someone who says, "I just saw your sign. Can I see the house?"

I haven't even taken off my jacket yet. The guy does a walkthrough of the house and states, "I'll take it."

I ask incredulously, "Are you for real?"

He is and I call up the real estate agent. "I just sold the house." My agent thinks I'm teasing him. So we see the condo on Sunday. Buy it on Monday. Then sell our house on Thursday. We are in love with the new place.

The kids hate it.

Ross declares, "This is the worst thing ever. How can you sell our house?"

My daughter sees the condo and feels the same. "This is ugly. Dad, Mom, how could you sell our home? I wanted to walk down the stairs and get married there!"

I point out, "You're not even going out with anybody right now."

Both kids are very upset.

We buy it without their approval, move in, and live happily ever after.

Lynn and Ross Going Forward

The reason we are able to downsize is there comes a time (as has been true for generations) when your children leave the home to venture forward on their own. When I am growing up, young people have a few different options. Go to work for someone else. Start your own business. Join the military. For me, it was go to college. The first in my family to do so.

By the time we have kids, the typical path is college. No doubt about it. At least, that's how *we* see it.

This is exactly the path that Lynn takes.

Lynn: Transitioning to Independence

Among Lynn's many wonderful traits, one that we see early on, is decisiveness. Sometime in the middle of junior high, Lynn declares, "I am going to go to Berkeley and I will be a teacher." Such conviction at such a young age surprises us. My sense is she may be fascinated by teachers at school. Or admires one particular female teacher and Lynn feels that will be a good career for her too.

Turns out, just as she predicted in junior high, Lynn gets accepted to Berkeley and plans to go! We are excited.

Yet some of our friends caution, "Are you nuts? You're sending your daughter *to Berkeley*? With all the crazy stuff happening there?"

It is true that protests and drugs and counterculture activities are still common at Berkeley during this era. So I contact a professor-friend at Berkeley (who I meet in the civil rights movement) and ask about the environment there. His astute reply: "There is a constant parade of all kinds of people up here at Berkeley. Your daughter will simply get in that part of the parade she is most comfortable with." Hearing this is comforting to me, as I believe Lynn will make smart decisions.

However, even when it is the right school, transitioning to college can be hard. And not necessarily just for the child. Lorraine and I drive Lynn up to Berkeley and help move her into the dorm. We get her all settled and then Lorraine and I drive back . . . and Lorraine bawls for the next six hours.

Being away from home for the first time can bring up needs for students too. I don't necessarily mean a need for parental reassurance. Sometimes it simply has to do with *supplies.*

Knowing I own the pharmacy, Lynn calls to ask, "Dad, can you send me some shampoo and sanitary napkins?"

Naturally, I send cases. Lynn sees the excess and decides, "What the hell?" Lynn starts *selling* the surplus!

Truly the daughter of an entrepreneur.

Unexpected Challenges

Before she heads up there, I warn, "You know, there are going to be a lot of really smart people at this college. In your high school, you were among the few who stood out in class. But at Berkeley, *everybody is you.* Everyone there comes from that kind of elite group."

Lynn discovers this pretty quickly. Even though she's a good writer, she takes a writing class and gets a C. Lynn has never gotten a C before in her life! It is traumatic! But this is college and that first C kind of slaps you right in the face.

She calls us up sobbing. "I'm going to flunk out!"

I say, "Welcome to the real world. But you are not going to flunk out. It's simply a different ballgame you're playing now. Just hang in there. You can do this. I have confidence in you."

Lynn hangs in there . . . and does really well.

Lynn having happy days at Berkeley

Mel Encourages: "You can do anything."

In truth, I feel Lynn can do anything that she sets her mind to and I tell her this starting early on as she is growing up. While my intention is to inspire her confidence and to follow her dreams, she interprets it as kind of an expectation that "she must accomplish great things."

Ross takes the other approach. When I tell him he can do anything, he sees it as liberating. Freedom! But Lynn's hearing it like "she *should* do great things" causes her to feel a lot of pressure. She always ends up the ace student in high school.

This is probably why it is *especially* difficult when she gets that C.

Fortune Teller

Lynn starts at Berkeley when I'm still traveling throughout the state for the California Alcoholism Foundation. Whenever that brings me to the Bay Area, Lynn comes into San Francisco and we meet at Sam Wo Restaurant in Chinatown, a well-known, multistory eatery that has been in the same location since the early 1900s. They still even use the vintage dumbwaiter (a mini elevator) to deliver meals to the upper floors!

When it's time to open our fortune cookies and look at the little slip of paper inside, Lynn's messages always predict a positive turn of events or offer some philosophical guidance. When I open mine, I always exclaim, "You won't believe what my fortune says: 'Help, help, I'm being held prisoner in a Hong Kong Noodle Company!'" For me, that joke never gets old. In fact, I later send Lynn a huge canister of fortune cookies—with every one of the fortunes saying this same thing!

A couple times when I'm up there, I visit Lynn at her apartment, where she serves me banana bread that she makes herself. I find out later that Lynn is trying to impress her father by showing him she can cook!

Well, it works. That banana bread is delicious!

Getting More than an Education

While at Berkeley, Lynn starts to date Darrell Friedman. The Friedman family are friends of ours in LA. In fact, we have traveled with Darrell's parents and even gone on a cruise with them, so we know Darrell pretty well. The kids are the same age and attend the same Sunday school growing up. While never friends, they do know each other. And when Lynn goes to Berkeley, so does Darrell. As they grow close, we think it is a match made in heaven.

Meanwhile, Lynn is agonizing over her career plans at Berkeley. Though she's wanted to be a teacher from an early age, she now questions if this is a sellout for today's modern woman. Teaching and nursing have always been the conventional woman's roles. At Berkeley, she is exposed to many new possibilities. She struggles with it, ultimately deciding that teaching is still her calling and she will follow that dream.

Lynn marries Darrell. We are thrilled. Darrell is going into business with his dad. Yet I get this sense that Darrell and his family want Lynn to be a stay-at-home mom, while Lynn wants to be a career woman.

Lynn and Darrell move back to LA after graduating Berkeley and she goes to UCLA to get her teaching credential. She participates in their University Elementary School—an innovative facility associated with UCLA's Graduate School of Education. A combination elementary school, research lab, and teacher training center, it advocates for progressive ideas on education. She studies under Madeline Hunter, renowned in the field and called one of the ten most influential women in education, having developed a teaching model widely adopted by schools nationwide. Lynn learns a tremendous amount from her. Upon once being asked if she could distill Madeline's approach into a single sentence, Lynn replies, "As an educator, you have a professional responsibility *to take the students wherever they are* and get them to the next level."

Earning her credential, Lynn is immediately hired to teach at Parkview Elementary in Simi Valley, where she will teach (at her request) each of the different grade levels during her years there—quite unusual for an elementary teacher. Yet she still feels a tremendous amount of pressure from Darrell and his family *not* to be a career woman.

Eventually the marriage comes to an end. After ten years together, she and Darrell divorce when their son Jack is two-and-a-half. To their credit, neither Darrell nor Lynn ever speaks badly about each other to Jack. They spare him much of the pain of divorce that I witnessed from my mom's constant complaining about Al.

Lynn moves out, buys a house, and starts a new life. She eventually meets someone—a principal at another school in the same district as hers (Lynn is a principal by this time too). One day, Lynn calls to tell us that she has become super serious with this guy. I say, "That's great news, Lynn! What's his name?"

"Phil Ross."

Let's remember that "Phil Ross" is also the name of Lorraine's dad . . . so *that* takes some getting used to!

They get married. Lynn keeps her name as Lynn Baron Friedman since people know her professionally as Lynn Friedman.

Ross: A More "Complex" Path

When Ross becomes a high school senior, we are worried. He doesn't seem motivated to go to college. This is in sharp contrast to Lynn. Like I've said before, with Ross, we never see schoolbooks. I'm sure he also cuts a lot of classes that we don't know about because he's out surfing and pursuing other diversions . . . likely with Mabel (his truck).

We start asking him, "Ross, what do you want to do?"

This he doesn't know. But he *is* certain that *he already knows everything that he needs*. He doesn't require college.

At this point, we're just praying he graduates high school! It becomes a source of much anxiety and discussion between Lorraine and me. Fortunately, Ross ends up graduating and we convince him to go to Pierce Community College. What a relief!

It lasts less than six weeks.

Ross drops out before he finishes a semester. He gets a job at a gas station. But that doesn't last long either as he realizes it may not be the best occupation. He next tries selling kitchen knives door-to-door . . .

but soon that doesn't seem like a budding profession either. Things aren't looking good career-wise.

But this isn't even our biggest issue with Ross.

Man of the Church

On a Super Bowl Sunday, Lorraine's sister Sharon calls to say, "What are you guys doing? I need to come over and talk with you."

We have no idea what could be so important as to interrupt Super Bowl Sunday!

Ross has gone to a pal's house to watch the game, when Sharon arrives to say, "This friend of mine told me, 'I heard your nephew speak at church. He's fabulous. He gave this incredible sermon.'"

Sharon responded to her friend, "I think you must be mistaken."

But her friend persisted, "Well, isn't his name Ross Baron? I'm telling you, he gave an incredible talk. He's a member of the church."

Now Lorraine says, "No, that can't be possible." Yet Sharon insists.

We get on the phone and call Ross. "You need to come home right away."

"I'm watching the game."

"We understand that. But we need you home. It's important."

So he returns home and we confront him with the story that we heard from Sharon.

Ross reveals, "Yes, I have joined the Church of Latter-day Saints." (At the time, this is also known informally as the Mormon Church.)

We are in shock to say the least. There is lots of upset. Lots of tears.

Then Ross responds, "If it is going to be a problem, maybe it's best I leave the house."

At this instant, I may have my wisest moment of my life. I say to him, "If you choose to leave the house, I want you to know our door will always be open. We will always love you no matter what."

It could have gone a very different way. Some Jewish families would be so horrified by a child leaving their faith for another that they disavow any connection to them. They actually sit shiva as if the child has died. For me, the thought of not having my child talk to me or be a part of my life is beyond anything I can comprehend. That is more precious and important beyond all else. There is never any question whether I will welcome him back.

Ross's Great Search

Yet at the moment Ross leaves the house, we are beside ourselves. We let Lynn know what's happened. This is while she is away at college and she doesn't understand it any better than we do.

Frankly, Lorraine and I are embarrassed. We don't know what to say to anybody else, especially my mother. We look at each other and ask, "What did we do wrong as parents?" Lorraine gets on my case that I have been too permissive as a father. Is she right?

Fortunately, we share what is happening with a few supportive friends. One of them is a psychiatrist who spends a lot of time with us, explaining, "Think about it this way: he's making a decision for himself. You gave him permission to be a free thinker. You gave him that ability. To think for himself." Lorraine and I consider everything our friend says.

We learn it is during high school that Ross becomes involved with the church. The father of one of his best friends is a bishop. Yet we wonder what motivates Ross to make such a change. As we think further about this, Lorraine comes to believe the biggest piece of this puzzle begins when Lorraine's mother died years earlier. Always so very fond of his grandmother, a young Ross asks Lorraine, "Where's Grandma?"

"She has died."

"But where is she?"

Lorraine says, "If you're Jewish, we don't know where she goes. We have no answer for that."

Well, the Latter-day Saints have an answer for that. They speak of the afterlife, of joining with past members of the family. They have many answers for things that we don't have in Judaism.

We believe Ross sought to learn more and that the religious portions of the Latter-day Saints speak to him in the deepest way. Time will prove that this is not a misstep for Ross at all. Now 63, he remains deeply involved with the church that he joined when he was 18.

Clearly the right decision for him.

The Mission

Not too long after we have our conversation with Ross, he informs us that he is leaving on a mission for the church. He's just 20 years old.

We ask, "What does that mean?"

Like in the play, *The Book of Mormon*, when you're on a mission, the men wear a white shirt and tie, with a suit depending on weather. Basically, you go door to door, asking people to listen as you tell them the virtues of the Church of Jesus Christ of Latter-day Saints, with the goal of getting them to join the church themselves.

In preparation, Ross attends a mission training center. They want him to cut his hair. That is a big deal to him! He resists at first, but this is important enough to him that he agrees. They teach him everything else that he will need, including immersing him in Spanish. Once his training is complete, he is sent to Argentina for two years.

We are once again besides ourselves. We don't know what to expect. Worse, when someone is on a mission, you are not allowed to visit them. You cannot speak with them. This is long before the days of Zoom calls, the internet, or even cell phones.

Instead, we get letters. Every week, Ross sends us what I call "sunshine letters." He reports everything is great and wonderful. The best experience! We only find out much later that Ross is sick and the circumstances are anything but easy.

"He's a Norman"

We tell very few people what Ross is really doing. But while he is away, my mother asks, "Where's Ross?" We tap dance around the answer: "Oh, he's gone off traveling."

She later asks, "When do you think he's coming home from his travels?"

We continue sidestepping straight answers with many family members, *especially* my mother. Eventually, we decide to tell her that Ross has joined the Church of Jesus Christ of Latter-day Saints.

She thinks about that a long moment, and finally smiles. "Oh, so he's a Norman."

And that's the end of the conversation. Apparently, he's not Mormon; he's a Norman. I have no idea if my mother really has a concept of what we try to tell her or not. But we leave it at that.

The Return of Ross

After two years, Ross comes home.

We go to the airport, eager to pick him up and have him back. But I cannot recognize my son. He has lost so much weight, and he's wearing a suit borrowed from somebody else (his being threadbare) that's far too large for him now. His worn-out shoes have holes in their soles, with cardboard stuffed inside to help provide structure.

We bring him home. We go shopping in Santa Monica to buy him a sweatsuit that fits. We grab lunch while we're out and what does Ross want to eat? Lox, eggs, and onions.

The Jewish boy who becomes a Latter-day Saint wants lox, eggs, and onions. Go figure.

After he's home for a while, Ross says, "I think maybe I should go to college."

"What? What?? . . . What a wonderful idea that is."

Ross has seen how hard life can be. On his mission, he lives in poverty in southern Argentina. Such conditions there are commonplace. He doesn't have a lot to eat. They are only allowed so much money and we can't send him anything. The weather can be brutal. To say it is a Spartan life would be putting it kindly. Ross wants something better for himself.

Since he is a returned missionary, he gets accepted at BYU (Brigham Young University). I have no problem with Ross choosing a school owned by the Church of Jesus Christ of Latter-day Saints. I am thrilled that he is going to college! By this time, Lorraine and I have accepted this is his path and given ourselves permission to tell others that he has joined the church.

Ross loves it at BYU far more than he has ever liked school before! But life-changing experiences aren't happening only at the college. At home on a break from his studies, Ross meets Kathleen at church in Santa Monica. They fall in love, get married, and she joins him at BYU as his wife.

Ross majors in finance and business, and when he graduates, he gets an offer to go to Houston and be involved in real estate and property management.

Ross and Kathleen's new lives have begun.

✦ ✦ ✦

CHAPTER 39

Lorraine Goes Back to School

I've returned to USC to teach part-time. Our kids are soaring off on their own pathways of greater learning. Yet the three of us are not the only ones embarking in new directions of higher education.

While we are still living in our Valley house (before moving to Santa Monica), Lorraine says, "The kids are going to be out of here pretty soon. What am I going to be doing?"

She is Mom and running the household, but feels there's got to be more to her life than that. Her experiences at Everywoman's Village give her the courage to now take a class at UCLA, similar to an extension class in that you are not enrolled at UCLA itself. This one is designed around women in careers, where different women entrepreneurs talk to students about their professions and offer guidance to people like Lorraine.

As part of class, they give the students an aptitude class and a mock UCLA entrance exam.

Lorraine doesn't have much of an educational background. Many years earlier when she starts LA City College, she only stays between six months and a year. It just doesn't do it for her. She does take a few business school classes to acquire some skills. But that's pretty much it.

Turns out, Lorraine scores really high on this UCLA entrance exam! Her aptitude test shows her to be a highly compassionate person with an innate capacity to care for and coach others. The result is she gets this lovely letter from UCLA asking if she'd like to join their community by volunteering in a counseling center at UCLA. Advising kids and helping at the office.

But Lorraine dismisses its significance. "I think everybody in the class got this letter."

I wholeheartedly disagree. "Lorraine, trust me, everybody did *not* get this letter. They want you there. You should do it."

She takes the position and quickly discovers some very substantial people are with her, including the wife of Sid Caesar (renown comic actor/writer and pioneer in 1950s live television) and Lucy Hubbard, the wife of John Hubbard, president at USC. They and others there are high intellect people, working in an elevated atmosphere. What's more, Lorraine is totally comfortable being in there with them.

Her experience shifts her beliefs about her value and who she is. Growing up, Lorraine's parents never encouraged her to make something of herself. They were the typical: "Marry a nice Jewish boy. Raise kids. Be a housewife."

Yet at this point in life, Lorraine realizes she's pretty damn smart!

At the same time, Professor Bill Williams of USC (the African American professor she initially meets at Everywoman's Village, who also encourages me toward my public administration degree) has developed a University Without Walls program for USC with Shaw University, an all-Black school. It is designed for older adults like Lorraine, rather than be a traditional undergrad program for eighteen-year-olds. She signs up.

Lorraine earns her bachelor's degree.

From her positive experiences advising and guiding UCLA students, encouraged by her aptitude test showing her to be gifted in this area, Lorraine is interested in becoming a therapist. She enrolls in a graduate program through Azusa Pacific University.

Just as Lorraine does for me when I attend pharmacy school, I enthusiastically support her new pursuit. I read some of her books to know what she is studying and understand the terminology when she talks to me about what she is learning. I go to some of her seminars and listen to the speakers.

We always support each other when either of us explores new things. Even when Lorraine is at Everywoman's Village, I go there as well, meeting the people she's interacting with (it's how I first meet Bill Williams).

Helping Others

Lorraine has always been kind and caring. It is one of the many traits I absolutely love about her.

As an example, when she and I move into our first house on Whitaker, Lorraine reaches out to a residential agency that assists young women who become pregnant out of wedlock and are then shunned and thrown out of their own family households. Called Hamburger Home, the Hamburger Family first finances this residence in 1928. Their mission is to place these young mothers-to-be in another family home that is stable, with a mom and dad and some kids. Someplace where nobody is drinking or throwing things, and people sit down for dinner like in *Ozzie and Harriet* (a 1950s TV series that epitomized the wholesome values of the period). In a sense, a role model for what a "normal" home can be like.

Lorraine is the force behind bringing these young women into our home (just one at a time). While here, they provide light housekeeping and some babysitting. Our kids are young, between kindergarten and second grade. In exchange, we feed and house them, and give them a chance to be part of a family that shares meals and a home without fighting. When the young woman is ready to give birth, Lorraine takes her to the hospital. Once the child is born, the agency assists these young mothers to move on with their lives. We help a couple of women in this way.

Many years later, a young man finds us and asks if we remember a particular woman who lived with us—and do we know whatever happened to her or where she went?

This young man is the son that she put up for adoption after giving birth and who is now looking for his birth mother. Unfortunately, we don't know what happens to his mother after she leaves us. But Lorraine asks him, "Would you like to know about your mother?" He eagerly says yes, and Lorraine shares the best that she can recall, about who this woman was when she stayed with us. The young man is very moved to hear that his mother was such a lovely woman.

Lorraine's deep caring is something that others recognize too. People will come up and just start talking to her. We can be in a market, a post office, anywhere. It's like there's a sign on her head that flashes, "You can speak to me." It is a true phenomenon! Trust me, people are not coming up to Mel Baron and telling him their story—*that* doesn't happen.

Licensed to Heal

After she earns her master's degree, Lorraine becomes a marriage and family therapist with a private practice at Sepulveda and Ventura in Sherman Oaks. This changes everything for her. She blossoms even more. Lorraine loves this new chapter of life and her time as a therapist is incredibly fulfilling. She sees herself as a professional woman. Somebody who gives deeper meaning and support to people's lives.

To her surprise, Lorraine now is also seen differently by others. When I'm later at Bard Corporation, Lorraine and I socialize with all these corporate people. They are polite, but indifferent to the women who are housewives. But when she informs them that she is a therapist, everybody is interested: "Well, let me tell you about my kids. . . ."

Now with her license, Lorraine is even more qualified to offer others guidance—including family. So much so that our children sometimes complain, "Mom, can you just be a mom and forget all that psychology crap?"

Raising kids can be tough!

Volunteering Again: Beit T'Shuvah

A new opportunity to help people presents itself to Lorraine.

A lady friend who went to high school with her is a volunteer at Beit T'Shuvah and says, "Lorraine, this would be a great place for you. With your being a licensed therapist, why don't you think about volunteering at Beit T'Shuvah?"

It's 2002 and Beit T'Shuvah is an alcohol and substance abuse rehab on Venice Boulevard founded by Harriet Rossetto. Lorraine has never worked with substance abuse patients. Her practice is focused on marriage and family counseling with mostly middle- to upper-middle-class clients. But she goes to meet the people at Beit T'Shuvah and is fascinated. She volunteers as a therapist there one day a week, seeing individual patients as well as running support groups.

Most of those she sees also reside there—Beit T'Shuvah has a 120-patient live-in facility. But occasionally people walk in for therapy. Some of these patients have ended up on the street even though they come from Encino and Beverly Hills and Brentwood—with the majority of her patients being Jewish (she sees African American and Hispanic clients too).

Even though I've worked with the California Alcoholism Foundation, I make sure I don't impose myself on Lorraine's involvement with Beit T'Shuvah. This is *her* place. I take a supportive role in the background. I am Lorraine's husband and Lorraine is the star.

Sometime after she is working there, Lorraine decides to retire from her private practice after seventeen years. She continues volunteering at Beit T'Shuvah.

While initially established to administer their rehab program, Beit T'Shuvah eventually creates its own synagogue, after Mark Borovitz, the husband of the rehab's founder, becomes a rabbi. Mark's background is not typical for a rabbi: he's an ex-con and recovering alcoholic. How he turns his life around is pretty fascinating.

Harriet Rossetto is a social worker, hired to visit prisons and work with Jewish inmates to help them during confinement and prepare them for once they are released. Mark is one of these people. While working with him, she tells Mark of her dream to create a rehab center. He says, "When I get out, I'll come and help you." Of course, Harriet doesn't think any further about this. People say lots of things.

Fast-forward, Harriet now has a little house by MacArthur Park with five rehab residents, trying to follow her dream . . . when Mark shows up on the doorstep.

"Here I am to help. Like I promised."

He dives in and starts helping. Sometime after, she says, "Look, if you're really wanting to help me, you need to become a rabbi."

Mark actually goes to Israel and becomes a rabbinical student! Of course, along the way, they fall in love and get married. He later writes a book on his odyssey, *The Holy Thief: A Con Man's Journey from Darkness to Light*.

Moved both by their stories and what they have created, Lorraine and I make Beit T'Shuvah our synagogue. We are still there today. It is not a traditional synagogue, as those running it are not traditional. It is an amazing story of how people can overcome their struggles and flourish. They now get 300 to 400 people for Friday night shabbat services. It is astounding.

Diagnosis

While she is working there, Lorraine gets diagnosed with chronic myeloid leukemia (CML). She begins treatment.

We've been through this before. I have prostate cancer and surgery in 2002. She and I support one another through each of our illnesses, just like we support each other through everything else. It is challenging and scary stuff, but we make it through, with the love of our family encouraging us. Lorraine has been cancer free for eight years now and I am as well.

Yet before either of us get sick, our daughter Lynn has cancer too—melanoma—and recovers. As will be discussed later, Ross also gets diagnosed. So Lorraine and I, Lynn and Ross, all have one form of cancer or another and all survive it.

Giver Keeps Giving

Both during and after Lorraine's illness, she continues working at Beit T'Shuvah. This really says a lot about her strong and generous nature.

Her time at Beit T'Shuvah is an important and satisfying chapter in her life as she helps many struggling individuals. She continues there for eighteen years, "retiring" only a couple of years ago just before COVID.

✦ ✦ ✦

CHAPTER 40

Mel's New Venture: Home Care Infusions

As enormous changes are occurring in Lorraine's life, as well as in those of our children, big developments are simultaneously occurring in my business world.

In 1982, my former student, Danny Gelber, is a pharmacist in our store. He is a quirky little guy, and brilliant. One day he says, "Mel, you know what? I've been working at the VA hospitals. Why don't we try doing infusion therapy in people's homes?"

I respond, "Danny, are you crazy? I don't know anything about that."

Truth is, practically *no one* knows anything about it because nobody is doing that in homes at this time. Infusion means the intravenous (IV) administration of drugs, typically in a hospital or clinic setting under very careful conditions. It simply isn't being performed in homes and certainly not by a pharmacy. It's a nutty idea.

I also realize something else—that many of the things we are *already* doing are not done by others either. Things that initially have people reacting, "You can't. It's not possible. That's a terrible idea." I also think back on all the times my father successfully entered professions he didn't know anything about.

I tell Danny, "Okay, let's look into it. But I want you to develop all of the policies, procedures, and set-ups needed to do this."

What we're considering isn't a small endeavor. It includes administering hydration (saline solution), antibiotics (intravenously), and total parenteral nutrition (special forms of food/nutrition given intravenously).

Danny starts developing protocols. A lot of challenges need to be overcome. For one thing, preparation of the IV fluids must be done under very controlled sterile conditions. At the back of our building, we build a second upstairs to create a "clean room" where we can properly prepare infusions with required ingredients. We purchase all the needed equipment. A full-time infusion nurse is hired to do this.

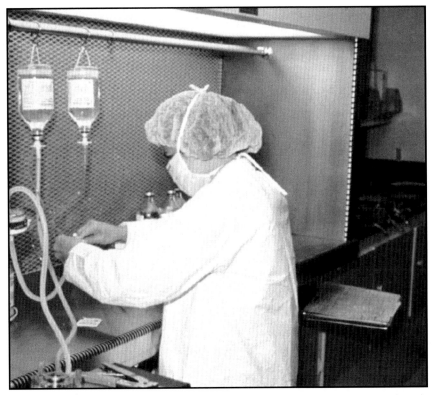

Our clean room where infusions are prepared for administration in homes.

Convincing Others

Performing home infusions means that once everything is prepared, a certified nurse brings it to the patient's home to run the IV. In many cases, this nurse also checks the patient's health status while they are there.

As I've said, all this is typically performed at some kind of medical facility. We have to convince hospitals to release patients to go home for us to take care of them there. Not only that, because this approach is new and unique, there are no procedures in place on how we get reimbursed. Importantly, we must convince *insurance companies* to pay for it.

We explain to doctors and hospitals that patients will be much more comfortable at home than having to endure long stays in the hospital or come into the medical facility every time to receive their IV. We focus on convincing insurance companies that we can save them money. In a way, the insurance companies will be the driving force to our success in this new venture. Let's face it, for them, it's about money. It's always about the money.

Both hospitals and insurance companies are initially skeptical. They are concerned that we might cause sepsis and even kill people if what we do is not performed correctly. There is certainly some risk involved for the patients—and a great deal of risk for our business. Still, we are certain that we can do this safely and place patients back in the comfort of home, as we save money for health insurers and in many cases for patients too.

Though this whole concept is highly innovative, we ultimately persuade insurers and doctors. We start this new service . . . and safely deliver on everything we promise.

An enormous new business begins to grow.

TPN or Booze—You must choose!

In many ways, this service involves us in patients' lives. After all, we are now *going into their homes.* That sometimes means encountering unusual circumstances. One of our patients receiving TPN (total parenteral nutrition) at home is using a certain number of bags per day. We realize that she is no longer ordering the TPN bags and no one is being scheduled to her home. Yet she needs this nutrition to live. What the heck is going on?

When we cannot reach her by phone, we send someone to her home—and I go with them. The patient can't be getting the TPN from another source. You can't buy it over the counter. It is formulated specifically for each patient—and must be kept cold, with most patients keeping two to four bags in their refrigerator at a time.

Arriving at her house, we find that she is alive (our first concern) . . . but there is a problem. Her husband is an alcoholic and totally out of it. We check the refrigerator—it is full of beer cans. There is no room for the bags, so she couldn't order any! She is already too weak to "resolve" this dilemma on her own—and only getting weaker.

This is absolutely insane! So we buy a used refrigerator and give it to her, and she once more has a place to store her bags.

Expanding Again . . . into the Computer Age!

Our new facility is a huge success. Our business is really expanding. And believe it or not, we are running out of room. Again. But what are we going to do?

I realize the lease is coming up on our tenant next door. "Let's just pray they forget to renew their lease."

Sure enough, they forget to exercise their option to renew. After several months pass, we tell them that we are not extending their lease. So now we take over the entire building—18,000 square feet including the mezzanine that adds its own 3,000 square feet. The new additional space gives us more room for inventory and shipping.

And for keeping track of everything going on in our business. To accomplish this, we get into computer systems. We create a giant computer room staffed with IT people. These computers are nothing like those we have today. These are a series of five-foot tall machines, running reel-to-reels of magnetic tape on which data is stored. These machines also generate a lot of heat—and we must keep them cool. We build a floor with a cooling system beneath it. As big as they are, these computer systems are pretty archaic. My iPad of today probably has more computing power than all these machines combined!

But we need them, along with our additional space for storing and shipping. Yet we *still* run out of room *again*—and end up leasing another building two doors down with another 15,000 square feet!

We keep expanding—and not just facilities. But also into new areas of business.

Board and Care Facilities

During my involvement in civil rights, a lot of the African Americans that I meet own "board and care homes." These house people that require assisted living services. Yet they are not large skilled nursing facilities. A board and care home may simply be a husband and wife who take in four or five people at their house, and have a board and care license. Those who reside there might have some mental or simple physical health issues, but have no other place to stay and shouldn't be in a hospital.

Local African Americans own quite a number of these . . . and who do they know that has a pharmacy? Mel Baron, of course.

We create a whole Board and Care Division at Shield. We're filling prescriptions. We're providing underpads, incontinence supplies, and the like. The majority of these patients are on Medicaid, and providing for them eventually becomes a major part of our business. Most pharmacies are only aware of skilled nursing facilities where there may be fifty or sixty residents and everybody competes for that market. Nobody knows this board and care business. So while starting small for us, this area grows rapidly.

We are thriving in all these different areas. At one point, we have 72 employees! A huge increase from a small neighborhood pharmacy with three people. Even *we* think it is unbelievable.

Apparently, we are not the only ones.

✦　✦　✦

CHAPTER 41

Bard Buys Shield

As Shield HealthCare, we are purchasing a lot of equipment and supplies from a corporation called C.R. Bard. It wholesales products to pharmacies and medical supply companies, and their "Home Care" division carries ostomy, incontinence, and related skincare products. They clearly are aware of the many ways in which we have been growing.

Bard sales reps visit us frequently since we are a huge purchaser. One day, they are accompanied by Mark Bruder, the Home Care division president. He knows the growth of our business and now sees the pizazz of our facility. He explains that Bard is interested in expanding beyond being only wholesalers—by buying our business and building it even larger. Bruder asks us to consider it.

After they leave, Fred tells me, "We are not selling this business. Not a chance. I don't want to be part of any big corporation. These guys wouldn't know what the hell to do with it anyway."

Magic Number

I'm not in agreement with Fred. Obviously, the money is a big attraction. You work all this time, build up a business. When do you cash in the chips? There's no guarantee you will ever be able to cash in. No guarantee that at any other point in time, someone will say, "I want to buy your company." So when that does happen, I think you should pay attention. Fred and I aren't sophisticated enough to have developed "an

251

exit strategy." I mean, that's not even a term we would think about. We are just doing what we are doing.

I'm also feeling, "Okay, I've built Shield HealthCare. I've done that. What's next? What new challenge can I take on?"

But I know Fred and there's no way I'm going to convince him to even consider it at this time.

So we continue doing business while I continue thinking about this. One day I say to Fred, "Fred, is there a magic number? Just some magic number that if Bard is willing to pay, you'd be willing to sell? You don't have to give it to me now. Just think about—if I could get that number, would you sell?"

"I'll think about it."

Some time later, Fred comes back to me and gives me his magic number. But I want to make sure we're both clear on this. "So you're saying that if I can negotiate this number, you are going to do the deal?"

"Yes."

I contact Mark Bruder at Bard. "We will entertain an offer."

Jumping Through Hoops

Of course, this is a Fortune 500 company on the New York stock exchange. We are not just selling to some individual. They start asking for information and data. *A lot* of information and data. They want inventory, sales figures, costs, projections. They want our business plan.

Well, Fred and I don't have a business plan. We're nothing but a couple of gunslingers who open our business doors every day and figure out how to get to the next day. We don't even know how to make a business plan!

So I say to Bruder, "You know what? Do me a favor. To make sure we provide you with the appropriate information in the format you prefer . . . could you send us some kind of template that we can follow?"

Sure enough, they send us a template. We meet with our accountant and I ask, "Can you help walk us through this? We know things in our heads. We have some data. Can we put this all together?"

Yet Fred is hesitant to reveal so much to this outside company. I turn to him and say, "Fred, we need to come clean. We have to give them everything they need and do it totally honestly. This is for real. I don't know if they'll ultimately do the deal, but we've got to provide what they ask."

So Fred and I (and the accountant) put together our very first business plan. Along with that, Bard is asking for a narrative to our story—the "Shield story" of how it all came into being.

We put all of that together . . . and they agree to our magic number!

But we want more. We are two young guys, only around fifty. What are we going to do now if we sell it?

We decide: "Let's negotiate an employment contract with Bard for us to oversee their new Shield acquisition and whatever they build from that. And let's tie some incentives to it so if this new business venture really takes off for them, we can make some serious money from that too."

But will Bard go for it?

Fred Thinks "Ahead"

Long before Bard is ever interested in us, Fred, in his brilliance, forms an organization. He figures at the time, "Let's get together with other people around the country who might be offering some ostomy services like us."

Fred convenes a meeting in British Columbia and invites enterostomal therapists and a half dozen people who own stores selling ostomy equipment at some level, similar to what we're doing. Some of them have drug stores, some only sell medical supplies. But Fred puts together this ostomy association.

It turns out to be one of the best things we ever do. We have great fun with it, and more and more members join the association. Every six months, we go to one of the member's pharmacies or facilities and learn what they are doing. We form a coalition and use that leverage to buy equipment more advantageously from wholesalers around the country.

Bard now knows of this association and that we are its leaders. They look at this as access: "We could purchase a number of these other places and put together a company nationwide." They see possibilities.

They agree to buy Shield—and hire us after the sale to oversee all this.

Big Payday

The day comes for all of us to sign papers and make it official. I tell Fred, "We've got to really dress up for this."

It is a big moment. I buy myself a new suit and a Montblanc pen. Lorraine purchases a new outfit as well, and we're there along with Fred and his wife, Marilyn. We meet with the reps from Bard in a huge conference room at an attorney's office. We sign the documents. There are hugs and kisses and handshakes all around.

They have previously asked us, "Do you want to take stock in the company instead of some of the cash?"

This is not an uncommon approach. Yet we have heard all kinds of terrible stories about taking stock in a company. We say, "Thank you, but we prefer the cash and not the stock."

We are now getting all cash *and* an employment contract for four years with incentives. By "cash," I mean cashier's checks. In fact, we ask that it not all be in just one check for each of us, but rather, a bunch of checks in $100,000 increments.

In our heads, we're thinking to buy $100,000 Certificates of Deposits at different savings and loan banks since these will earn some interest and be federally insured.

The Bard reps start handing us stacks of $100,000 cashier's checks.

Spreading the Wealth

By now, it is noontime and we've got all this money. Lorraine and I drive to different savings and loans and open these accounts in hundred thousand increments. Fred and Marilyn do the same.

After a number of bank visits, Lorraine says, "You know what? It is crazy to do this all at once. We're tired. We're hungry. Let's have lunch." So we eat a celebratory meal and then distribute the rest of the money over the next couple days. But Fred . . . he doesn't give up his mission! He goes that whole first day from bank to bank to bank. It could almost be a cartoon comedy, these two couples running around town to all of these banks and making their deposits.

A comedy with a very happy ending. We feel great!

◆ ◆ ◆

CHAPTER 42

Sadie

While Lorraine and I are raising our family and I am building Shield, my mother is living her own life.

Once I am married, my mom stops running the boarding house in the duplex she has been renting. She and my sister move into an apartment, where the two of them live until my sister leaves to get married herself.

Both my sister and I encourage Mom to date again: She is only 45. But she never does. My mom lives the rest of her life independently in her apartment. She keeps her place absolutely spotless and whatever she has is never tattered. If she doesn't have money to buy new, she has it reupholstered or refinished.

Though I can eventually help her financially, she wants to work. She has jobs most of her life in food service, but never really progresses due to poor writing skills. Though embarrassed by this, she never improves them. Even being a waitress writing down a clear food order would be too challenging for her *and* for the cooks. At Fisher's Hamburgers in the Town and Country Market (a shopping center across from the original Farmer's Market), she provides food service from behind a counter. Places like Fisher's have no waitresses or waiters. Customers go to the counter, place an order, and then pick up their meal from my mom at the counter when it's ready.

She works at eateries at Town and Country and the Farmer's Market almost to the end of her life, becoming a known "fixture" at many of these places. Someone might see her at a wedding or bar mitzvah and say, "Oh, there's the lady who works at Fisher's."

Outside of work, her time is spent with family and some lady friends. But she never gets involved at the synagogue or the Jewish Center despite our encouragement.

When we live in the Valley, she lives in the Fairfax area, so as I said earlier, she sees our children only when we visit her or we take her back to our home to spend a few days with us, since she doesn't drive. While I wouldn't describe my mother as "playful" with our kids, she is a very loving grandmother who truly cares for the children.

For one brief period, my mother lives with us. We're in our first house and the kids are very young when my mother has breast cancer and surgery. She recuperates in our home, so the kids have that "live-in time" with Grandma at our house. She asks them about school and encourages them to do homework. Sometimes she tells them stories about her life in Russia when she was a young girl. I imagine they find those fascinating. I always have.

At some point in her seventies, Sadie stops working. Her health suffers after that, and a few years later in 1983, she goes to the hospital on Mother's Day when she is not feeling well. We don't think she is that ill, but after a week passes, it looks like she won't survive. The doctor has a conversation with us about feeding her through a tube to keep her alive. But my mother makes the decision not to move forward with it. My sense is this is not what "dignity of death" looks like to her.

I call Ross and Kathleen: "You need to come and see Grandma. I think this is it." They fly out with baby Joshua, who is maybe a year old. We are all at the hospital as Ross and Kathleen bring Joshua up to Sadie's room. Sadie is so happy to see him! It's wonderful to see her face light up. Yet the next day when we come back again and ask, "Do you want to see Joshua?" She says "No, no."

So I go downstairs to a lower floor waiting area with Ross and Joshua, while Lorraine and Kathleen remain at my mother's bedside. Suddenly I hear a "code blue" announce on the PA system to all the staff. Somehow, I know it's my mother.

Ross and I come running upstairs with the baby. But Mom is gone by the time we get there. She must have known this was to be her time and she did not want the baby to see her die. Yet it is a very touching moment for Lorraine and Kathleen to be at her bedside as she passes. We join them. Though I am not surprised by her passing, it is still devastating when you lose your mother.

Lorraine feels a deep loss as well. My mother and Lorraine enjoyed a loving relationship. Sadie knew how wonderful Lorraine is as a wife and mother, and Lorraine really appreciated my mom too. They spent a lot of time together.

Sadie is buried separately from Leo. He is at Home of Peace in Boyle Heights, while my mom is at Mount Sinai. She is buried above ground in what is called a garden wall. She chose a space in this wall because she wanted to be at eye level. She didn't want anyone looking down or up at her.

Fortunately, before Sadie passes away at 78, she is able to see a lot of who we become . . . my sister getting married . . . our kids growing up . . . Lynn graduating Berkeley (we take Sadie up for the event) . . . Ross having his first child, Joshua . . . my building and selling Shield to Bard. Important milestones for all of us to share with her.

My mother continues to remain very much in my mind. Whenever I go to the Farmer's Market, I still imagine her sitting there in her camel coat, sipping coffee, watching all the assortments of people around her.

I miss her.

✦　✦　✦

CHAPTER 43

The Sisters

Both Lorraine and I have one sibling each—a sister.

My relationship with mine remains as caring big brother to adoring younger sister. I'm always looking out for her, and she is always cheering me on.

In her late twenties, Maxine marries Harvey Jessel. They are together for a ton of years, but it is not a happy marriage. When we live on Julie Lane, Maxine would show up at our door with a suitcase to stay with us while they experience some difficulty. Lorraine and I sit with her and suggest, "Look, if you want to divorce this man, we've got enough money to help carry you through."

Fortunately, even with her marriage challenges, Maxine always has a cadre of gal pals. She forms close relationships with a number of girls while at Louis Pasteur junior high school and they remain close over the years. Maxine has one child, Nikki, who is married and divorced, and has a son, Drew—my sister's beloved grandchild.

Maxine works hard during her forty-something years as a teacher's aide at Riverside School. She also is employed by a company called Paper Pushers where she does party planning. At one time, Maxine has three different jobs. So she ultimately does pretty well even though she barely gets out of high school and doesn't go to college since our parents never steer her in that direction.

Sadly, Maxine passes away on Christmas Eve of 2021.

Sharon and Artie

Lorraine's sister, Sharon, is nine years younger than Lorraine. In fact, when Sharon is a teen, we often take of care of her when her parents go away for vacation.

Sharon later marries and has three children with Mark Shaw. Who is Mark Shaw? Mel Baron's first delivery boy at Shield Pharmacy! Delivering medicine to my in-laws' house is how he and Sharon meet. So you might say that from the start, Mel Baron's pharmacy is a full-service business. Whatever you may need, we deliver it right to your door!

Unfortunately, their marriage doesn't work out. Sharon has subsequent marriages that are not successful, but more recently, she marries Artie Butler, a really nice guy and well-known musician, arranger, and songwriter whose long career has him involved in many hit records with performers like Barbra Streisand, Frank Sinatra, Bette Midler, Barry Manilow, Louis Armstrong, Joe Cocker, Neil Diamond, Liza Minelli, Dionne Warwick, Gladys Knight & The Pips, Bob Dylan, and many more (the list seems endless). Artie has been awarded over 60 platinum and gold albums!

Sharon now has a stable and nurturing life that is a joy to behold . . . which shows it is never too late to find happiness!

She just turned 80. A youngster.

◆　◆　◆

CHAPTER 44

Life at Bard

Old joke: "So these two Jews walk into a Bar(d) . . ."

After Fred and I sell our company to Bard, we are invited to their headquarters in New Jersey. As we're flying there, I say to Fred, "You know, they have all our figures we came up with and our story of how Shield developed. Do you think anybody really reads all that crap?"

Fred replies, "I have absolutely no idea."

I agree, "Me neither. Maybe we ought to review what we wrote and all the numbers—just in case anyone asks us about it. We don't want to start off there on the wrong foot."

The next day we're in Bard headquarters and it's like out of a movie: super-plush corporate office, conference room with a high-gloss table, rich leather placemats in front of each chair, multiple water pitchers. Everybody in the room is male, White, and lean. Wearing a crisp blue suit, flawlessly knotted tie, and perfectly polished brogue shoes.

We walk in—these two Jewish guys. Fortunately, I predicted to Fred, "These guys are going to be dressed up, so let's not embarrass ourselves." Fred and I come in decked out in sharp suits ourselves.

All fifteen of these Bard people are six feet plus. An Irish Catholic company where everyone is named McCarthy, Maloney, McFarland, McMahon. In walks this short guy, Mr. McCaffery, President and CEO. A hush immediately comes over the room as we all sit, Fred and I at one end of this long conference table.

As requested, we have prepared a presentation for all of these higher-ups. I run a slide projector (this is 1983—long before PowerPoint) while Fred narrates the story as we're showing the figures.

Turns out, not only did these people read the documents that we sent—*they know every word and every number and come at us with question after question.* They've invested a lot of money and are interested in building a chain of these Shields around the country. They're trying to challenge us and poke holes in our story. I'm starting to sweat and feel, "Oh, my God. What are we doing here?"

Fred finally leans over the table, looks at them all and says, "Hey, guys. No matter what, you ain't getting the money back."

The whole room breaks up! It relaxes the tension for them and certainly for us. We get through that day and I spend my next four years with Bard (Fred spends an additional four years there after I leave).

Building Bard's Shield HealthCare

At Bard, I help acquire other businesses similar to ours in order to create a chain operation of facilities throughout the country. To do this, I travel around the nation and work with legal counsel to make offers to buy these other businesses, using my insight to determine what a particular site may offer and how it can fit into our overall plan. Since the businesses I approach include some in the Ostomy Association that Fred Bray created, I already know many of these people. When I go in there with Bard Corporate execs, it is a little easier since I'm a friendly face. I discuss Bard's goals to create this chain and convince them that each party can complement the other. In many cases, we purchase the business and the people already running it stay on. I help mold them in the direction we are heading.

Of course, for most of these business owners, the biggest appeal is the same as it is for Fred and me. Like us, most small entrepreneurs don't have what we call exit strategies, so when there is a chance to cash out and maybe even to stay with the business, that is highly attractive. They recognize this is a once-in-a-lifetime opportunity because not many companies would ever purchase theirs. Some competitor in the area might offer to buy them out, but nothing at the financial level we're offering. After they join our chain, we have their operations provide much of the same services as Fred and I developed, with user-friendly facilities.

Playing with the Big Boys

Bard is corporate America. Big time stuff. Fred and I still work out of Los Angeles, but fly back and forth to their headquarters from time to time. On one of these occasions, we are at a meeting in New Jersey and it's getting time that we need to catch our flight out of Newark to go back home. But they still have more to discuss.

Somebody suggests, "Let's see if we can get you out of Kennedy."

They book us on a flight out of Kennedy Airport . . . and then *heli-copter us* from Newark to JFK. Just so they can spend a little more time with us. This is heady stuff.

During my time at Bard, I am aware this is a unique and special period. I want to really enjoy it. This is a new world with all new rules. There is a lot of stress with a lot to do and many new things to think about. But I am happy since we are getting a lot of money and I'm excited to find out, "Can I fit in this corporate world? I'm a small entrepreneur running a business but these are the major leagues. Are these people smarter than me . . . or can I hold my own in this group?"

I'm aware by this time that I like new challenges. Shield was built because we were willing to expand into new areas—new not only for us—but also new for the field. Now am I able to succeed in corporate America?

I'm flying around the country, working with pharmacies and medical supply companies, making *company acquisitions* and turning them into nationwide home health-care centers under the Shield banner. I work a lot with the only other Jew in the company, their attorney. We have a great friendship.

Fitting In

Now in their world, I realize I need to talk and dress like they do. I remember once sitting in a room of Bard execs while someone comes in to make a presentation. As he's setting up, one of the Bard people leans over to me and whispers, "Look at that guy's briefcase. He's a lightweight."

This guy is judged as a lightweight based on the type of briefcase he has. That's their reality and the corporate culture at Bard. These people are always impeccably dressed. If you travel on a plane for Bard, you wear a shirt and tie. Once we flew to a meeting in Vegas and are met at the airport by the president of Bard at that time, George Maloney. One of the guys with us from Shield is in a polo shirt as he comes off the plane. George Maloney sees him and the guy is terminated right there.

I quickly learn the game and how to play it. In fact, George Maloney becomes a great friend. Everyone is afraid of him, but after we join Bard, I realize, "Hey, these are really regular people." Yes, they have demanding dress codes, specific ways to behave, and to be successful there, you play by their rules. But when it comes down to it, they're still people.

While all of this is going on at Bard, I continue teaching part-time. USC sees this as advantageous: I'm now a professional working at a Fortune 500 corporation *and* I'm a USC professor.

Corporate High Life

We are flying around the country and eating in fancy restaurants. They make us play golf a couple times, even though Fred and I have never lifted a golf club before. It's not so much about creating camaraderie. These guys play for money and they know they can take us! After Bard, I never play golf again.

Overall, I think it's actually a bit easier for Fred and me at Bard than many of the others working there. We already have all this money. These other guys are trying to build careers and so feel a different pressure. They have greater need to constantly impress people than we do.

In the corporate world, a lot of money is floating around. I mean, flying on helicopters to save a little time? Fred and I are not at the level to travel on their corporate jet, but they treat us with respect. There is social time with lots of dinners. After a meeting, we go to some swanky restaurant with expensive wines, cocktails, and steaks.

We learn to blend in on those occasions too. One night out at dinner, the waiter brings a big silver platter of desserts.

"What would you like?"

Fred confidently says, "Leave the tray on the table. We'll take it all."

Where's the Caterer??

As I said, Fred and I continue working from LA. I tell Bard at the beginning that I won't move. But I am traveling around the country, making acquisitions, and going to meetings.

Lorraine flies to New York with me while I'm having meetings there. She dresses up in fur coats. We stay at elegant hotels and enjoy lavish meals with the Bard people. This is a whole new lifestyle for us. Even though I make money before Bard, we do not live such an indulgent existence.

Bard's corporate people also occasionally leave their New Jersey headquarters to journey west . . . sometimes with unforeseen results.

In 1984, the New York Giants are playing in the Super Bowl, held at the Rose Bowl in Pasadena. Most Bard people are big Giants fans, so they all come out. Lorraine and I live in our condo at 323 San Vicente and invite them over on Saturday night—the night before Sunday's game. We invite George Maloney and everyone flying out with him. We add a few of our family and friends. We cater the event.

But everybody is arriving and the caterer is nowhere to be seen. We're calling them but no one answers. Meanwhile, we're pouring drinks to keep our guests occupied.

I worriedly take Lorraine aside. "Where is the caterer? We have a house full of corporate brass that we're trying to impress and we have no caterer and no food! What the hell are we going to do?" This is well before restaurants are making food deliveries to homes, except for maybe pizza. Pizza won't do.

I remember there's a little take-out type place called Seventh Heaven on Montana Avenue. I say to Lorraine, "I'm going to run over there. We have to come up with something! We can't keep pouring drinks all night."

I rush to Seventh Heaven, go in and say, "Thank goodness you're open. I have a home full of starving people. I need anything you can give me right away."

"I'm sorry, sir. It's almost seven. We're closing."

I respond, "What? You can't close. You can't. I don't care how much it costs. Bring me some food on platters to make it look nice. Bring me appetizers. Bring me desserts. Bring me anything!"

They reluctantly agree to come up with something and I return home. By this time, everybody there knows what's going on and is rooting for us (they're also really hungry). They don't know what to expect at this point . . . and neither do we.

The only entrance to our place is through our front door (no back entry) and suddenly the bell rings. I open the door—and in marches the crew from Seventh Heaven carrying platters of food. It's a little hodgepodge of this and a little of that—anything and everything they can come up with. But we don't care. Our guests applaud as the group parades in!

So what happened to our food? The caterer calls us on Sunday, eager to bring over our food and set up for the party.

I say, "Party? What party? The party was *yesterday*."

When we initially talked with the caterers, we told them we are having a party on Saturday to celebrate Sunday's Super Bowl. But they didn't hear the Saturday part and only remembered the Super Bowl part—so Sunday is when they were going to deliver us the food.

So the end result of our party? Well, what looks like a disaster becomes one of those stories that people at Bard talk about for years. An example of something that seems to be the worst possible circumstance . . . turning into something great (at least memorable). Everybody at our 1984 Super Bowl party has a wonderful time . . . even if it is a nightmare for the hosts!

Lasting Friendship

My friendship with George Maloney continues to this day.

Part of that friendship has been a running ten-dollar bet on all major sporting events: World Series, NBA championships, college championships. The specific team does not matter. I get whatever team is West Coast. He gets any team East Coast. No points. Our bets are simply ten-dollar bills in little envelopes that get passed back and forth depending on which team is victorious. I just got back my winnings (George has been way ahead of me)—four ten-dollar envelopes. George never spends any of it, and now returns them to me with a beautiful note honoring our friendship.

Who would expect this highly revered (and feared) head of a huge corporation, and Mel Baron who is only at Bard four years, would develop a friendship that lasts forty years?

George is a gentle man, Catholic and very religious. He and his wife have always been very kind. I thought he ran the company really well and I learn a lot from him. He is someone who says to me, "It doesn't matter how big our company becomes or how high we personally rise in its ranks—we're in the people business. It's always about people."

That always remains a critical piece for me.

Original Founders

During my time at Bard, I help acquire eight independent businesses that become part of their chain of health-care centers. Interestingly, they don't acquire too many more after I leave because Bard ends up selling their Shield HealthCare division three years later in 1990 to a Japanese company, Kobayashi Pharmaceutical. In turn, Kobayashi sells it to American Management Company. Sometime after that, they move out of our facility on Valjean Avenue that we are leasing to them to go into a larger facility.

Even though Fred and I have been long gone from Shield for many years, we are not forgotten. At Shield HealthCare headquarters in Santa Clarita, there are two conference rooms named for us: the Baron conference room and the Bray conference room. In the Baron room is an oil painting of Mel Baron. It's like one of those oil portraits you see in banks of some founder who is a hundred years old. But I didn't pose for it and had no idea about it at all. When I left Bard after my four years there, they held a party where they presented me with this painting they commissioned. I certainly felt honored, but it wasn't really something I was going to hang over the mantel at home. So I magnanimously said, "You know what? Why don't we leave this at Shield?" It continues to hang in the Baron conference room, in part to answer the question: "Who the hell is Mel Baron?" for the people who now work at Shield.

Shield HealthCare continues to this day. In fact, its website says they have been in existence since 1957—the year I founded our company.

✦   ✦   ✦

CHAPTER 45

DASON: Rude Awakening

As my contract with Bard comes to a close in 1987, I am looking for new challenges. In my head now, I'm a pretty hotshot guy. I've been super successful my whole life. I've got money. Time for a fresh adventure.

By this time, Ross has graduated BYU, moved with Kathleen to Houston, and works at a real estate company. Our grandchild Josh is born and then Jonathan. Lorraine and I travel back and forth to Houston to see our new grandchildren.

Ross is doing property management and putting together real estate deals. So I say, "Ross and Kathleen, Mom and I would love you to come back to LA. Ross, why don't you and I merge your expertise with my money I got from Bard and become involved in property management? Maybe even get investors and buy some real estate?"

Ross and Kathleen see this as an opportunity to return to Los Angeles and be with the family. I am thrilled to have them back.

DASON is Born

I rent a high-rise office suite on Olympic Boulevard. So now with our new office space and new partnership, what do we call ourselves? We figure the company is a dad and son . . . so how about DASON?

Ross and I find investors to buy a shopping center and an apartment house. Our proposal says if they invest a certain sum, they can expect a financial return of this other amount over time, etc. Ross and I will be the general partners while the investors become limited partners, meaning we control the project and they remain silent investors. As we buy these properties, Ross and I also take a fee to manage them.

Though Ross and I work well together, I learn that being in business with family is different than with typical business partners. On one hand, it is wonderful. Being together and hanging out.

On the other hand, issues can arise like I come home and share with Lorraine: "Ross comes to work and doesn't even have his shoes shined."

I mean, it's stupid little things. Even though he's smart and enormously talented, there's still a father-and-son dynamic going on.

Lorraine Estates

Someone suggests we build a tract of homes in the Edwards Air Force Base area. About an hour north of Los Angeles, the base is expanding and there will be stunning growth there. Sounds perfect!

Yet I have a cousin in the real estate business who advises, "Mel, don't pursue this. You really don't know what the hell you're doing."

I don't listen. Remember, I'm riding high after a string of big successes! We invest only a little bit of money ourselves and bring in a couple of partners. We start building a tract of thirteen starter homes, all two and three bedrooms. We call it Lorraine Estates.

Ross is handling this along with our other real estate holdings, helped by a couple of employees. We have a lot going on, and there's about to be more.

Let's Buy a College!

Milt Chortkoff, the owner of that local cleaners I mention earlier who dances with my mom in the living room, has been pretty successful and wants to partner with me on real estate. He comes up with a brand-new idea: "Let's invest and purchase a college."

Merit College is a private, for-profit vocational college in Van Nuys that offers medical transcribing and court-reporting courses. Why is this of interest? Because we're at the brink of a technological revolution in this field.

Medical transcription is a big industry. It is how notes dictated by doctors and hospitals are typed and become permanent medical records. The entire medical field relies on such services. If you can type and transcribe at 60 words a minute, you're a sought-after typist.

Court reporting—those typists in courtrooms documenting every word spoken during a trial—is a bit different. To be a court reporter, you must pass a test where you can type at 200 words a minute on a stenotype machine (rather than a conventional typewriter). You type in shorthand— the only way one can keep pace in real-time with what's said during court. Yet most people never get to this speed. Even with Merit's courses, it is a struggle for students to stenotype more than 150 to 170 words a minute.

However, new computer-assisted technology has been developed so people can transcribe at faster rates, based on the stenotype shorthand. We'll use this new tech to teach a fresh population of typists that the world desperately needs and revolutionize the field!

I'm thinking this is a home run with the bases loaded!

We bring in the guys who created this cutting-edge technology. Together, we create a business plan that I show to an accountant friend I run with every day. He reviews it and responds, "Mel, this doesn't work. The numbers don't make sense. I would definitely advise against it."

I've been advised against the tract houses. I'm now advised against the Merit College purchase.

But my ego gets in the way.

I've already accomplished things in my career that people never imagined—or actively advised against. Ostomy care. Selling supplies to hospitals. Board and Care. Home infusion. I prove the "experts" wrong. I shine at Bard as well. I have been so successful in so many areas. I can make all of this work too!

At least, that's *my* thinking.

Calamity Ensues

This whole thing collapses. *Everything.*

The real estate market goes bust.

Our major contractor for the tract homes at Edwards Air Force Base gets arrested.

The Merit College goal is unachievable. The inventors of this new technology lie to us and it does not work anywhere near as well as promised.

I am carrying the financial burden of this and it's a gigantic disaster. We sell whatever we can to start paying off huge debts. When all is said and done . . . we no longer own anything.

Ross Continues to Manage

All of this is really my catastrophe and I don't want Ross brought down by it. He isn't a dollar investor in these things and he shouldn't suffer in the way that I am. I want him to continue with the management portion of our business—managing other people's properties that we don't own any part of. That portion of the business is still fairly decent.

I tell him, "This is yours—do what you can with it."

At the same time, Ross is super supportive and helps me determine how to get out of these failed deals. It takes a lot of work to clean all this up and he plays an integral role. This speaks to the strength of our bond—that our relationship survives quite well during this in spite of everything going on. In other families, that could go very differently.

Barren Baron

I'm broke.

We're in such financial straits that Lorraine says to me one day, "Are we going to lose the condo—our home?"

I answer, "I don't think so. But it is possible."

We are now living on credit cards.

Lorraine has already begun her practice as a therapist by this time, so the bucks she brings in are quite helpful. But I tell her, "I only have this part-time teaching job at USC. It pays, but not enough. I think I can get a pharmacist job at one of the chain pharmacies. That would be full-time pay with health benefits. My friend, Michael Stern, has already agreed to let me work at his Dana Drugs pharmacy for free. It's been years since I've dealt with patients and I'm not up on all the computer systems that now support pharmacies. I need to refresh my abilities so I can apply for a full-time position at Thrifty Drug."

Lorraine listens to everything I have to say and all of my concerns. Then she looks at me straight in the eye and says, "I do not want you to work at Thrifty Drug. You have too much talent, too much creativity. You have too much to offer. Something will work out."

I never seek out that job. I listen to her and say, "Okay, things will happen. We'll make things happen."

Yet I'm not sure how.

This whole period is really difficult with lots of stress and lots of tears. But never once does Lorraine say to me, "You *should've could've would've* done something differently." She knows how much pain I am in. She doesn't need to remind me of the failures and fiascos. She is an amazing champion throughout this.

For me, the key to surviving this period is Lorraine. I remark earlier that we both are very supportive of one another. But this is the first time that support is really tested. I mean *really tested*. It is a pivotal moment—losing everything and thinking about bankruptcy. I've been riding this golden wave of success for so long and now it all comes crashing down. I'm so grateful when I reflect back on all her support at this time.

Hallelujah Honda

One day during this period, I'm driving home from my teaching job at USC in my big Mercedes-Benz 450SL. A pretty fancy car that comes with pretty fancy lease payments. I suddenly realize, "What the hell am I doing driving around in a Mercedes? I'm living on credit cards! Who am I kidding? This makes no sense."

I pull over into a Honda dealership.

Having come from USC, I'm wearing a suit and tie. I climb out of the Mercedes as a salesman walks up to me. Before he has a chance to say anything, I tell him, "I'm looking for the cheapest Honda you have."

The guy sees how I'm dressed. The 450SL.

"This Honda is for one of your kids?"

"Nope. It's for me. I can't afford this car. I want you to get me out of this Mercedes lease and into an inexpensive Honda."

Though surprised, he rolls with it and starts pitching me all the virtues of a Honda. But I stop him. "Look, you can't compare a Honda to my Mercedes. They're nowhere near the same—but I need the Honda."

I buy my Honda and am out of the Mercedes lease.

Besides a totally different driving experience between the two cars, I also take a hit psychologically. I'm tooling around in a Mercedes and the next day I'm behind the wheel of this little Honda. It takes some guts to do that. Especially as my ego has already been knocked down so much. But it's the right thing to do.

Barons at the Brink at the Bank

I'm behind on bank loans and they're putting a ton of pressure on me. They call a meeting and want Lorraine to come too.

Lorraine and I go into a room at the City National office building. Two other people come into the meeting—a young hotshot guy and an older man who seems kinder and gentler. The young hotshot rips into me: "What the hell did you think you were doing? You really blew this." He then lays out *his plan* of how I'm going to pay this money back.

I have already decided that I don't want to file bankruptcy. A lot of people advise us to file, but I think it's just not right for me and Lorraine. I owe this money. I made some mistakes. I'm going to pay it all back. Somehow I'll make everybody else whole and make us whole again.

Yet right now I'm in this meeting while this younger guy is a real jerk. I'm getting more and more angry at this asshole.

I finally interrupt, look right at him and assert, "Let me tell you something. If you make me sign these documents you want for the plan—I'll be forfeiting on this whole thing within 90 days. There's no possible way for me to pay this money in the manner and pace you've structured. If you let me tell you how I can pay this out, then you'll get your money back."

The older man listens to all this and helps revise those documents. I reimburse every nickel and we never file bankruptcy. We repay them and everybody we owe.

Heart of the Matter

My kids are concerned for me during this time. But mostly they are just supportive, like Lorraine. I never sense any criticism from them or get questions like, "Gosh, how did you get into this mess?" They know it happened and it is real. While I share with them what is occurring as the crisis unfolds, I don't share the amount of fear I have.

To call this a stressful time is a massive understatement. I am waking up in the middle of nights with the T-shirt I'm sleeping in soaking wet. The anxiety is unbelievable. And while Lorraine is not kicking me while I'm down . . . I am kicking the hell out of myself for having let this happen.

I'm really struggling during this and I develop some heart issues. I get an angiogram. I'm awake in an operating room while a very thin flexible tube with a tiny camera is inserted into an artery toward my heart to look for any artery blockages. It's a scary thing. I'm only in my fifties.

The cardiologist tells me, "Once we get in there and see, we'll make a decision whether to do open heart surgery or an angioplasty."

An angio*plasty* is where a tube is again inserted, this time with a small balloon at the end that inflates to open the blockage—still scary, but by far the preferred choice over surgery. I'm lying on this table while they do the first part of the procedure, waiting for them to make this decision. The doc finally says to me, "We'll perform the angioplasty."

They do the angioplasty, I survive, and the doctor reports to me after, "It went very well and now you'll never need to see me again." This procedure occurs in 1990 and I've not had another cardiac issue since.

Suffice it to say, this is a very unsettling period of strange moments on top of other strange moments.

◆　◆　◆

CHAPTER 46

The Resurrection of Mel

During this terrible period when DASON goes in the toilet, nobody knows about my circumstances besides my immediate family and a couple of close friends. I am still a part-time faculty member at the USC School of Pharmacy, but they have no idea. I teach there only a couple of days a week, with a little office down in the basement. But they keep asking me to do more and more things.

Like create a new pharmacy on campus.

One day, the dean, John Biles, asks, "Mel, I'd like your help on something. Could you help us design, organize, and open a pharmacy in a new medical building on the Health Science Campus?"

Of course, I say yes.

They already have two people working on this project. But neither of them has any experience whatsoever in owning or operating a pharmacy. You can imagine how well that is going!

I'm excited to help on this, though it is a lot of work. Aside from designing the space, there is a whole range of issues, from getting fixtures and the right equipment, to different types of licensing regulations, etc. But we make it happen and everything comes together beautifully. They actually have me in charge of running the place for a bit as well.

Our newly named "Plaza Pharmacy" is successful and necessary. It not only serves students and faculty on the health campus, but also patients receiving medical services. Plus, it is another place where pharmacy students can intern.

Magic Words

I'm doing this pharmacy project along with other added tasks at the school . . . while also worrying how in the world am I going to support Lorraine and myself. I need more money. I have to do something.

I make an appointment to speak with the dean. I go in his office and say, "John, you know I really like teaching here. But with my creating the pharmacy and everything else I've been doing, you really got me working full-time. Yet I'm only getting paid part-time."

I'm hoping John can get me some additional payment for all the extra work I'm putting in.

John does much more than that. He is aghast as I point out all that I'm doing for the university. "Oh no. You're right, Mel. That's totally unfair. Let me talk to the school. I'm going to insist you become *full-time faculty*. I have no doubt they will agree. Would you be open to that?"

"Would I be open to that?" John just said magic words to me. Magnificent words. A full-time job! Bigger salary. With benefits. Health care and everything I need at this time. It is a godsend.

I want to hug John. I want to kiss him! But I play it cool.

"Let me talk it over with Lorraine."

So in 1990, I begin as a full-time associate professor.

My Campus, My Second Home

Having a full-time academic position is a huge relief to Lorraine and me. HUGE. She was right—something better *did* come along. I so appreciate that she had faith and convinced me to believe in myself as well.

We can breathe again!

I think back to when I began teaching part-time. At first, it was a little intimidating to be among all these academics, especially the PhD researchers. I thought everybody was smarter than me. I was comfortable in what I could do, but I was a little in awe of this group.

Fortunately, I am pretty personable and they welcome me in. Plus, over time, there develops this myth that I sold my business to a Fortune 500 company for millions and millions of dollars. They never know the actual number, though my driving around in a Mercedes during those first years doesn't hurt that image. I never say if the story is entirely accurate, but I never discount it. I simply don't say anything about it. Yet the myth of Mel Baron grows, such that it becomes almost like *I am doing a favor to the school* by teaching there—especially now as a full-time professor.

As I said, no one knows of the collapse of the DASON business or my present circumstances. Here, back in my world of pharmacy and now full-time, I feel very at home, valued, and respected.

Birthing Another Pharmacy

Turns out the Plaza Pharmacy I help create as a part-time professor is not the only one being planned.

John Biles has another conversation with me. "Mel, now that you're here full-time, I feel more comfortable asking for your help. We want to relocate our Park Campus pharmacy."

When I attend USC in 1953, a pharmacy exists in a building basement on the university's Park Campus. Now, many years later, the department wants to move that pharmacy to the main floor of an administration building at campus center, next to the Tommy Trojan statue.

I join the team that's both planning this move and finding funds for it. A major project, it requires coercing AmerisourceBergen (a drug wholesale company) and Sav-On Drugs to pony up considerable cash to help us pay for this. Neither company will be involved in running our pharmacy. They donate simply out of goodwill . . . and Mel Baron's ability to schmooze.

As you may have noticed, I like pharmacies to look a little different than the norm. While I am pretty limited in what I can do with this pharmacy, I reach out to the dean of the Fine Arts School with an idea: "Let's do a project with your department to beautify this pharmacy and make it unique. We'll have a competition and select one student to create a huge painting to span across a pharmacy wall. We award the winner first prize, plus have second and third prizes."

Before they draw their proposals for the painting, I explain to students how a pharmacy functions. We then get their submissions, choose our top three, and pick the winner—a young woman who then creates a canvas painting twelve feet across that is mounted in the pharmacy. Turns out, she is a minor in fine arts while a premed student. Her concept's images illustrate pharmacy, medicine, and health care. It looks great!

(Many years later, I happen to be in that pharmacy on the Saturday of a USC football game. This woman, now a physician, is there with her family as she proudly reports to them, "When I was a student here, I created this!" This is a total delight for me to witness.)

Our mural addition turns out to be such a success that we decide to add a mural to the first pharmacy I helped design on the science campus. We hold another competition with the fine arts students, the thrilled winner now creating a large original painting for our Plaza Pharmacy—adding another eye-catching special touch.

My Playgrounds

As I describe earlier, when I am at Bard, the offices are like a movie set, and my jetting around in their corporate world a working-life fairytale. This doesn't seem real.

In a sense, the same is true with being a professor at USC. From the beginning, I do things my own way. I have small classes instead of large lectures. My classrooms are held in the round. My students dress for class. I innovate new curriculum and create projects (like the later fotonovelas).

But here's the thing that really boggles me: I have this fabulous, interesting pharmacy career, both from a pharmacist standpoint and also financially. Then I have this three-year bump in the road and I get sick and the whole thing looks like a disaster. Then in 1990, I launch into a new segment of my life as a full-time professor.

So I have two major careers in my life. And a lot of fun playing in both.

I look forward to my teaching job every day. It never feels like work. Even when I'm teaching the same classes year after year, it never gets dull because the students always change. And the way I design my classes doesn't have me giving the same lecture over and over at the front of a classroom or lecture hall. It is constant interaction with the students.

No two days are ever the same.

The students really challenge you, as do the cultural differences of who makes up our student body. Today, we have a lot of Asian and Middle Eastern students, along with some Russians. It is fascinating to see how even those from other cultures are influenced by my stories.

Running a pharmacy business and teaching are quite different from one another. Though both are challenging, there is a lot less pressure for me in being a professor than running a company in which I'm responsible for many employees, plus all the financial, selling, and supply issues, etc. As a professor, I do miss being directly involved in patient care.

But there are so many new possibilities to explore.

Storyteller

A big part of my success in life is due to my being a storyteller (something Leo excelled at too). I convey knowledge and ideas through my stories.

The same holds true at USC. I don't think I'd be a good faculty member if not for my thirty years in pharmacy. If you run and build a business, and then work in the corporate world, you have a vast breadth of experience about how and why things work (and sometimes don't work), about managing people, as well as dealing with money and finance. College students have long complained that many courses give them the academic understanding, but not necessarily how it applies in practical ways—the nuts and bolts of their chosen careers.

I'm changing that. I'm bringing in real-world, working knowledge. My conveying these experiences and what can be learned from them is a critical piece to my accomplishments as a USC professor.

I share a lot of my personal life with my students. It helps connect us. I tell the class how I meet Lorraine. Funny tales about my kids. I use the stories as teaching tools.

In the business class, I talk about the time Ross worked for me at the Shield warehouse. A woman named Mary Katie is supervising it. One day, Ross comes up to my office and says, "Dad, I need the next week off."

I say, "Oh, okay. But why are you telling me that?"

Ross says, "Well, you're my dad and you own the business. I want to take next week off."

I ask, "Who do you report to?"

"I report to Mary."

So I tell Ross, "Why don't you go ask Mary? Don't ask me. I have no idea about the schedules of people working in the warehouse."

"But you're my dad. You own the business."

"That doesn't make any difference. You report to Mary."

I'm talking about my son, but it's a teaching moment for students. Even when you are running the business, if you undermine a person managing parts of the business and/or employees, all control is gone.

Because I'm conveying these lessons as stories rather than as some "principles," the students remember them even better. These are the things that resonate and take on life as the students go forward.

I also have a talk in which I share about building Shield. This is to give them a sense that it can be done, though it requires a lot of risk taking and failure at times. I include all the things at Shield that we screw up and don't go well. I use slides to illustrate my story as I detail various transitions throughout that business. When you tell students all this—both the good and "the bad"—students see you as real. They genuinely listen.

I also share stories of situations that no one can really prepare for . . . to encourage their adaptability to the unexpected.

"Reach for the Sky"

This section title ("Reach for the Sky") isn't describing an aspirational message. In fact, it references something nobody would want: a holdup.

Pharmacies are prime targets for thieves, especially those who want drugs along with cash. A person may crash through our giant front windows late at night. The alarm rings, the police arrive, and I get a phone call from the alarm company. I drive down there to find trash and broken glass and missing drugs. We board up the broken window with plywood and arrange for it to get repaired. It is a real pain.

But worse is when a robber creates a more "in-person" experience. In truth, no one shouts, "Reach for the sky." An in-store robbery is more subtle. The robber doesn't wish to attract attention, and certainly doesn't want you raising your arms up.

One day, between noon and one, a guy walks up to the counter.

I smile and go, "How can I help you?"

This guy points a gun at my face.

"I want the cash. And the narcotics."

He has my full attention.

I reach into the cash register and slowly take out bills and place them on the counter. The whole time, I never take my eyes off the guy. In this moment, I figure that is safer than turning away, which might make the guy think, "Hey, what's this pharmacist up to?"

I'm staying calm on the outside, but I'm thinking the whole time how best to handle this. I don't make any jarring moves that might startle him, while saying to myself: "Please God, don't let him pull the trigger." I reach over to the narcotics cabinet to my left and bring out some of the drugs and put those on the counter.

Meanwhile, at the end of the prescription counter, my clerk, Rick Shub, is casually eating a sandwich since it is a little quiet at the moment. He's sitting there, entirely unaware of what's going on and I'm not saying much. Once I've put everything on the counter, the guy takes it and leaves.

I take a deep breath, turn around and I say, "Rick, we were just held up."

"What?!"

Rick jumps up and starts running after the guy. I yell to him, "Rick, stop, what are you doing? The guy's got a gun. Sit down!"

I fill out a police report and detail which narcotics are taken. Months later, I go to a lineup. Apparently, this guy has terrorized places throughout the Valley. I recognize him in the lineup. A drug addict, he looks terrible.

I don't know what eventually happens to him, but he gave me a moment of fear like I've never had before and haven't forgotten since. If you've ever been held up and somebody puts a gun in your face, it is major trauma.

This story becomes a teaching moment for my students. I emphasize that your personal safety is the most important consideration. Don't be a hero. Don't make any false moves. If you are asked to hand over anything while somebody points a gun at you—do just that. Whatever you're giving up doesn't mean anything. Your life does.

Relaying this story is another part of my "real life" teaching approach.

I paint another scenario for the students along similar lines: "There are times that you may be given a prescription slip and you know it is phony or stolen. You just know it. So how do you deal with that? You may be working a late shift. It's ten o'clock at night and you are the only pharmacist on duty. Do you fill the prescription, knowing it's a phony?"

I let them respond with their ideas. Then I recommend that one approach could be to pretend you are going to fill it. But when you check the shelf, you inform the phony patient, "You know what? We're out of stock on that. I can see it's on back order."

The next question: "Do you hand that prescription slip back to them or try to hold onto it?"

I suggest give it back to them. But don't say it'll be in stock tomorrow. Better: "It's on back order. Probably won't be in for a week." You don't want that person returning tomorrow. After a week's time, they will have moved on.

There are all kinds of teaching moments that I share with the kids, most fortunately much less dramatic than these.

Seeing Students as Real (with Real Lives)

Because of my background leading up to becoming a professor—growing up in a family with struggles, participating in the civil rights movement, earning a master's in public administration, and working for the California Alcoholism Foundation—I come to the classroom seeing my students as more than merely scholars.

These past experiences only enhance my success at the pharmacy as well as an academic, as they affect how I deal with patients, and now how I teach and treat students.

For example, when I witness one of my students having difficulties, I wonder, "What's going on?"

I am teaching one day when I look at one of my students. She has been in my class for some time and I can tell she's really in pain. I quietly ask her, "Could you see me after class?"

Once the bell rings and everyone leaves, I say, "Tell me what's going on. You're having some problems, aren't you?"

She manages to reveal, "Yeah I am . . . I'm getting divorced" and starts to cry. We talk about this and it seems to help her.

If you're really paying attention, you can pick up on things with your students. But you have to see them as people, not just pupils moving through my class to whom I need to impart certain information. Besides, personal issues can affect how well (or if) they can even absorb that information. Given what I've seen and experienced, I empathize when they're having a tough time. I want to help.

Many years later, I see this woman again. She is remarried and thanks me. She is now a pharmacist, and still remembers that day when I sat with her and we talked.

I think the true value I bring to my teaching is not just knowledge. But also caring and compassion. There is another piece to this as well: When I look at a student, I know in four years, that student will be my colleague. Why am I not treating them as a colleague now? Yes, they don't have the degree, but they will soon. I want to make sure that when you are my colleague is no different than when you are my student.

Sure, while they are students, I expect them to turn in their homework and take tests without cheating, etc. If they do something that doesn't meet my requirements or satisfaction, it needs to be addressed. But there are different ways for dealing with all of that depending on your attitude.

First Job

Not all steps I take beyond the scope of normal teaching are about fixing problems. Sometimes they are about opportunities.

On this other occasion, I'm watching this first-year student, Edith, coming in my classroom. Somehow, I know she needs to earn money *and* that she is a go-getter who would be an asset wherever she works.

I say, " Edith, would you like a job?"

She answers, "For sure. I can really use one!"

So I tell her, "I want you to head over to the Plaza Pharmacy and let Sherry know that Mel Baron said she needs to hire you."

Edith looks at me hesitantly, "Can I really do that?"

I clarify, "When class is over and you get up from this chair, go over and tell Sherry to hire you."

She does and Sherry hires her. Fast-forward, Edith gets the job and her degree. She is now a major faculty member at USC—a colleague—and doing fantastic work. She is smarter than I am!

Edith still occasionally tells that story at various events—most recently at a USC gala. It is just one of those moments in a person's life. I've come to know her husband and her children, and always look forward to seeing her.

Honestly, I'm pretty fearless in stepping outside the "typical boundaries" of being a professor . . . just like I go beyond what is "standard" in the pharmacy field. I don't think the school is going to fire me. I'm not worried about tenure because as a clinical professor, I can't even get tenure!

When I'm at the university, I get away with a lot of stuff. I just do it.

Moonlighting Mel

When I'm full-time at USC, a law passes in 1990 called OBRA '90. This is a Medicare-Medicaid law that says if a patient receives a new prescription, or there is a change to an existing prescription's directions or dosing, the patient needs to be counseled by the pharmacist.

The law lays out a list of things to be discussed with the patient. Unfortunately, most pharmacists prefer to be behind the counter, rather than in front. They want to fill prescriptions. They want to put pills in bottles. They aren't inclined to interact heavily with the public. But with new regulations in conflict with that insularity, how will pharmacists fulfill their duties?

Seeing this will be an issue, USC's John Biles, a visionary himself, hires Norman Sigband, a professor from the business school. Norman creates what he calls, "The Power of a Minute."

The essence is: "What can I tell you about your medicine in sixty seconds?" This doesn't cover all the criteria demanded by these new laws, but it trains pharmacists to ask open-ended questions as opposed to close-ended questions. That means not simply asking, "Do you know how to take this medicine?" because if the patient says "yes," the conversation is over. But if we ask, "How are you going to take this medicine?"—then we have an open-ended question that requires the patient to *prove* they know what to do.

Norman creates this approach, and then separately from USC, procures a paid contract with Longs Drug stores to train their pharmacists. He recruits me to go along with him to help conduct this program. The two of us travel around California, teaching pharmacists better communication skills. This revitalizes me too! It gets me out of the classroom and traveling again, going into pharmacies throughout California and interacting with professional pharmacists.

What I'm really doing is being innovative. Again.

For the actual training presentations, Longs rents a local hotel room and "orders" the area's pharmacists to attend as part of their work assignment. Though the training lasts just a few hours, it is pretty thorough. A group presentation, after which they break up into smaller groups and practice the communication skills they were just taught.

All this is a tonic for me. I also make a few extra bucks with it. Plus, I bring this back to my first-year students since it is all now legally required. As with the rest of my curriculum, I teach this in the round with thirty kids sitting in a circle—and me right in their faces: "Tell me how you're going to counsel the patient that you're giving this prescription."

The students learn pretty quick.

✦ ✦ ✦

CHAPTER 47

Lynn: The Teacher's Path

Lynn's journey in the educational field has many stages, each building on the one that came before as she rises in her profession.

As I touch on earlier, Lynn begins her teaching career at Parkview Elementary. Over her years there, she teaches each of the grades K through six at her own request. There are a couple of reasons for this. First, she likes change and trying new things (something I relate to). Second, even though she may not have been fully aware of it at the time, on some level she wants to be an administrator and

Lynn guiding Ross toward reading at an early age.

the more experience you have in different classrooms, the greater your credibility.

Lynn is a natural teacher. As a little girl, she loves to read.

As a mother, reading stories to her son Jack becomes a nightly ritual.

At school, Lynn really understands what children need. Not only that, her extensive teacher training gives her a lot of tools going in. Plus, she is a really hard worker. I have never met anybody more prepared! When Lynn gives a presentation, she is meticulous in her detail and planning and understanding her subject material. She would never just show up and wing it. *Mel Baron* would show up and wing it. But not Lynn.

I love visiting her school. While I certainly don't sit in on her classrooms, I meet her colleagues and appreciate how they respect her. She and I go to lunch so I can hear about her latest experiences there. Lorraine and I attend some of the school functions as well.

What's funny about all this is that during her early years of teaching, Lynn is worried at the end of every year that she won't be rehired for the next one. Lorraine and I come to expect this: "Okay, the school year is coming to a close. How soon you think before Lynn brings up that she's never going to get hired again?"

I tell her, "Lynn, stop that. You are for sure going to be rehired." And she always is. Eventually she outgrows these doubts.

After teaching a number of years at Parkview, Lynn moves on, becoming a coordinator working on curriculum at the county office. From there, she becomes assistant principal at Las Colinas in Camarillo, a combined elementary and middle school. This is her first real administrative type job and a wonderful experience. She is also expecting during this time, so the whole school gets to experience their assistant principal being pregnant and having a baby! Lynn makes some of her closest friends at Las Colinas too. So her time here is significant in both her career and life.

I even volunteer to come in to give a "career day" while she is there, talking about my business and some lessons I've learned that might be understandable and hopefully inspiring to these young students.

Marriage Break

Unfortunately, it's while she is at this school when Lynn's marriage to Darrell falls apart. It is a very tough time for her. Suddenly a single mother, she devotes herself to caring for Jack who is two and a half at the time, in addition to her school responsibilities. I really see her strength shine. Yet like many women going through this, she worries if she will ever find love again. "I'm working and raising a son. How will I find the next guy? *Will there be* a next guy?"

We feel our daughter's pain. We have Lynn over every week to spend a day together. I play catch with Jack on the grass in front of our place along with all the other fun things you do with little kids. We all go for walks. Have dinner together. I think Lynn genuinely appreciates it.

Principal Lynn

Lynn leaves her position as assistant principal to become the principal at Big Springs Elementary in Simi Valley.

She is the school's first woman to hold that position and only 35— very young for a principal. Many of the teachers there are older than her and make it very clear they don't approve: "Why are you the principal? I could be your mother. Who are you to suggest how I run my classes?"

I know this is challenging for her, though she doesn't really talk about the details with me. But I see her work ethic kick in: You get a job, you make a commitment, you figure out how to do the right thing for the people you serve. She and I talk about that.

Special Needs

Lynn eventually moves on to become principal at Garden Grove School, also in Simi Valley.

Garden Grove has a large population of special needs students with moderate to severe challenges. Some of these are medical, but there are also autism and behavioral issues. These demand special care in the classrooms, and even when holding events like assemblies. When visitors from the Music Center outreach program come in to play instruments, Lynn tells the performers there are children who may make various sounds and movements during the performance. So they should be prepared for that.

When Lynn arrives there, the school has ten special needs classes in addition to all the general student population classes. That's a lot and a big challenge, but also rewarding as Lynn relishes the professionalism of the staff. Their level of caring and commitment is inspiring! Lynn also realizes how blessed and fortunate our families are not to have these issues. The school kids really touch Lynn's heart, and she is proud to be part of an accepting community that creates such inclusivity.

Hearing all this touches me deeply as well, as it reminds me of the empathy I feel when working with civil rights and the California Alcoholics Foundation.

Recognition

Lynn's steadfast dedication to the kids at the school is noticed. So much so that she is given the Lew Roth Award for Administrator of the Year in 2002. This is particularly meaningful to Lynn since you must be nominated by your colleagues for the honor. Those people she works with most closely take the time to submit all the paperwork for the nomination.

The award ceremony is a posh affair with dinner at the Reagan Library. Of course, I love these kinds of events! Many of the teachers from Lynn's school attend along with the school secretary. This feels like true affirmation for Lynn. Sometimes you are trying to lead and hope there's somebody actually following you. These people appreciate Lynn's vision for the school and everything she brings to it.

Speeches are made and Lynn is handed a beautiful trophy. I'm so proud of her! I'm there with Lorraine, along with Jack and Phil.

Phil Ross

Being honored with this award is not the only "prize" that she gains when at Garden Grove Elementary. It is while she's there, that Lynn often crosses paths with Phil Ross at district meetings. He is a principal in another area school. By a certain point, Phil asks her out.

I speak about Phil earlier. The two of them grow close during their courtship—closer than even we realize! In 1999, Lynn and Phil elope to Brazil for a surprise wedding! Thrilled for our daughter, Lorraine and I happily host a party for the newlyweds at our home upon their return.

Director of Curriculum

After being a principal for thirteen years, Lynn is asked by the superintendent of the Simi Valley school district to become their director of curriculum instruction for K-12. In this key position, Lynn doesn't develop new curriculum as much as work with teachers and administrators to implement more effectively what already exists. In particular, to better adapt the curriculum for English learners (students for whom English is their second language). Whatever is presently being done in the district isn't working. Helping English learners becomes a passion for Lynn.

She eventually moves on to work in the Ventura County Office of Education as a curriculum and instruction director. Looking to further improve instruction, Lynn uncovers groundbreaking work being done at Harvard, particularly when it comes to English learners. She petitions her boss and receives approval to spend a week working with these Harvard researchers at their campus. It is an outstanding experience, from which Lynn brings back new strategies to apply to classrooms.

I really admire Lynn's devotion to improving education for students. In some small way, this reminds me of writing my letter to John Biles when I believe there are better ways that USC can be teaching pharmacy. Like father, like daughter?

✦ ✦ ✦

CHAPTER 48

Ross at USC: the Next Generation

As I describe earlier, before I join USC full-time, most of the DASON business that I create with my son collapses. At that point, Ross takes over the remaining property management portion of the company while I leave it entirely.

Though he's probably earning $150,000 yearly or even more, Ross comes to decide that being a property manager is a really boring business. Yes, you make good money. But it's just handling details of maintaining the property: if there is a problem with someone's toilet or appliances or leaks, you send somebody to fix it. Or you execute leases for new tenants.

He chooses to instead get involved with the church in a new way. He becomes an Institute Director and Coordinator in the Claremont area about 35 miles east of Los Angeles. The Institute is part of the Latter-day Saints church's presence at their various colleges, similar to a Hillel (for Jewish students) or the Newman Club (for Catholics) that have their centers on secular university campuses. It provides a place for students to hang out. Ross is in charge of various activities between male and female students, and also conducts classes there about the Book of Mormon and the church. Ross is kind of a lay teacher and counselor to students, encouraging and helping them academically and in life.

I'm supportive of the change, though concerned this is a significant drop in income for him and his family. But he loves his new calling and thrives.

Then at a certain point, he tells me, "Dad, I think I should go back to school. I need to get an advanced degree."

I love the idea. "In fact, now that I'm full-time at USC, it's a freebie if you study here."

That's what Ross does, enrolling in a master's program. He's in it only a short time before they accelerate him into the PhD program for comparative religion and social ethics.

This all sounds ideal, but life isn't always ideal. During the latter part of his PhD studies, Ross is diagnosed with lymphoma and Hodgkin's disease. This is a huge shock to everyone. He starts treatment: surgery, radiation, chemo. He has so much on his plate: recovering from cancer, studying, raising seven kids by this time.

Fortunately, treatment results are working. In fact, one week prior to graduation is his last chemotherapy treatment. Knowing he is weak from all the medications, I ask, "Ross, can you make it to the graduation ceremony?"

He replies with certainty, "Dad, I will be there."

Ross's health improving and his graduating USC with a PhD is incredibly meaningful to all of us.

Particularly for me, as I am able to participate in his graduation. Separate from the normal graduation, there is a hooding ceremony for doctoral candidates where a faculty member places the doctoral hood over the head of the graduate to signify their completion of the program. Standing alongside his department chair professor, I am allowed to hood Ross. Talk about emotion. Ross's face is puffy from all the cortisone and drugs, but he's there. What an experience for both of us, accompanied by tears of joy. Lorraine and Kathleen are present when I get to hood my son.

Ross's family is now living in Claremont. Kathleen is a stay-at-home mom. One day, we get a phone call. Ross and Kathleen want to get together with us. I have to wonder why?

Ross informs us, "I've been offered a job as a professor at BYU-Idaho. We're moving to Idaho."

Since they've been local, we've been seeing them and the grandkids all the time, with grandchildren even staying over at our house. It feels like a big loss to have everybody move away. Yet another change for us. And for them.

Another Professor Baron

Ross and family move for Ross's professorship at BYU-Idaho. This is not the main BYU campus, which is a university with graduate programs and professional schools. BYU-Idaho is a newly commissioned school that was previously a two-year junior college (known as Ricks College). The Church decided to turn this into a four-year undergraduate liberal arts college.

I have to reflect on Ross's path to get there: He starts as this kid who doesn't even think college has a purpose, to becoming a lay teacher counseling students, and eventually becoming a professor himself. Remarkable.

Not long after Ross starts at BYU-Idaho, I am to visit him there in 2005 while the school is inaugurating its new president, Kim Clark. They invite me to march in the inauguration procession and represent USC. Flattered, I still contact the USC protocol staff and say, "I'm a professor, but not anyone really big at the school or part of the administration. Can I really represent USC?" Fortunately, they answer yes. And off I go!

Ross and I march in the processional together, wearing our USC red robes. I really enjoy this! It helps me feel part of Ross's world at the college. Yet this is not my only involvement at BYU-Idaho.

A Latter-day Saint Seder

Within the first year or two of his being there, Ross calls up to ask, "Dad, would you like to do a Seder at BYU-Idaho?"

Naturally I reply, "What in the world are you talking about?"

"We can do a Passover Seder with the president of the university."

Though intrigued, I'm more than a little skeptical of this plan. "I don't think Mom is going to schlep all the kinds of food and cookware that we'd need there along with everything else."

But Ross assures, "No, no. BYU will take care of all that. The president and his wife, plus a colleague of mine, all want us to do it. You just bring the family Haggadah."

So Lorraine and I and Lynn put together our own Baron/Friedman family Haggadah. The somewhat *abbreviated* version.

Lorraine and I fly to Idaho. In a private university dining area, the president of the university and his wife, a professor friend of Ross's and his wife and daughter, Lorraine and I, Ross and Kathleen and a couple of our grandkids—all sit down to a Seder that the university has prepared. Right down to the gefilte fish!

The people serving the meal watch this unfamiliar Passover supper in awe. Yet they have put the dinner together perfectly. The only exception being that instead of dipping the parsley into salt water, they have sugar water.

At the end, the president's wife asks, "Can we keep our Haggadah?"

I answer, "It would be our pleasure."

Now whenever we visit Ross at the college, we always have an audience with whoever is the president at the time. Kim Clark is there ten years and we've met two additional presidents since him. We always have great conversations.

I also come to realize that Ross must be very proud of his parents, or why always take us to see the presidents? And they must think highly of Ross to agree to it. Ross is so well known there. He teaches courses on the Old Testament, the New Testament, The Book of Mormon, and also philosophy classes. Lorraine and I have sat in on his classes and he's freakin' amazing as a teacher and speaker. Frankly, this blows both of us away. We had no inkling of this ability.

A few years ago, Ross is invited to teach in Jerusalem for a year. BYU has a facility there called The BYU Jerusalem Center for Near Eastern

Studies. You can't proselytize there as that is against Israeli law. But if you're a Latter-day Saint student who wants to travel abroad and study in Israel, they offer a program that lasts one semester. When we visit him in Israel, we find that Ross now speaks Hebrew, which also floors us. Yes, he was bar mitzvahed when he's thirteen, but you forget that stuff soon after. He has since learned Hebrew and can interpret the Bible. He knows the Old and New Testaments practically by heart. It's mind-blowing.

There is always a blending of the two religions in our family. Ross's kids come to our Seders when they are young and break the fast and know Yiddish expressions. Lorraine and I have been to baptisms and Sunday church services. Our love for each other, and for being together as a family, overcomes any obstacle that we might have expected could be in our way.

Ours is really a love story of family.

Jack at USC—The Next Next Generation

Much like when Ross goes to grad school at USC, I'm thrilled when Lynn's son Jack chooses to attend USC as an undergrad. It is a super fun experience having a grandson at the college where I am a professor.

We're on two separate campuses—I on the Health Science campus while he is at the Marshall School for entrepreneurs on the University Park campus. I drive over and we meet at the faculty club for lunch. Or just meet to have coffee. Or go off campus to one of the local eateries. We attend all the games. And when it becomes his turn to graduate from USC, I am able to hand him his diploma! Just like I was able to with Ross.

Another Dream Becomes Reality

As a huge USC football fan, one of my dreams has long been to go down on the field of the Coliseum during a USC game. A nice fantasy.

Then one day about seven years ago, I get an USC email that says for a donation of $1,500, I and a guest can go through the USC tunnel and dash out onto the field with the team at a game.

"Oh my God!"

I immediately call Jack and practically shout, "Jack, we can run out on the field—the USC football field—with the team as they enter for a game!"

Naturally, Jack says, "Papa, you're kidding me, right?"

"No—and we're doing it!"

I give the donation and arrangements are made. When the day comes, we are waiting in the tunnel that leads to the field, talking with coach John Robinson while the players gather there—along with Traveler the white USC horse mascot that is at all USC home football games. I am so excited!

I feel the momentum building. They tell us to get lined up behind the players. We look like midgets compared to these guys! The music

Jack and me about to go into the tunnel

playing out on the field gets much louder—and suddenly it's time to go! The team comes racing from the tunnel onto the field—with Jack and me running right behind them. Lorraine, Lynn, and Phil see us on the stadium's big video screen as we come out . . . while Jack is secretly praying, *"Papa, please don't fall."* Because the team is coming out, there is this massive roar from the crowd—and we're there feeling it with them.

Mel Baron has never had this big of an audience!

What a night.

✦ ✦ ✦

CHAPTER 49

Worst of Times Becomes the Best of Times

As you move through life, you learn many lessons along the way if you pay attention (the label "wise old man or woman" is given for a reason).

One huge lesson in my life is realizing that a seemingly awful and unwanted situation . . . can turn into an opportunity for something truly great. It practically becomes a theme in my life! Yet most of the times when I am experiencing the worst part, I am not envisioning the upcoming best part. Until it happens.

Several times.

College of My Dreams

From an early age, I dream of going to UCLA. When I apply and get accepted there, I couldn't be more thrilled!

But when Leo gets very sick and our family faces enormous financial hardship, my mother suggests I go to USC instead. That way I can still live at home and help her with the auction house business, while putting money that would have paid for my UCLA dorm housing toward my USC tuition.

"Okay. I'll apply to USC."

So I am accepted and start USC. Yet here's the thing: my ending up at USC absolutely alters my entire life as an adult in the most positive way possible. The education, the profession I enter, the people I meet—my whole career *depends on my attending USC.*

UCLA does not even have a pharmacy program. They still don't. While that isn't something I'm thinking about at the time, I end up enrolling in USC's pharmacy program—which happens to be one of the best in the country. It launches both of my careers—in business and later academia.

All the wonderful things that happen throughout my professional life—are due to my enrolling in USC's School of Pharmacy.

Ross Finds His Path

Growing up, Ross seems like a lost soul in some ways—a person without a purpose or plan—who is adamantly against going to college.

When Ross is eighteen, he becomes a member of The Church of Jesus Christ of Latter-day Saints. Lorraine and I don't know what to expect. All we do know is it feels like a very dark time for us. A painful time.

Yet it is after going on a mission for the church that Ross enrolls in college, gets married, and starts a sensational new life, eventually teaching at BYU-Idaho. We get to witness the wonderful man and family and life that he creates. One that Lorraine and I could never have predicted, but wholeheartedly embrace and admire.

It is yet another example where what first seems like a catastrophe turns into the best thing ever. Ross travels a path from being this kid who doesn't even think college has any value, to becoming a college teacher counseling students and eventually a professor himself.

Mel, Come Home!

When my traveling for the California Alcoholism Foundation becomes a threat to my marriage and forces Lorraine to put her foot down that I must end my involvement with them and stay home, it causes me to really focus on my business along with Fred Bray (who I hired to allow me to travel)—and build Shield into the wild success that it becomes.

DASON Collapses

I start my DASON business with Ross after I sell Shield to Bard. Yet DASON fails spectacularly, causing me to lose all of Lorraine's and my money . . . and enter the most difficult period of my life.

Yet it is because of this failure that I am able and eager to take up John Biles' offer to become a full-time professor at USC. I end up teaching from 1981 through June of 2021: an extraordinary experience where I spend time with fantastic people, make lifelong friends, and learn as much as I teach. A far more rewarding experience than if DASON had been successful and all I concentrated on was making money.

Even though such turnabouts occur a number of times during my life, they almost always catch me by surprise. I become more aware of the "phenomenon" during my later years as I can clearly see this pattern of weird happenings: that what seems to be the worst of circumstances . . . turns into the best possible outcome.

You Never Know Who Can Change Your Life

In addition to realizing that terrible situations can transform into great ones, it is also fascinating to recognize how those you cross paths with can turn your life in wonderfully unexpected directions.

I originally bring Fred Bray into Shield so I can earn my master's degree in Public Administration and travel for the Alcoholism Foundation . . . yet he becomes the key to the success of Shield. I hire my former student, Danny Gelber, to help with our day-to-day running of the business . . . and he ends up suggesting the home infusions that significantly contribute to our expansion and Bard purchasing our company. It is John Biles' responding to my letter about changing the pharmacy curriculum . . . that leads to my teaching career at USC. As you'll read later, my sitting next to Dr. Robin Clark at a breast cancer conference in Norris Cancer Center . . . results in a twenty-year phase of my life during which I create fotonovelas.

I find this pattern to be such a profound part of life that I talk about it in class: "How do you know that someone you meet in the next minute, next day, or next week—won't change your life?" In this discussion, I reflect back on many of my own serendipitous examples.

I encourage students to be open, alert, and willing to take chances and say *yes*. "You just never know who may step in and turn your world in a new positive direction."

✦　✦　✦

CHAPTER 50

Mentors and Father Figures

Speaking of people changing lives, I relish my new full-time role at USC where I can educate, inspire, and mentor young adults and launch them on careers in pharmacy. In truth, there are many times throughout life when most of us can greatly benefit if we are lucky enough to have mentors to help guide and encourage us.

As I reflect on my life, I realize I've long had my own need and desire for mentors—and for father figures. My earliest recognition of this latter yearning occurs in a rather startling way.

In the late 1960s, I'm still in my thirties when Lorraine and I are in a couple's therapy session and the therapist says to me, "Mel, can you be sixteen years old right now?"

I'm not sure what he is getting at, but he gets out of his chair and comes over and embraces me. My face crosses his face with its stubble, and I begin to bawl. He doesn't say a word. At that moment of our faces touching, I am sixteen years old again with Leo.

I don't know how much of my life shifts from this experience with the therapist. But it eventually becomes clear for me that I've been constantly looking for this fatherly figure, a mentor.

But it's more than that. I'm looking for my father not just for guidance, but also to give him my report card. I never have that opportunity with Leo because he dies so young. He never gets to see the man I become: the successes in building a career and creating a family. Business-wise and academically, I probably win every award in the world of pharmacy.

Mine is an incredible career and one I'm very proud of. Yet I wish there was a chance to tell Leo: "Hey, I did really okay."

Because of this desire—both for fatherly guidance and for someone to report my achievements—a number of men have filled these roles at various times in my life. They provide advice and direction, or allow me to offer an accounting of what I have accomplished: attaining an advanced degree, getting married, raising a family, creating a thriving business, becoming a full-time professor. Many milestones.

Learning by Watching

Looking back, I think this desire starts around the time I get my pharmacy internship job. It is 1953 and only two years after Leo passes away. I never get to tell him that I'm studying to become a professional pharmacist or that I have my first internship. Yet when I later get a job at Major Drug, I see the owner Joe Rosslaw as something of a father figure and guide to my new life ahead. Joe Finkelstein, a USC pharmacy grad, is there as well, but he's younger than Joe Rosslaw. Joe Finkelstein helps me along in school, but it is Joe Rosslaw that really resonates for me in this way. Something about his age and character that has me feel this connection.

With Joe Rosslaw, I witness his sense of caring in how he treats the patients coming to the pharmacy. Plus, if someone is sick at a hospital, he visits on his way home. This impacts me as a health-care professional in how I attend to people. I may not be fully aware at the time, but his approach influences my entire career.

In truth, I learn some of this dedication from Leo too. Though he isn't in a profession that helps people, he is very devoted to his family.

Fatherly Father-In-Law and More

Perhaps fittingly, another father figure for me is Lorraine's dad. Phil Ross is gracious to me from the beginning, aware that I recently lost my father. In addition to being supportive, he and his wife loan us money to buy our first house. I don't refer to him as Phil. I call him Dad.

Yet it is my next job that becomes my biggest turning point, while working with my next mentor and fatherly figure. During my final year of pharmacy school, I have my internship/job at the hospital pharmacy run by Bill Behrns and his wife. About halfway through my senior year, Bill mentions there is a doctor constructing a medical building in Van Nuys that wants him to put in a pharmacy. This is when he asks me that most unexpected (and life-changing) question I could imagine: "Do you want to partner in this with me?"

After I come up with the needed $5,000, Bill and I open Shield Pharmacy. He is certainly my mentor since I don't know how to run a business, borrow money from a bank, or even order from a wholesaler! He guides me through every step. Though partners, I'm really running the business. Think about it: I am out of school just six months, recently married, a baby born last October, and this man has enough confidence in me to trust that I can pull this off. Remember, he's risking his money too.

That means a lot.

I vividly remember how fatherly he is as he guides me. Actually, he's not just guiding me—he is encouraging me forward. Everything with the new business goes so well, that after three or four years, I say to Bill, "Can I buy you out?"

He looks at me knowingly . . . and grins. "Yes."

From there, the business expands tremendously, becomes Shield HealthCare, and eventually sells to a Fortune 500 company.

Professor/Dean/Father (Figure)

Though he is a professor when I first get to know him at USC, John Biles becomes dean of the pharmacy school—and integral to my life.

I've written that when we create the Shield HealthCare Center, John is right there at our grand opening, walking down from the second-floor mezzanine with tears in his eyes. He is witness to my "report card"—acknowledging he has never seen such an outstanding, innovative place. It feels absolutely great to hear this from him!

In fact, John is the one who persuades me to become a faculty member at USC, and later asks me to be a full-time professor. Innovative in pharmacy as well, John endorses the many new approaches I bring to my classes. We have numerous discussions about where I think pharmacy should head and the advancements we can introduce into the field.

Loss Magnifies the Need

All of us desire praise, for someone to pat the top of our head and say, "Really good work." But when somebody loses their dad as early as I do, before ever having a chance to show who I am, that desire is all the stronger.

I always have that kind of approval from my mother. She thinks I can walk on water! Yet that's not satisfying. Her regard is not in response to something I achieve or who I become. But getting the genuine thing from a male, after losing my father, is meaningful in a different and profound way.

My decision to meet with Al is so I can give him my report card: married to Lorraine, two teenagers, a lovely home, success at Shield Pharmacy. It is a pretty good report! Though I'm not entirely aware of it at the time, in my head I'm thinking, "Hey Al, this is what you missed out on."

I believe I go to see Al a second time *not in spite* of my first visit with him being so unsatisfying—but *because* of it. I want to try again. My desire is that strong. But the next visit is just as awful as the first. After this second disaster, I'm, "Okay, you're obviously just not interested and never will be. So the hell with you. I'm done."

310

The Company of Men

That pull toward male figures continues. Even now, as Lorraine and I travel, we meet other couples. They're mostly my age so it's kind of strange, but I am still drawn to some of the men in a sense. Yet they are not really mentors at this point and I don't think of them as father figures.

The draw may be simply to the company of men.

I am in a men's group that goes back to the early eighties. Creating this group is the idea of my business partner at Shield, Fred Bray, and a dentist in our building at the time. They ask if I want to be in it.

I'm not so sure. I caution, "Fred, it may not work since we're partners in business. It sounds like personal kinds of things will get discussed."

Even though there is risk that it could shake up our working relationship, Fred wants to try. It turns out to be very beneficial for Fred and me—as business partners and friends. And for more beyond even that. One of the things that comes from such groups is camaraderie. When we are young, we may find a kind of male camaraderie on a sports team. Or as part of a fraternity. Or if you are in the military. As we get older, this isn't commonly available in our culture. When men do get together, talk is typically about business and sports and those kinds of things. More personal discussions about family relations, children, etc.—not so much. That's different from women who have more intimate kinds of conversations with their girlfriends.

In our men's group, there is sharing about marriage, illness, work, sex, different fears—all the many pieces of life that affect men. All shared with confidentiality so we feel free to talk. It is a powerful thing that you can only do with just men.

Not only can you gain better understanding and answers, but you also come to realize some of the issues you face are not as unique to you as you might imagine. They are common to other men too. Realizing that most everyone has some of the same worries and doubts as those burdening you, provides both deep comfort and insight.

Even though I am already around fifty when I start in this group, it is very helpful as I continue to grow and mature. Our group continues today, though we are down to five people. I'm the oldest in the group. The youngest is eighty. We're still together after forty years. I think that says a lot about the need that men have for one another.

◆　◆　◆

CHAPTER 51

Broadening My Teaching

Much like I look for ways to expand Shield when I build my business, I find ways to "widen" the breadth of my teaching beyond the mandatory freshman classes I establish when first hired at USC.

Class on Special Populations

Though I don't create the pharmacy school's Class for Special Populations, I do help develop some of its curriculum, and team teach the course with other professors.

Key for me, and the reason I love this course, is that when you practice pharmacy—especially in a place like Los Angeles with patients of every religion, culture, ethnic group, and language—how do you adapt to these differences among patients? How do you best communicate? This is not only in regard to language. Different cultures also bring different points of view to the interaction.

Sometimes people from other countries have various old-world remedies for how to deal with health and medicine, from ways to cure the common cold to whatever else that Grandma knows how to do. So how will that integrate—or conflict—with Western medicine? You've got Eastern medicine, folk medicine . . . plus all kinds of boogeyman ideas and beliefs.

Special Populations is all about how you deal with different peoples. One example: People from certain cultures don't like for you to get too near or touch them. They're not interested in close contact. They want space. Understanding the patient's culture is even an integral piece to the fotonovelas I develop that I'll address later.

One issue that comes up in communicating to *any* patient is that many students like to "show off" that they know a lot. They choose to use medical jargon and may ask a patient, "Have you voided today?" But some people will not know what you mean. You need to ask, "Have you urinated today?" But even that may be too sophisticated at times. You may need to say something like, "Did you pee today?" Whatever wording gets the answer is the right way to go. You have to determine the level at which to speak to the patient.

Codirector of the PharmD/MBA program.

The USC pharmacy school has created a number of dual degrees. One of them is the opportunity to earn a PharmD *and* an MBA through USC's Marshall School of Business. For the PharmD/MBA dual degree, I take on the role of codirector, even though I don't have an MBA myself. But I have extensive experience through my own business.

Participants in the program get both the PharmD and MBA degrees in five years straight—instead of a more typical route of getting a PharmD, going out and working, and then spending another two years on the MBA. They end up with a pretty cool dual degree that is very helpful to their careers.

The Clerkship

My clerkship is essentially an independent study with me, an elective intended for a fourth-year student. I take one student at a time for six weeks. They have reading assignments in business books and spend time in my office each week. They participate with whatever I'm involved in at the moment. It could be on a project I'm doing, or going with me to visit a community clinic or surgicenter (private surgical facility for minor outpatient procedures instead of a hospital).

Another focus for the clerkship student is learning what it takes to open a hypothetical pharmacy from scratch. The student has to find a suitable location. If they are to lease the space, how much will that cost? The student must speak to an actual real estate agent to learn the answers.

Plus, how will you finance it? Bank loan? Borrow money from a family member? The latter is a whole different game plan than borrowing from a bank. Banks don't care what you do in your personal life as long as you make payments every month. But borrow money from a family member—suddenly they want to know how you're living. "What do you mean you bought a new car? Took a vacation? You still owe us all this money!"

I ask the student, "What are your plans for the pharmacy itself? What services will you provide? How will you market the grand opening? How do you differentiate yourself from other pharmacies in your area? What is your staffing? If starting as a one-person operation, waiting on people is humongously difficult. What if someone wants a flu shot while more people are waiting and 20 other things are demanding your attention?"

Suddenly their "dream" faces a reality check. During the six-week course, I work with the student on all of this. Essentially me translating my world of experience to them.

The student's final exam is to create a business plan to present to a bank in order to ask for a loan to open their pharmacy. They create a personal financial statement, three years of projected income, as well as profit or loss forecasts. They also need to present themselves professionally.

For this final, I role-play the loan officer. The student is coming to *The Bank of Baron*. I critique their pitch from a loan officer's point of view and from Mel Baron the pharmacist's point of view—what do I think about their plan. It is an intense and valuable learning experience for them!

A part of my success with clerkships is due to my access to community clinics and surgicenters where I can bring students . . . which comes out of a little side gig I have at the same time that I'm teaching.

Side Business: PharmaCom LLC

Though I'm very happily teaching at USC, my entrepreneurial spirit hasn't gone away. All that's needed is an opportunity.

One day, I receive a phone call from a safety net clinic—those types that cater to underserved populations. This one is putting together a small dispensary at their facility and they are wondering if I might come by to see if I can help them organize it.

Though I don't know much about this type of operation that is a dispensary rather than a pharmacy, they are still doling out medicine. They also have a lot of regulations. I research background on it and conclude, "Yes, I can help set you up, clarify regulatory requirements, and outline what you need to do."

Once I consult there and the necessary tasks are all completed, they ask, "Could you come by regularly to check on us—see how we're functioning and if we're meeting our regulatory obligations?"

I continue doing this for them in my spare time, and before too long, I'm getting calls from similar facilities referred to me by this first clinic. After one of these new places sends me even more referrals, I realize there is a real opportunity here! Most clinics don't understand how to effectively run dispensaries or the laws governing them. I memorize all the regs and how clinics must meet them. Now I'm going into clinics and instructing, "These are the things you need to do and this is the paperwork you must fill out."

Turns out their permit requires that a pharmacy consultant advises them at least quarterly. So I "formalize" my new business and the fees I'll charge. Before I know it, I am consulting for a significant number of these clinics, visiting them on my way to USC or going home afterward.

I also approach surgicenters, figuring they dispense medications too and can use my consulting services. In addition, I start working with a number of pharmacies that are on probation with the State Board of Pharmacy for one reason or another. This opportunity traces back to that first guy I meet at the School of Pharmacy, Herb Weinberg, who after being a pharmacist for many years, then goes to law school and starts practicing law—in the field of pharmacy. He helps people buy and sell pharmacies, *and* helps people who are under the gun with the State Board of Pharmacy when not meeting some regulations. A good friend ever since school, Herb refers these pharmacies to me since the pharmacy board requires they meet with a consultant regularly—part of the stipulation for not taking away their license while they stay on probation for three to five years.

This becomes a substantial part of my business too.

Side Benefit

I use this business to also further my teaching. When I visit a community clinic or surgicenter, I may bring along a clerkship student as an educational exercise. I ask the student, "Let's say you are a consultant to this clinic. What are you doing in that capacity? What abilities must you have? What legal issues face you and the clinic? If you come across some glaring errors at this clinic, how will you convince them to make the necessary changes? What kinds of reports would you send them? How much do you charge for your services?"

I am again exposing students to real-world considerations.

Too Big for One Person

PharmaCom continues growing such that a person could do this full-time and earn quite a nice living! But it is too big for me to do alone and still teach—and I want to teach. So I need help. Plus, I know that at some point, I may want to think about retiring.

I bring on and train two other pharmacists who were students of mine. One is Raffi Svadjian, who is now also a faculty member at USC. The other is a more recent student, Oscar Tello, who has been working at CVS, but now will be helping us full-time. It's the three of us, plus secretarial support.

We are now seeing over 250 clinics, a dozen pharmacies, and three different surgery centers! PharmaCom has contracts with some fairly large organizations. In addition to Los Angeles, we have work in Simi Valley, Lancaster, Palmdale, and San Diego. This is a big business.

In truth, what we actually do is not all that hard. It's not magic. If you know the rules and regs, you are simply helping clients follow the guidelines. But you also have to be careful how you speak to these people. You don't talk down to them. You try to keep them out of trouble and get those on probation through their "crisis." In the case of clinics, the problems are not usually with the nurses or doctors, but the lower-level staffing. You don't want to make them feel stupid. No matter what their blunders may have been, you are respectful as you guide them.

Just like George Maloney at Bard points out to me years earlier, we are all in *the people business* regardless of the setting or specific tasks.

PharmaCom continues today. While I no longer personally consult or visit clinics and pharmacies, I do send out monthly newsletters to the health-care community. Primarily short articles about what I would call community-pharmacy-type issues like diabetes, hypertension, and obesity. Aside from being informative for them, it serves as marketing for PharmaCom as we stay in front of their faces. Rather than send an email newsletter that can all too easily be ignored or deleted, I make the choice to send out a hardcopy newsletter as first-class mail. Some places actually post them at their clinics for patients. This works well for us—and for those people coming into the clinic.

◆ ◆ ◆

CHAPTER 52

Fotonovelas

While I am attending a seminar on breast cancer at the Norris Cancer Hospital, the woman sitting next to me starts a conversation. She is Robin Clark, an MD geneticist concerned about the Hispanic population, since they have twice as many birth defects as any other ethnic group.

Yet we don't know why.

As she and I continue our conversation, we discuss that one of the ways to prevent birth defects is having prospective mothers take 400 micrograms of a folic acid supplement daily. Robin is trying to develop programs to educate physicians on the need for this. She wants any woman of childbearing age to take folic acid as it can help prevent 85 percent of these birth defects.

I say, "Truthfully, I think you're focusing on the wrong area to promote this. The Spanish population that you're looking at is generally not going to the doctor until they're ready to deliver the baby. Too late. I'm not so sure they really get much prenatal care."

This is disappointing news to Robin. Then I add, "But you know, you ought to try pharmacies. That's really the most accessible health-care provider for this population. They go to drug stores and in a way trust the pharmacist. That's the place to do it."

She agrees this is a good idea and I want to help. So we write a few grants to get funding and begin a continuing education series for pharmacists to tell the story of folic acid and birth defects. We are fairly successful. But the process is really slow. Though a good idea, it's not making the impact that we want.

I happen to mention this to someone else and they ask, "Do you know what a fotonovela is?"

I have no idea. They explain, "These are little Spanish booklets. Often written in English and Spanish, though mostly Spanish. They are comprised of a series of pictures that tell a story along with text and dialogue. Some are like soap-opera or romance stories, and can get kind of racy."

Robin and I look at some and I wonder, "Could we integrate a health message into something like this?"

We again write grant proposals to seek funding. But using a "fotonovela" to disseminate medical information to the Spanish community doesn't make any sense to those people who fund grants. Fortunately, we are able to get some initial backing from USC's Good Neighbors Campaign that helps serve communities around the university.

Realizing we'll need help to create a fotonovela, Robin and I find Greg Molina in another department at USC. He speaks Spanish and has developed a comic strip for *La Opinion* newspaper. He agrees to collaborate. Once we raise sufficient additional funding from a variety of sources, we begin creating our fotonovela. Called "What My Girlfriend Didn't Know," it is essentially a black-and-white comic book-style booklet with a provocative color cover. Sort of like those romance novel covers that feature a lusty woman. In our case, the woman is sitting on a guy's lap. It tells a kind of melodramatic soap opera story within which we integrate our message. Each fotonovela is in both Spanish and English.

I am fascinated to be part of this. It's like nothing I have ever done.

It is also *revealing*. While creating it—*we discover one of the reasons* for the elevated numbers of birth defect cases in the Hispanic community!

Mystery Solved

While one can buy a separate folic acid supplement, most people get it as part of a multivitamin. But when we do focus groups to figure out how to best tell our story, we find out a lot of people in the Hispanic community believe a myth that if you take vitamins—you're going to get fat.

This is eye-opening and clearly a problem we must resolve. But how are we going to dispel this myth? Not only that, how are we also going to convince a mostly Catholic population—to take the supplement *prior to getting pregnant?*

Medically, the supplement is needed because the embryo's neural tube closes between the 17th and 30th day after conception. This neural tube later becomes the baby's spine, spinal cord, brain, and skull. But if the neural tube fails to close properly, a defect occurs. Folic acid can prevent this. The problem is, it can be too late to start taking folic acid only after *you know* you're pregnant. A woman often won't realize she is expecting until *after* the time frame when the supplement is needed.

The answer is that any woman of childbearing age should be on folic acid—before she is even certain she has a need. That's where we come up against the myth that vitamins make you fat. What woman wants to risk that—especially if she's not even aware that she is pregnant and needs the supplement?

We have challenging issues to face.

Working really hard, we create approaches that overcome all these issues. Incorporating them into our story . . . we produce the fotonovela. So what is the response?

People think it is fabulous!

Promoting with the Promotoras

Our next focus is, "Where are we going to distribute this? Only in pharmacies? Who is going to help us? And how do we train these people who may then be asked questions about it?

We decide the key to all this are the *promotoras*—people in the Hispanic community who are lay health workers. Basically, they tell stories to educate the public.

We put together a series of training programs for promotoras, giving them kind of a toolbox of questions and answers, and ideas about how to tell the story in addition to what is presented in the booklets. Though our training programs help give them information, the promotoras are inventive in coming up with their own ways to reach the public. They go to laundromats, stores, bus stops—and talk to people—while handing out our fotonovelas.

This entire project is very stimulating to me. What did I know about fotonovelas or promotoras or such myths within cultures?

An incredibly difficult learning curve . . . and also incredibly fun.

Book Two

Since our first book is highly successful, we figure, "Let's do another." We launch the second fotonovela on diabetes.

This subject is much more complicated. As we think about how to compose it, I use what I learned from Bill Williams when I got my master's in public administration. His area of study is about communicating messages.

I suggest, "We need to write the story from bottom up, not top down." That means write it somewhere between fourth- and fifth-grade reading levels. It must be simple since our reading audience could include people from a variety of educational levels. I want subjects that might intimidate or put off some people to be presented in ways that can be readily and easily absorbed." (While fourth- and fifth-grade levels might seem extremely low, in reality, many novels and newspaper articles are written around eighth-grade reading levels.)

We also need to know if there are any beliefs our target audience already has about this diabetes topic. Focus groups help us again—and surprise us again. We find out that a large percentage of this population thinks that insulin is the cause of the blindness and amputations that can actually result from diabetes.

This is crazy making. We know insulin is a godsend, but we're hearing just the opposite!

When we speak to physician practitioners in the community, they verify this fear is predominant. People think insulin is worse than the disease. We have to dispel that myth right at the beginning while we also make our story entertaining. If the reader is bored after page one, they'll put the book down. The story must compel them to turn the page, then the next page, and the next. . . .

Again, we make the cover provocative. It doesn't say anything about diabetes (just as the first cover doesn't mention birth defects). Our lessons have to sneak their way in.

The title of this second book becomes *Sweet Temptation.* That is both enticing and still hints at the actual subject.

Words and Pictures

Of course, it is not just words that convey our stories. We are creating loads of pictures with actors to illustrate our messages. A lot of thinking goes into this: "How do we shoot the photos to help tell the story? What kind of layout artists do we use to create this?" The pictures must have a good flow to them, and by the end of our tale, both the story and the photographs should model good behavior.

We also create a Q&A section that kind of tells the story again and repeats our messages. We use a picture of a person's face as "their dialogue" poses a question. Then a picture of a nurse or doctor (or me as a pharmacist) as the "talking head" that responds with an answer. All to further clarify the information we are sharing.

As you can see, there are *many* pieces to this puzzle!

Fotonovela on Hypertension
Spanish Version   English Version

Each of these big projects takes nine months to a year to produce with a budget around $100,000. So there is always a lot of grant writing and securing funds from foundations, health-care insurance companies, etc.

Once each fotonovela is produced, we then must figure out where to distribute these books. What kinds of establishments will best reach their target audience? We place them in local pharmacies, safety net clinics (that provide health care to underserved populations), and health fairs.

After a lot of hard work, our second fotonovela becomes highly successful as well! We continue producing more of them.

We also create three *audio-video novellas.* Using the same pictures we already have for the booklets, we produce videos with voiceover in both English and Spanish (along with added sound effects and music). People can now watch the story on their screens. Some medical facilities play them in their waiting rooms.

Out in the World

To date, we have distributed over a half million copies of our fotonovelas.

But even more people are seeing them than these numbers would indicate. Apparently, people don't throw them away after reading. They pass them along to others. The data shows that on average, four people read each booklet. We are definitely getting our messages out there!

And overseas as well. A university in the Netherlands pays us to translate the diabetes fotonovela into Dutch, and uses it in the Netherlands and in South Africa. They write a peer-reviewed article on this "experiment," reporting that even though the pictures and storyline are designed for the Hispanic community—the fotonovela resonates and is accepted in these other cultures as well.

Over the years, we receive more requests to translate fotonovelas into other languages.

Giving Credit Where Due

While I get a lot of praise for the fotonovelas, my colleague, Greg Molina, is the creative genius behind it all and has the background, speaking both English and Spanish, and having grown up in the neighborhood.

Greg is like Fred Bray at Shield: He is making it happen. Along with Robin Clark, my secretary Roseann Cadena, and the rest of the people I surround myself with. They *all* make it work.

The fotonovelas bring a ton of recognition to the university and the School of Pharmacy. The booklets educate a portion of the population that normally doesn't get this information, and leads to dramatic improvements in patient care. No one in pharmacy has done something like this before.

Trusting the Trustees

As president for twenty years, Steven Sample is a driving force in transforming USC into an elite university.

Right after we launch our first successful fotonovela, Steven asks me to speak to the trustees about our project. Trustees are like the university's board of directors. I prepare what I'm going to say, and when the day comes and I'm awaiting my turn, the person before me is speaking to the trustees about cutting-edge stem cell research. I mean, it is as sophisticated and groundbreaking as it could possibly be. And I'm to follow this guy to talk about a fotonovela we produce at a fourth-grade reading level?

I think to myself, "This is way beyond comical."

I explain our project, figuring no one is going to be very impressed. But I'm wrong. Some of the trustees think it is remarkable: "You are telling a story with an important message—and as it resonates for the reader—lives will be positively affected."

Their response boggles me. They totally get what we're doing!

Continuing the Education

From our auspicious start in 2000, *we are still producing fotonovelas.* We now have eleven fotonovelas covering a wide variety of conditions, including birth defects, diabetes, breast cancer, pediatric asthma, childhood obesity, dementia, hypertension, depression, immunizations (in which we add an insert on COVID-19 vaccinations), and more.

My team has sent out 50,000 copies of our new COVID-19 immunization edition. We have 40,000 of these inserted into the pages of the *La Opinion* newspaper—so when readers open their paper, they find our booklets. Another 10,000 will be distributed through clinics, schools, etc.

Getting to this point has, at times, been extremely challenging. Yet the benefits to the communities make all our efforts worthwhile.

✦　✦　✦

CHAPTER 53

Road to Full Professor:
Paved with Teamwork

Because I'm a clinical professor, I never become a tenured professor. But even if you're not tenured, there is pressure at USC from the start to be promoted—to rise from assistant professor to associate professor to full professor.

Yet my road to full professor doesn't begin right away after I become full-time. Despite the push to advance, I am just doing my thing and enjoying it. But before too long, my competitiveness kicks in. I say to myself: "Okay, if I'm going to be here—then I'm going to play this game."

To really participate, you have to understand what the game is and the university culture, and what you must do to be part of it. I seek out others' counsel on how to best propel myself forward on the full professor track. It is not determined by how long you are teaching at the school. In fact, I learn that to move from one level to the next entails steps beyond teaching entirely: it requires research and being published. This is especially true in research institutes like USC or Yale or Harvard, etc. The value to the university for requiring this is that when a professor gains attention and recognition, it adds prestige to the school and faculty. (In contrast, Ross at BYU-Idaho—a four-year liberal arts college—has none of this pressure to research or publish. His role is to teach and he is a full professor.)

I also learn that you cannot really do these steps alone. I search out others with whom to collaborate so we can help one another. You need teamwork to get you there.

We join together to create peer-reviewed articles. "Peer reviewed" means other professionals (not involved in your study) literally review your completed article to decide if it is worthy of publication. In fact, some publications *only* publish peer-reviewed articles. On my own, I publish a number of articles in trade journals and receive some "credit" for that. But the university doesn't hold those in the same regard.

When you look at peer-reviewed articles, you typically see five or seven authors listed. Each of them has various strengths or areas of expertise they bring to the project (even including how to compose such articles). So together with these other researchers, I produce a number of research studies that bring me further along this professorship path.

Finally, to decide whether to make you a full professor, the university assesses *all* of your contributions to the field. They may also select an additional five or six people outside the university who do not know you (and so avoid favoritism) to receive a package of all your work, along with your personal statement, curriculum vitae, etc. These evaluators are asked, "Would you promote this person to full professor if they were at your school?"

It all is quite a process.

Fotonovelas Take Me over the Edge

Though I never predicted this when we began them, I think producing the fotonovelas is what makes the final difference in my professor track. They are an innovative and creative approach to communicating health information for people who might otherwise never receive or accept it. The fotonovelas's success and international attention put me over the threshold to be awarded full professorship (and also lead to my receiving the 2011 Pinnacle Award).

Mel Baron is now a full professor at USC.

◆ ◆ ◆

CHAPTER 54

Life is a Team Sport

I am good at business strategies. I am willing to take risks. I can look ahead at what might be possible. I have loads of information that I can teach students.

But my success really comes down to being able to work with people. Another way of saying it—and this is among the remarks I give at my USC retirement party—is that *life is a team sport*. It's not about me doing it all on my own. It's not simply about me being the leader of others. It's about *all* the people on a team that make things happen.

I realize that throughout my life, I move from team to team to team. I join my first team in 1932 as an infant. My *family team* expands when my sister is born. In many ways, me and my buddies growing up together are a team (a far better term than "gang"). Then there's Mel and the Meltones. In high school—classmates are really teammates. We're in it *together*.

In 1950, I enroll on the USC team with "coaches" (professors) guiding my way. I later join a USC auxiliary team called the School of Pharmacy in 1953. I'm on a team at my first pharmacy job. Then, in 1957, I get a whole new team—at a startup called Shield.

It continues from there.

There's Operation Bootstrap, Bill Williams and USC again when I get my Public Administration degree, the California Alcoholism Foundation, the Fred Bray and Mel team, Bard and its corporate team, USC's teaching team, the research team that writes peer-reviewed articles, the fotonovelas team. Even that men's group I join with Fred Bray is us banding together to support one another through life.

The list goes on, with many smaller teams mixed in among those.

Of course, though I am mostly naming the specific organizations and places, my teams are really the people at each one. Be it my parents, Johnny Shambra and Lazar, Bill Williams, Fred Bray and Danny Gelber, John Biles, Greg Molina and Robin Clark, Roseann Cadena—all important teammates without whom I would never have the successes or the life that I am blessed with. They all make it look easy for me.

I'm a constant team *builder* and a constant team *player*—even when I'm the leader. I don't lead in isolation. I recognize what others bring and embrace how those talents enhance whatever we undertake together.

Strengths and Weaknesses

My sense from early on is that I'm a B-student at best. Certainly not a scholar by any means. In fact, if you ask my former pharmacy students: "Do you think Mel is brilliant?" I predict their answers would be: "Not even close."

Yet I am able to succeed in life. In college. In career. Eventually becoming a full professor at a highly ranked university. It boggles my mind.

Perhaps reading this may prove inspiring to those who may think, "Oh, I'm not super bright, I won't amount to anything" or "I will just have a midlevel job." Being brilliant may not be the most important criteria for achievement. There are plenty of brilliant people who aren't successful.

I believe I excelled because of other innate abilities. Most important, understanding what are my strengths and also my weaknesses. I surround myself with people who make up for my weaknesses.

My teams.

They make me look good. They help make things happen. At the same time, it is through my leadership that I select those people around me and help guide them to make it happen.

Even in the band, Mel Baron and the Meltones, Johnny Shambra is critical to our success. He's a really talented musician who arranges our music, while I'm kind of the producer/manager who arranges everything else: solicits the clients, books the job, pays the players, etc.

When I think about Shield HealthCare becoming really successful, the genius is my partner Fred Bray. I may create the concepts. I create the sales. But he is the detail guy—the guy that makes sure we have everything in stock, that we collect the money, that we pay the bills. I am the one "out front:" Mel Baron and Shield. But without Fred, the whole thing would be a disaster. Similarly, when Danny Gelber joins us, he designs the protocols for our innovative home infusion program that amplifies our success and helps catch the eye of Bard who buys us.

At USC, I'm the face of the fotonovelas and make that happen—but Greg Molina and Robin Clark are the real keys to it along with Roseann Cadena, my assistant/secretary/confidant for twenty years who supports this and many other projects. USC researcher Jennifer Unger designs some of the studies cited in my scientific papers. Sandy Jean, my secretary at PharmaCom for over 25 years, also gives critical help to my USC projects.

I tell my students that you don't have to be the smartest, most knowledgeable, or most skilled to be highly successful. By surrounding yourself with those people who shore up your weaknesses, you then can take more risks and play the bigger cards.

The Revelation

Truthfully, even though I instinctively value having good people around me from early on, much of my awareness of this doesn't come to me until much later. After I sell my business to a Fortune 500 company.

While I'm working for this corporation that buys Shield, they send me to a management seminar in Santa Barbara. There are fourteen attendees from different companies. By this time, I've got a ton of money and with it a pretty big ego. Mel is wonderful!

That is about to get shaken up.

Those putting on this management conference take the opportunity beforehand to interview the people who report to each of us attendees, and the people we report to. When I get to the conference, pairs of giant posters have been set up around the room. Each pair of posters has one titled "Strengths" and one titled "Weaknesses"—reflecting the information acquired by interviewing the people we work with. Nobody's name is on any of the posters. We are instructed to walk around the room to see if we can identify which set of posters describes ourselves.

As I go through the room, this one pair of posters jumps out at me. I look at it and think, "That is me."

The guy running the seminar now has us all sit down and asks, "How many of you recognize your set of posters by your weaknesses?"

I raise my hand because it is glaring to me . . . and now I'm depressed. But then he says, "None of you got this far on your weaknesses. You got here on your strengths."

I think about that and recognize he is right. Somehow, I realize early on that some of my weaknesses may not be "fixable." So instead, I focus on my strengths throughout my life—including leading and inspiring and enabling those people around me to do their best. I reflect back on how I have always surrounded myself with people who cover my weaknesses so I can play to my strengths. In a way, we each support one another—to create something together that none of us could on our own.

In my clerkships at USC, I teach students about the real world of pharmacy. But I also want them to *learn about themselves* and what enables them to achieve.

I instruct them: "Take a piece of paper and draw a line down the middle. On one side, write all of your weaknesses. On the other side, list all of your strengths."

Then I ask, "Do you want to improve some of your weaknesses? *Can* you? *How much* do you want to change those?

What can you do with your strengths? How can you make the best use of them? How can you offset your weaknesses?"

My self-assessment exercise becomes something the students think about the entire semester.

What Game Am I Playing?

In any sport, success on the field comes out of truly understanding the game and what is required to prevail.

Life makes the same demand. One of my strengths has always been to answer this question: What game am I playing? I call every arena or endeavor a game. Business is a game. Corporate America is a game. Academia is a game. How do you play in that particular world? What skills are most needed? What are the goals? Who are the key players? What "costume" do you need?

The word "chameleon" could be used to describe me. I can fit into whatever arena I'm playing. I succeed in corporate America even though it is a whole different playing field than I am used to, requiring a different costume. By "costume," I'm really describing persona more than actual clothing (though clothing counts too): your dialogue, your conversations, how you carry yourself.

Academia is another whole world. The stakes are different. The game doesn't operate the same. I'm able to see all of that and how to play in it.

The constant question is, "How do you 'win' in whatever environment you're part of?" That's what you have to figure out. I am successful in junior high school, high school, my careers—all by these same basic means. Yes, I make some mistakes in business and fall on my face a couple of times. But that isn't because I don't understand the playing field. It is because my ego gets in the way and subverts my gamesmanship.

The Game of Love and Life

As I think about this, much of what I describe here helps to explain the success of my love story with Lorraine.

Lorraine has so many wonderful attributes. Traits and abilities that offset whatever weaknesses I have in the relationship. Likewise, I feel I have done the same for her. It is, I think, what makes a good marriage. A love partnership. Not just one leading and the other following. Both lead at different times. With the absolute support of the other.

My *most important team* officially starts in 1953 when I commit to "The Lorraine and Mel team." Together, we navigate life, through all kinds of challenges and achievements.

Now as I finish forty years of teaching at USC, I am looking at a *new* team called the "retirement team." One on which Lorraine will join me again since what we sign in 1953 is a *lifetime* contract.

Yet she won't be the only one on it besides me. Like in every other stage of life, I'm sure we'll have plenty of other teammates participating!

◆ ◆ ◆

CHAPTER 55

Pharmacy Progresses

Just like many of my life's twists and turns have astounded me over the years, I marvel at the radical transformations that have taken place in pharmacy during my lifetime.

I already mention that our pharmacy school today has a student makeup that is 70 percent women, with the medical school being 50 percent women, and many more foreign-born students as well.

Yet even more dramatically, the pharmaceutical field itself is totally changed.

There are no antibiotics prior to World War II—no significant anti-infective agents other than sulfa drugs. Fortunately, penicillin enters the mainstream in the early 1940s. This is the starting point to developing the many antibiotics that we have today.

In the beginning of my career in the early 50s, pharmacists are the ones compounding different substances together into capsules and bottles. Today, we have a vast array of "packaged" medications that help us care for patients. In fact, we're at a point where we can target a particular disease with a specific medicine. As example, when Lorraine is diagnosed with chronic myeloid leukemia, the doctor says to her, "You have this terrible disease, but you have it at the right time because there is a drug called Gleevec that targets that type of leukemia." She does really well on that drug for a while. Then when she can no longer tolerate it, she goes on another drug called Tasigna. She has been cancer free for over eight years. The drugs know exactly where they need to go.

Such pharmaceutical breakthroughs are one of the reasons we see so many people living longer today.

The *responsibilities* of pharmacists have dramatically changed too. First, the number of medications we must know has grown exponentially! We also do far more than dispense medications. Pharmacists are now giving immunizations, taking blood pressures, and managing osteoporosis.

Yet, in my opinion, we are still underutilizing the profession. One example is when they release the COVID-19 vaccines. They should have gone to the pharmacies right from the get-go. We are the most accessible health-care profession in the country. Pharmacies and drug stores are everywhere. People trust them. They go there all the time. Yet the pharmacies don't get the vaccines until way later. Instead, people are lining up for hours at Dodger Stadium and parks. People could have been going to their local pharmacies just like we do with flu vaccines. It could have been much easier from the beginning.

Safety Net

In addition to all our routine responsibilities, pharmacists today also serve as the last line of defense in making sure patients get the proper medications and dosages. This is a major issue. As a pharmacist, you are the final person looking at the prescription given to a patient. Is it the proper medication? Is this the appropriate dosage? Is the patient on some other medicine for which this new med is contraindicated? Is it a duplicate of something else they are already taking?

Remember, people go to different physicians. Most of those doctors do not coordinate with one another in terms of the patient's care. Do they always know all the other medications that patient is taking? Does the doctor know how two medications could interact? Might he or she make an error and prescribe a toxic dose? How might the side effects of this drug affect someone?

On top of everything else that doctors do, and with so many drugs out there today, how well versed are they about a particular medication?

It gets complicated. The pharmacist plays a key role in safeguarding the patient.

In fact, some pharmacists who work in places like a clinic or Kaiser may even have prescriptive authority. That means they could actually see you and prescribe your medicine. Or change the dose of your existing prescription or frequency that you take it. That is quite a change.

With their vast knowledge, today's pharmacists could do even more than they are now. Yet some of that gets political. Doctors may feel we are trespassing on their turf. Still, pharmacists will most assuredly take on greater responsibilities in the future, given how far things have progressed already.

✦ ✦ ✦

CHAPTER 56

Recognitions and Retirement

I have been blessed with a wonderful second career as a professor at USC. A new world where I discover fresh ways to contribute. I know I've affected many lives there, while mine has changed for the better as well.

I get to hood my son, Ross, when he graduates USC's PhD program. On top of that, my grandson Jack gets his bachelor's degree in 2010 while I'm there. *Three* generations!

During my time with USC, I am honored by the university and other organizations. Now, I am the first to admit that I only can do what I do with the help of many other people. Still, the awards are satisfying as they attest that the work I have done is valuable.

While I am particularly proud of receiving California Pharmacist of the Year, the 2011 Pinnacle Award for Individual Achievement from the American Pharmacist Association is probably my single biggest honor. Just one person receives that during a year. I get it largely because of the fotonovelas. The award is presented in Washington, DC, on their headquarters' beautiful rooftop overlooking the city. Lorraine, Ross, Lynn, and her husband Phil all attend with me. Being honored there with my family watching is so exceptional and emotional for all of us.

Being inducted into the Half Century Trojans Hall of Fame in 2012 is perhaps my other most prized honor. It celebrates those who received their USC degree at least 50 years ago and have since demonstrated achievement and leadership in their field. As far as I know, I am the only pharmacist. So receiving this award is very satisfying . . . and also kind of funny.

In Washington, DC, receiving the Pinnacle Award.

As the ceremony day is approaching, I tell Lorraine that we should plan to arrive at the event by 11:30.

She questions this. "You mean 11:30 in the morning? Are you sure? Nobody holds important award ceremonies in the middle of the day."

"Well, these people do."

When that day arrives and it is my turn to speak to the audience, I introduce my speech by first describing my conversation with Lorraine.

"I let my wife Lorraine know that we needed to be here by 11:30 for a twelve-noon start. 'Why so early in the day?' she asks me.

"I tell her, 'This is the *Half Century* Trojans Hall of Fame. Who do you think is going to be there—it's a bunch of really old people who need dinner by five and don't drive at night. You cannot hold an evening event. These people are eating the early bird special and then they're home!'"

Everybody laughs, largely because it's true. A fun opening to my speech.

It so happens that seven years later, I am also inducted into the California Pharmacists Association Hall of Fame. Someone congratulates me and then says, "So . . . one hall of fame wasn't enough for you? Mel needs *two*?" I suppose it's an embarrassment of riches.

A Long History

I begin teaching part-time at USC in 1981 when I'm around 49. Now at 89, a lot of years have gone by. I'm not certain, but I may be the oldest full-time faculty member ever to teach at USC, even though most students and staff may not realize how old I really am. I continue to be passionate and energetic. I've led a life that has always been stimulating, challenging, and has kept me young.

Plus at USC, I'm around young people—innovative students and faculty members—doing phenomenal things! I find it invigorating. The previous dean would call me "the Energizer bunny" because I have a lot of vim and vigor. It is true—that is exactly me when I am enthused and excited.

By now, I'm almost a fixture at USC. As I walk around campus, people know me. They wave hello, including those from other disciplines at the school. USC is my special home away from home.

So Why Retire Now?

There are a couple of pieces to the puzzle of why retire now. As I am nearing ninety years of age, I'm no longer driving anymore. I struggle with my eyesight.

Plus, with COVID, the last year's classes have pretty much all been on Zoom. For me, my love of teaching is being on the campus with my students and colleagues. Having to instruct online doesn't have the same feeling. So I start thinking, "This has been amazing. I've loved it! And maybe now it's time."

With my secretary's help, I bring in a crew of five to help me clear out my office. There is a lot of memorabilia from my many years there. But I make a decision not to take home a ton of stuff and then have to figure out what to do with it all. So we really purge the place—and once we do, I say, "We're done."

Lorraine asks how I feel about this? It doesn't seem traumatic at all. This is the right time. I feel the university will continue to be part of my life. But I'm done grading papers. I don't want to make another syllabus. I don't want to take another mandatory sexual harassment class. I'm done with all that.

I'm mentoring several students. Recently, two others—a former and a current student—ask if they can meet with me for advising. So I am still involved. I will attend events. But I don't have to do the heavy lifting of running classes, which I'm happy about.

Forging Futures

There is an astonishing benefit to teaching that I did not anticipate when I began: seeing the fruits of my labors.

One of the biggest pleasures in raising children is watching them grow and thrive on their own. That has certainly been my great joy with Lynn and Ross. Yet I realize now that I have countless other "kids" too. So many of our graduates end up in incredible places doing wonderful things, many becoming leaders in the field. I might be at a meeting on campus or attending a conference, and one of my former students is up there giving a presentation. The bulk of our current faculty in the clinical department are my former students. In fact, my department chair was both my student and my intern at Shield. Now I'm reporting to him!

In 2022, the USC School of Pharmacy has their gala at the Langham Hotel in Pasadena with over 300 people in attendance. They give a half-dozen different awards to former students who are now part of the pharmacy and health-care communities. For me, it is wonderful being there with Lorraine to see colleagues and former students, many coming up and giving me hugs. You always hope to be appreciated for what you do.

Then as they hand out the awards, two of the recipients specifically thank me for the role I played in their careers. When something like that happens, you get a little emotional. At least I do. I still get emails and notes from former students too. Ongoing validation of the work I have done.

Such acknowledgment can happen in very unexpected ways as well. When my niece learns that her husband-and-wife neighbors are physicians at USC, she asks this couple, "Do you by chance know my uncle, Mel Baron?"

The wife-neighbor looks back at her and exclaims, "Are you kidding? Of course I do. He's a legend!"

My niece phones to tell me this and asks, "Uncle Mel, do I now have to call you *The Legend*?"

I say, "No, of course you don't have to. . . . It's entirely optional."

The reality is that when I see former students today, they blow me away. Some are so impressive. Truthfully, I feel privileged that I perhaps played a little part in who they've become.

Retirement . . . Almost

Just as my careers take many unforeseen turns throughout the years . . . so does my retirement. Barely a year after I officially retire from teaching, USC is officially asking me back! They want me to come in one day a week starting July 1st, 2022 to continue working on the fotonovela health literacy project for the next year.

Of course, I say yes.

I've already started—and I am loving it.

Family of Teachers

As I think over my academic career, I realize something else: teaching is kind of a "family tradition." Everyone in our immediate family become educators in one fashion or another.

Lynn starts the ball rolling, knowing in the eighth grade that she wants to be a teacher. Later I start my own teaching career at USC. Ross then becomes a professor. And Lorraine, in her own way as a therapist and volunteer at Beit T'Shuvah, teaches people how to live better.

What's also wonderful is that all of us really enjoy it! I mean, some people have teaching careers and can't wait to retire. But each of us is really passionate about it. I think we all have a giving nature—wanting to help others. Teaching provides a great avenue for that.

✦ ✦ ✦

CHAPTER 57

Legacy: Grandkids and Great-Grandkids!

It is both a thrill and a wonder to see the evolution of our children as human beings, from their marvelous careers to raising their own families, to witnessing them become citizens of the community. For me, this is the greatest blessing. I have the same sense about our grandkids, and expect I would be able to say a similar thing about our great-grandkids. Does Lorraine's and my participation in their lives play a role in any of this or would they have done it all without our influence? I mean, we'd like to give ourselves *some* credit for contributing to them.

Yet I realize something unexpected: I learn early on that my children are smarter than I am. Now I have grandkids even sharper than their parents! I'm in awe of their intellect, their skills, and the things they do. I feel they will leave this Earth a little better than it has been before. A hope I have for myself too.

But from a parent's perspective, witnessing all this in your children is a pretty cool, phenomenal life journey. We now have our two children, eight grandchildren, and *nineteen* great-grandkids! My eldest grandchild is Joshua at 39. Zachary is the youngest at 27.

The family has been busy!

We are fortunate to have all our grandchildren live in Los Angeles when they are young. There is something surprising about being a grandparent: It is way more fun than I ever imagined.

Not being *their* parent, I feel no responsibility! Far different from raising your own kids. We can spoil grandchildren big time. In fact, it is *our job* to hug and love and spoil them. That's the grandparent formula. My son Ross will complain, "It takes us three days to get them back to being organized and in a routine once they leave your place!"

He's right, of course. When they visit, we say, "We're grandparents. Eat what you want. Watch whatever. Stay up late!"

Lorraine comes up with a brilliant idea to make visits even better. We do what is called "Special Day." Grandkids don't visit us as a group. One comes over at a time, usually on a weekend, and gets a special day and sleepover at our home. We go out to whatever restaurant they want, whatever stores, etc. If you're one of seven children like in Ross's family, it is nonstop at your house. So coming here and being alone with Grammy and Papa really is a magical time. The grandkids talk about it even today. I mean, they're married and have their own children and they tell us, "I still remember my Special Days!"

Staying in Touch

Today, my grandson Jack is the only one who lives in Los Angeles. Everybody else is in Idaho, Utah, or the state of Washington. We fly to see the grandkids after they move away. But as it becomes harder for Lorraine and me to travel so much, we now find simpler solutions, like flying our grandson, Jonathan, in from Spokane to visit us with his wife.

We stay in contact the best we can. I probably text my daughter every single day and I think Lorraine speaks to her almost daily. Plus there are my Sunday Zooms with Ross. I text my grandkids and my great-grandkids. Yet even that can be a challenge—with *nineteen* great-grandchildren.

One thing we do is make a big deal out of everybody's birthday. With so many descendants, Lorraine has a chart to keep track of everyone's date. They get a present. They get a phone call. And most important—they get serenaded by Lorraine and Mel with "Happy Birthday."

The best present of all!

It is more than a little startling to realize that Lorraine and I are the origin of all of these amazing people—our offspring and all the offspring's offspring *and* all the offspring's offspring's offspring.

We couldn't be happier about it!

An appendix in the back of this book shows a family tree, starting with my and Lorraine's grandparents all the way through our grandchildren, followed by a listing of all our great-grandchildren . . . so far!

✦ ✦ ✦

CHAPTER 58

Lorraine and Mel: The Love Story

Though I've focused much of my writings on Lorraine and me in regard to our multifaceted careers, the bringing up of our family, and ways we help others—so much of my story is really a love story. All the career successes, volunteering, and even raising of children, would not be anywhere near as gratifying and enjoyable for me if not for Lorraine.

We have been together for over seventy years, and when I say "together"—I mean really together. After our first date, I never date anyone else. She is the only woman I ever love romantically.

While a lot of my time focuses on work and a lot of *our time* centers around the children—Lorraine and I also have our own life together. We both are people persons, with very active social lives. You could say our parents are role models for this when we are young. Lorraine's parents enjoy going out with friends to dinner and clubs, as well as traveling, especially to England. My parents also love to entertain, including when relatives (such as Al and Goldie Canter) visit from back East and always stay at our house. My dad and mom love taking them out to nightclubs.

Actually, my parents just love going out. Often with many of those same people . . . who are so important in my life as I am growing up (as seen in picture on next page).

Dining at the lavish Cocoanut Grove nightclub, Los Angeles' premier night spot.

Left Side, Front to Back	Right Side, Front to Back
Al Canter	Goldie Canter
Betty Winnick	Sid
Phil Winnick	Pebe
Sadie	Leo
(unknown man)	(unknown woman)

Lorraine and Mel Out on the Town

Especially once our kids leave the house, Lorraine and I have more time to enjoy day- and nightlife. We are both interested in jazz and other music starting from our early days when we go to a lot of clubs. We love attending theater and other live performances.

Of course, there are also sporting events, like football. Lorraine is such a champion. She goes with me because she is aware how much I love football. She doesn't know a thing about it, but becomes a pretty good student of the game, learning all the key players. We have USC season tickets since forever. Yet the football games are not just sporting matches, but also social activities where we bring our kids, relatives, and friends since we always have four tickets. A social function with lunch beforehand. The game itself is almost a backdrop to our spending a fun day together. We also attend cultural and intellectual events revolving around USC.

For Lorraine and me, it's not like, "Oh, you can go to the game (or other event) and I'll do something else." That's not who we are. We do most everything together as a couple. Some people wouldn't want to live that life.

But it works great for us.

Lorraine and Mel on the Road

After Lynn and Ross leave the nest to create their own lives, Lorraine and I do more traveling on our own. We visit all the Scandinavian countries. We go to Russia. We visit China. We go to Malaysia. I teach in Japan. We go to Alaska. We take cruises. There are still a couple of places that I would love to go, but probably never will at this point. Safari in Africa. Australia and New Zealand. But for the most part, we have glorious opportunities to see the world.

Even with globetrotting to so many fascinating places, we don't buy knickknacks as keepsakes. But we do collect art. Almost all of the artwork in our condo comes from places visited around the world. Yet, on our travels, we acquire something even more precious: people from all over the globe who become lifelong friends.

In England, for example, it is the Kaisers—a lovely couple with three kids. We are upstairs at a restaurant, where Lorraine is smoking these little cigars that are popular at the time. The Kaisers think we are Hollywood people! It turns out they are Jewish, live in Miami Beach, and are extremely personable. We become fast friends and travel Europe with them. We go to Alaska. We travel to all three of their kids' weddings. He is a pediatric thoracic surgeon and she is an artist. Some of her artwork hangs on our walls.

Mutual Support from the Get-go

People sometimes ask how the two of us have stayed so happily married for so long, even with our going through a variety of challenges. There are many parts to that answer. One is how we relate to one another. Unlike some couples who like to argue and bicker and find fault, we look for the best in each other, and endeavor to *bring out* the best in one another too.

As I've said, we really are a team. A great marriage team. We are deeply supportive of each other from the start. When I am faced early on with deciding whether to go to pharmacy school after my plans for dentistry fall flat, I call Lorraine. We're not even married yet. She encourages my decision to move forward. Then she helps me through school. She helps me study for exams, using those little three-by-five cards that I create to quiz me: "Tell me about this drug. What is the dose? What is it used for?" She works a job so I can focus on my studies in addition to my part-time employment.

Of course, not all attempts to be helpful work out exactly as intended.

When I open the pharmacy, Lorraine decides it is time to cut expenses. She helps in the pharmacy because the business isn't busy enough to support a staff yet, and we need clerical help and someone to answer phones and wait on customers. One of my wife's many wonderful traits is her warmth, her caring, her ability to make everybody feel comfortable all the time. So when she's at the pharmacy and cousin so-and-so calls up to order something, Lorraine is schmoozing with her (or some friend or good customer) on the phone.

But I'm anxious about the business and yell, "Why are you on the phone so long with so-and-so?"

After I speak to her that way, Lorraine is in tears and I feel terrible. I realize I'm really uptight about getting this business going and she's kind of loosey-goosey. Not that she isn't helpful, she is. But it's not working for me—or for our marriage. Recognizing this too, she says, "We have two choices. Either I stop working, or if I stay here, we're getting a divorce. What do you want?"

I don't hesitate. "Stop working here."

Her illustrious career at Shield Pharmacy is brief.

Though no longer physically at Shield, she supports me in other ways. I might come home and talk about my frustrations with something going on at work—I may need to have a difficult conversation with an employee or a supplier or vendor. She is a good listener and can offer insight on how to best deal with it.

Of course, I support her as well. After our involvement in civil rights and Lorraine goes back to school to get a degree, I totally encourage her. I attend a number of her seminars and listen to speakers that she is excited about. I meet her classmates. I read some of her class books. The same kinds of things she would do for me.

We don't view our individual pursuits as separate from one another. We truly are a team.

Along the same lines, if we ever experience difficulty in the marriage (all couples go through some), we don't shove it under the carpet to let fester. We face it together.

At the time we choose to do marriage counseling, therapy has become a more popular kind of thing for both couples and individuals to work through issues. Since we know other people in therapy, we decide, "Why don't we join this couple's group and explore some things for us?"

If there is still any stigma to doing therapy at this point, we don't care. What we care about is each other. Turns out, the time we spend in therapy not only helps our relationship, but also each of us individually.

Born Optimists

A lot of success in marriage comes from the personalities of those who enter that union . . . and who you develop into during the marriage. Hopefully, you only become better!

We are very fortunate. Born only a day apart, we share many traits, while others complement each other. Lorraine is optimistic. That doesn't mean she's Pollyanna. Given cause, she can be more circumspect about a person than maybe I will be. But overall, her outlook and overall view of the world and life is upbeat and positive. We are not opposites in this respect (some couples are). I am mostly optimistic as well.

Another of Lorraine's wonderful traits is her willingness to express her deepest thoughts and feelings. Probably more than me, though she also prompts them from me and then often has a bit of insight to add. This only becomes enhanced, of course, after she trains as a psychologist. She has a whole new wealth of knowledge and information to share.

Mel the Romantic

I consider myself a romantic in how I express kindness (along with flowers and surprise gifts), in how I speak with Lorraine, and the affectionate names I call her. I have a pet name of "Putchie" that I use with people I love. I don't know where it comes from, but I use it with my kids and especially her. I think I'm actually more romantic than Lorraine. She is loving, but I make the more outward kinds of gestures.

Her romantic actions come out more in her caring for our home and especially for me. She's always there when I need to talk or am going through a rough patch. She doesn't back away during tough times. She has real conversations and confronts me with things she feels I need to look at. We are equally romantic in that we put our relationship before pretty much everything else. That deep caring continues even now after all our many years together.

Today, if Lorraine is going to run an errand nearby, I'll invariably say, "I love you. Be good. Just drive very, very carefully." She will not leave the condo if I do not say that. It is a showing of love and affection, and also a little reminder that, "Right. I'm going to be in a motor vehicle. No matter what else is going on, I need to pay attention."

She would say a similar thing to me. I don't drive now, but if I'm going out for my walk, she says, "I love you. Be good. And be very, very careful." We do this not because we worry so much, but because we care so much. The other person's well-being is every bit as important or more so than our own.

Of course, when I am away from her—out for a walk or anywhere else—Lorraine can always call me on my Apple Watch, which is an extension of my cell phone. I like keeping up with the latest trends . . . though it actually recalls the comic books from my childhood where the great detective, Dick Tracy, uses a "radio wristwatch" to communicate to others.

Now, if I can just find my decoder ring. . . .

Faith in One Another

I'm not referring to religious faith. I am talking about belief in each other.

I've taken many business risks in my life and Lorraine has always been there believing and encouraging me. Even when times are hard. That's when you really know who's with you. As we lose all that money after DASON fails, she has genuine worries. "Are we going to lose the condo? Am I going to be a bag lady sitting on a bench on Fairfax Avenue waiting for a bus?"

Many wives would feel a lot of anger toward their husband and even threaten divorce. She never does that. She never berates me by saying, "What the hell were you doing?" She understands that my ego got in the way and I made a major mistake. A huge turning point in our lives, this is when I'm thinking I should take a normal full-time pharmacist job to bring in income. Lorraine disagrees. "I know there is a better future for you. We just have to hang in there."

I have just as much faith in Lorraine as she has in me. After she takes that mock UCLA exam and is invited to volunteer at UCLA, I wholeheartedly encourage her to accept, knowing she is super smart and this invitation is not a fluke. Then later when she wants to go back to school to become a therapist, I'm again her biggest cheerleader. I have absolutely no doubt that she will be successful in her new profession.

Trust In All Areas

We count on each other, and trust we are making right choices together as we go through life. Given that, we don't overanalyze or overthink things. Even something as simple as getting a refrigerator. We go to Best Buy, see a refrigerator, decide together it's the right one and buy it. We don't consult *Consumer Reports* or go to twelve stores looking at twelve kinds of refrigerators and talking it over with twelve salesmen (and each other) until we can't stand it anymore. We presume we are making the correct selection and move forward. This may seem like a small example, but in truth, it illustrates a good way that one can live life.

"You want to go on a vacation?"

"Sure, where do you want to go?"

"How about this place?"

Again, we don't research it endlessly. We make a decision and we go!

Even when the issue of cancer comes up for each of us, it's "Okay, we'll get treatment. We'll get through this." We have faith that it is going to work. We don't see twenty different specialists getting first, second, and third opinions and so on.

When we get sick, it also doesn't bring up any crisis of faith in God. We don't feel sorry for ourselves. We simply don't entertain those thoughts. Again, it's "Okay. We're sick. We don't know how we got it. But we're in it, so let's deal with it." That's not to say we don't have tears and fears. But we also have a belief that, "We're together and together we'll make it through."

And we do. Twice. (Four times if you include our kids.)

Mel Baron's School of Finance

On a perhaps lighter note, I suppose our faith is demonstrated even in how we approach our financial lives. Even though money can sometimes be tight, especially at first, Lorraine and I never put a budget together. We just wing it. That's who we are.

Someone might ask, "What's your strategic plan?" Well, there is no strategic plan. We never sit down to create a five-year or ten-year plan. We keep moving forward and if a financial issue comes up, we deal with it. That's not to say we are not focused. From the start, I know I'm going to finish college and will work hard on my business. But in some ways, we are simply taking the next steps and trusting that we'll be okay.

When our kids grow up, Ross especially finds this pretty astounding. "Dad, you have the Mel Baron School of Finance. You're in another world from most of us." This is particularly noteworthy to him since his church preaches the importance of budgets and encourages couples in that direction.

Yet it's not that we're being irresponsible. I always inform Lorraine of where we are in terms of our finances, and she will always ask, "Can we afford this?" before making a significant purchase. Admittedly, life is simpler in some ways when Lorraine and I are first married. We are not using credit cards and getting ourselves into trouble (credit cards don't even exist!). Almost everything is cash for us. As Lorraine puts items into the grocery store cart, I'm adding up prices in my head, pretty confident we have enough to cover it. But, if on occasion, the total at the checkout stand is more than what is in our wallets, we remove two or three items and say, "Sorry, we're not going to take these." There's no embarrassment about this. It's simply what we can afford.

We spend our entire lives without a budget.

Like a Fine Wine: Better with Age

Though we are now both turning ninety, in so many ways, the girl I fell in love with is still the woman I've been with for seventy years. Lorraine is caring, kind, understanding, insightful. A wonderful companion and partner.

Some people change as they get older. They become disinterested. They lose their passions. They become cranky. But our wonderful youthful traits that drew us to one another remain strong.

We've been through trials and tribulations like in every marriage. Having children and arguing over how to raise them. Our family's different cancers. My losing a ton of money during one period and us hanging by a thread. But as we make our way through all these turns, each of us is right there for the other person. With no loss of commitment or interest.

Romantic couples at the beginning of their lives often wish, "We want to grow old together." Well, Lorraine and Mel *have grown old together.*

We have our wish!

✦ ✦ ✦

Conclusion

Moving Forward

Early in July 2022, Lorraine and I celebrate our 90th birthdays (a few weeks early) with our extended Utah and Idaho clans in Salt Lake City. Gathered in a private room at Valter's Osteria Italian restaurant, we have a fantastic time together—full of warmth, joy, and lots of love. Each of the grandchildren speak and there is a slide show of our family throughout the years.

Our Utah-Idaho Gang

Lorraine and I also hold private get-togethers during our five days there with smaller family groups—allowing us to also give special time to those great-grandchildren too young to attend the main event. That experience fondly reminds me of our *Special Days* from many years earlier, when just one grandchild at a time would visit our home.

Our partying repeats on July 30th when Lorraine's sister Sharon and her husband Artie throw us *another* 90th birthday bash for our Los Angeles family members—at Il Moro restaurant's lush patio with its koi pond and small stream—a little oasis in West LA. Another beautiful and loving evening.

Our Los Angeles Gang

It is a thrill to be with all our progeny at these celebrations—the next three generations following Lorraine and me. That really gets me thinking, especially about our two amazing children, Lynn and Ross. When I think of what they have overcome and accomplished, it's nearly beyond my understanding.

Lynn Expands Her Reach

In addition to her position as a curriculum director for Simi Valley District, Lynn starts traveling to Sacramento to advance English

Learner curriculum on a statewide basis. All in all, she enjoys an exceptional 40-year career in education, only recently retiring in 2019, two years before me. I joke with her, "So you're retired—*and your dad's still working?*"

The truth is, Lynn isn't retired. She consults for Californians Together, a statewide advocacy coalition for English Learners with a focus on immigrants and refugees. She continues to feel passionate about serving marginalized students as well as supporting fellow educators. The wonderful thing about semiretirement is she gets to pick and choose the work! On a more personal scale, she also consults for her son, Jack, who is the founder of Study Smart Tutors.

I'm so delighted for her. Lynn is this awesome woman who gets divorced, raises Jack through a rough period, is now 23 years into a loving marriage with a wonderful man, and has a booming career that distinguishes her in the field.

Lynn and Phil

Besides all of this, I don't know if anyone could be a more caring and involved daughter to us. She and her husband Phil come over every Monday to have lunch and prepare dinner for us, so Lorraine doesn't have to cook anything.

What's more, Lynn gave great input, support, and encouragement to me in the creation of this book.

Ross Expands His Horizon

Just like my mother calls Lynn a genius, I think Ross is truly one as well. His memory is beyond belief. He speaks multiple languages. I mean, I reflect on the transition from before he is a Latter-day Saint to becoming a highly valued professor at BYU-Idaho. The metamorphosis is *huge.*

Ross and Kathleen

Together, he and Kathleen raise seven terrific children. Though a stay-at-home mom when the family lives in Claremont, after they move to Idaho Falls and the kids are older, Kathleen gets her doctorate at the University of Utah and becomes a nurse practitioner working with clinics as well as teaching.

We recently learn Ross is making yet another dramatic career change. He and two colleagues at BYU-Idaho are moving to the main BYU campus in Provo. It is a significant promotion, with the three of them tasked with furthering innovation at the university.

Though Ross doesn't live near Los Angeles, we Zoom together every Sunday to chat about family, career, life. A profound pleasure that will certainly continue after his big relocation.

You Really CAN *Do Anything*

After learning of his new BYU promotion, Ross says something very meaningful. "Dad, I'm where I am today because of what you and Mom would always say to me: 'You can do anything. The world is open to you.'"

I am deeply touched. Apparently, Ross really embraces the advice I offer to empower him. As I think about it, even though Lynn contends our telling this to her when she is young feels burdensome (like she *must* accomplish great things), if I look at her life and all she's done . . . I have to believe she takes it to heart too.

The truth is a lot of parents offer all kinds of "guidance" to their children. They don't always necessarily believe what they're saying, but they think it's a good thing to impart.

But my "You can do anything" are not just empty words. I know they are true. Why? Because I have *seen* it.

My mother's peasant family leaves the only world they know to make an incredibly arduous trek to America to start over. Leo repeatedly dives headfirst into all kinds of businesses for which he has no skills or training, and almost always succeeds. I witness how they *"can do anything."*

And then I do it myself.

I transform a neighborhood pharmacy into a huge multifaceted business with innovative services that is purchased by a Fortune 500 corporation. I get involved in Civil Rights even though not an activist and make a difference—and also inform much of what I later do in my professional life. I transcend a probable life-crippling failure (DASON) to create an immensely fulfilling forty-year career as a professor at one of the top university pharmacy schools, pioneering programs and receiving recognition for my contributions to helping others.

My children know all of this. They know my story. They know Leo's story. They know my mother's story. It isn't just me casually saying, "Oh, you can do anything." They see the *proof* this is true—that they can do anything. They believe it.

And then they do it too.

And now, my memoir offers *this same proof* to all of my grandkids, great-grandkids . . . and beyond.

Fantastic Journey

There's one more thing I want to add. While I enjoy the fruits of my labors, it isn't just reaching the final goals of my successes that has been so satisfying.

It's more like the old adage: "Enjoy the journey."

I really have enjoyed my many journeys. In my careers. With Lorraine. With my children. It wasn't just about the goals. In fact, in pretty much every case . . . I never foresaw the end result that was coming.

Like I've said—everything turned out far *beyond my dreams.*

It all truly has been a wonderful journey. A great journey. An incredible journey. So I encourage my offspring, my offspring's offspring, and the offspring of my offspring's offspring: "*Go enjoy your own journey.*"

Move with courage toward your dream.

✦ ✦ ✦

Appendix

FAMILY TREE

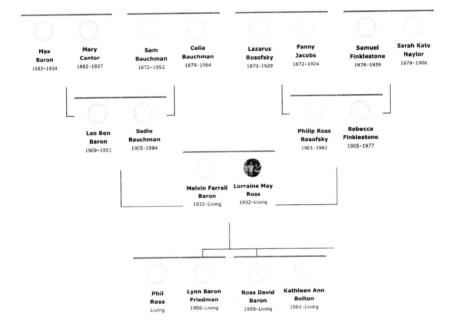

GRANDCHILDREN

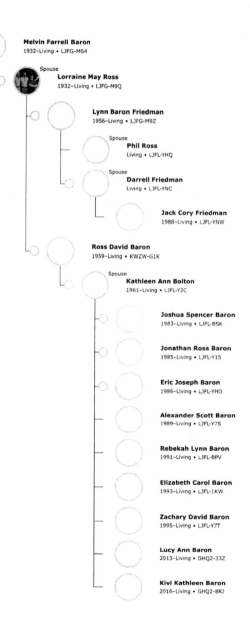

Melvin Farrell Baron
1932–Living • LJFG-MS4

Spouse
Lorraine May Ross
1932–Living • LJFG-M9Q

Lynn Baron Friedman
1956–Living • LJFG-M9Z

Spouse
Phil Ross
Living • LJFL-YHQ

Spouse
Darrell Friedman
Living • LJFL-YNC

Jack Cory Friedman
1988–Living • LJFL-YNW

Ross David Baron
1959–Living • KWZW-G1K

Spouse
Kathleen Ann Bolton
1961–Living • LJFL-Y2C

Joshua Spencer Baron
1983–Living • LJFL-BSK

Jonathan Ross Baron
1985–Living • LJFL-Y15

Eric Joseph Baron
1986–Living • LJFL-YHD

Alexander Scott Baron
1989–Living • LJFL-Y7S

Rebekah Lynn Baron
1991–Living • LJFL-BPV

Elizabeth Carol Baron
1993–Living • LJFL-1KW

Zachary David Baron
1995–Living • LJFL-Y7T

Lucy Ann Baron
2013–Living • GHQ2-33Z

Kivi Kathleen Baron
2016–Living • GHQ2-8RJ

GRANDCHILDREN & GREAT-GRANDCHILDREN

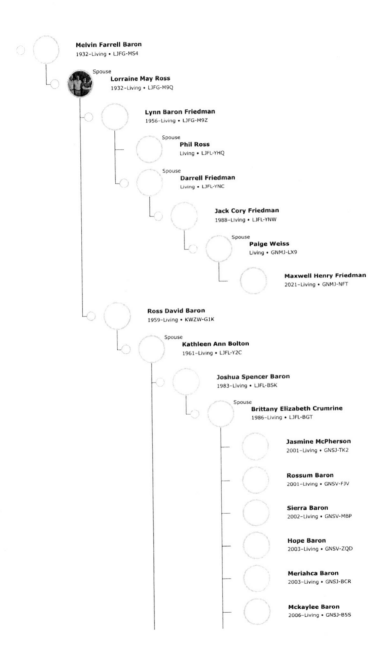

Melvin Farrell Baron
1932–Living • LJFG-MS4

Spouse
Lorraine May Ross
1932–Living • LJFG-M9Q

Lynn Baron Friedman
1956–Living • LJFG-M9Z

Spouse
Phil Ross
Living • LJFL-YHQ

Spouse
Darrell Friedman
Living • LJFL-YNC

Jack Cory Friedman
1988–Living • LJFL-YNW

Spouse
Paige Weiss
Living • GNMJ-LX9

Maxwell Henry Friedman
2021–Living • GNMJ-NFT

Ross David Baron
1959–Living • KWZW-G1K

Spouse
Kathleen Ann Bolton
1961–Living • LJFL-Y2C

Joshua Spencer Baron
1983–Living • LJFL-BSK

Spouse
Brittany Elizabeth Crumrine
1986–Living • LJFL-BGT

Jasmine McPherson
2001–Living • GNSJ-TK2

Rossum Baron
2001–Living • GNSV-FJV

Sierra Baron
2002–Living • GNSV-MBP

Hope Baron
2003–Living • GNSV-ZQD

Meriahca Baron
2003–Living • GNSJ-BCR

Mckaylee Baron
2006–Living • GNSJ-B5S

Continued over the next two pages

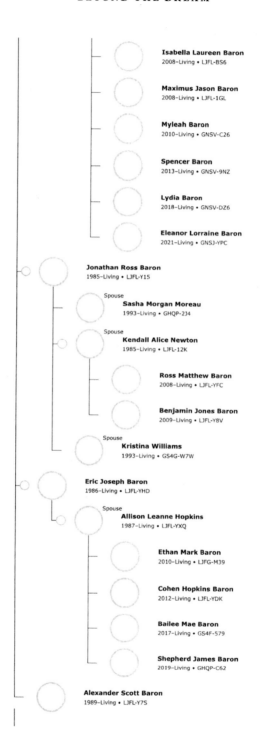

Isabella Laureen Baron
2008–Living • LJFL-BS6

Maximus Jason Baron
2008–Living • LJFL-1GL

Myleah Baron
2010–Living • GNSV-C26

Spencer Baron
2013–Living • GNSV-9NZ

Lydia Baron
2018–Living • GNSV-DZ6

Eleanor Lorraine Baron
2021–Living • GNSJ-YPC

Jonathan Ross Baron
1985–Living • LJFL-Y15

Spouse
Sasha Morgan Moreau
1993–Living • GHQP-2J4

Spouse
Kendall Alice Newton
1985–Living • LJFL-12K

Ross Matthew Baron
2008–Living • LJFL-YFC

Benjamin Jones Baron
2009–Living • LJFL-Y8V

Spouse
Kristina Williams
1993–Living • GS4G-W7W

Eric Joseph Baron
1986–Living • LJFL-YHD

Spouse
Allison Leanne Hopkins
1987–Living • LJFL-YXQ

Ethan Mark Baron
2010–Living • LJFG-M39

Cohen Hopkins Baron
2012–Living • LJFL-YDK

Bailee Mae Baron
2017–Living • GS4F-579

Shepherd James Baron
2019–Living • GHQP-C62

Alexander Scott Baron
1989–Living • LJFL-Y7S

Rebekah Lynn Baron
1991–Living • LJFL-BPV

Elizabeth Carol Baron
1993–Living • LJFL-1KW

Zachary David Baron
1995–Living • LJFL-Y7T

Lucy Ann Baron
2013–Living • GHQ2-33Z

Kivi Kathleen Baron
2016–Living • GHQ2-8RJ

Photograph Credits

p. 6, Photograph. Courtesy of University of Southern California, on behalf of its USC School of Pharmacy/Photo by Ed Carreon.

p. 184, Photograph. Courtesy of University of Southern California, on behalf of its USC School of Pharmacy.

p. 301, Photograph. Courtesy of University of Southern California, on behalf of its USC School of Pharmacy.

p. 324, Photograph. Courtesy of University of Southern California, on behalf of its USC School of Pharmacy/Photo by Walter Urie.